T0156546

ODD WORDS

FOR CROSSWORDS AND PEOPLE IN PUZZLES
(THIRD EDITION)

Bentley Bougard

iUniverse, Inc.

New York   Bloomington

**Odd Words for Crosswords and People
in puzzles (Third Edition)**

Copyright © 2009 by Bentley Bougard

*All rights reserved. No part of this book may be used
or reproduced by any means, graphic, electronic, or
mechanical, including photocopying, recording, taping or
by any information storage retrieval system without the
written permission of the publisher except in the case of brief
quotations embodied in critical articles and reviews.
The views expressed in this work are solely those of the author
and do not necessarily reflect the views of the publisher, and
the publisher hereby disclaims any responsibility for them.*

iUniverse books may be ordered through booksellers or by contacting:

*iUniverse
1663 Liberty Drive
Bloomington, IN 47403
www.iuniverse.com
1-800-Authors (1-800-288-4677)*

*Because of the dynamic nature of the Internet, any Web addresses or
links contained in this book may have changed since publication and
may no longer be valid. The views expressed in this work are solely those
of the author and do not necessarily reflect the views of the publisher,
and the publisher hereby disclaims any responsibility for them.*

*ISBN: 978-1-4401-1616-2 (pbk)
ISBN: 978-1-4401-1617-9 (ebk)*

Printed in the United States of America

iUniverse rev. date: 1/15/2009

A hobbit - BILBO

A little, musically - POCO

A people of Mexico - SUMA

A sound - SCHWA

A thousand years - CHILIAD

Abalone - ORMER

Abandoned calf - CADE

Abbot's staff - CROSIER

Abnormal loss of hair - ALOPECI

Aborigine of Japan - AINU

Abounding in shrubs - BOSKY

About 1.3 cu.yds. - STERE

Abraham's wife - SARAH

Abruzzi bell town - ATRI

Absolute rule - IMPERIUM

Absorbed-dose units - RADS

Abstract artist - ARP

Abstract being - ENS or ESSE

Abstract painting - OPART

Abusive phrase - EPITHET

Abyss - ABYSM

Acacia tree - BABUL

Acclimation - ECLAT

Accustomed - WONT

Achilles' victim - HECTOR

Acid in tone - ACERB

Acid of apples - MALIC

Acidity - ACOR

Acorns coat - TESTA

Act of God - FORCE MAJEURE

Actual being - ESSE

Acupressure - SHIATSU

Adding machine inventor -
    PASCAL

Address the moon - ULULATE

Adriatic peninsula - ISTRIA

Adriatic seaport -
    ANCONA,BARI, RIMINI
    or TRIESTE

Adriatic wind - BORA

Adroit, generally - HABILE

Adult doodlebug - ANTLION

Adult insect - IMAGO

Advantage - BEHOOF

Adventure tale - GEST or GESTE

Aegean area - IONIA

Aegean island - DELOS or
    SAMOS

Aerospace material - BERYLIUM

Aesir ruler - ODIN

Afghan city - HERAT

Afloat - NATANT

Afore - ERE

African antelope - ADDAX,
    BONGO,ELAND, GNU,
    IMPALA, KOB, KUDU,
    NYALA, ORIBI, ORYX,
    RHEABOK, STEENBOK,
    TETEL or TORA

1

African arid region - SAHEL

African badger - RATAL

African caftan - DASHIKI

African capital - ACCRA

African evergreen - COLA

African fever - LASSA

African fox – ASSE or CAMMA

African gorge - OLDUVAI

African ground squirrel - XERUS

African knife - PANGA

African language - SWAZI

African lemur - MACACO

African lily - AGAPANTHUS

American lizard - AMOLE

African lute - OUD

African mammal - RATAL

African monkey - GUENO

African musical instrument - MBIRA

African nation - DJIBOUTI

African nomad - BERBER

African ox - ZEBU

African palm tree - RAFFIA

African plant - ALOE

African pullover - DASHIKI

African river - UBANGI

African rodent - HYRAX

African ruminant - OKAPI

African shirt - DASHIKI

African sorcery - OBEAH

African spear - ASSEGAI

African spear tree - ASSEGAIS

African stork - ARGALA or MARABOU

African tableland - KAROO

African timber tree - ODUM

African tongue - RUNDI

African tree - SHEA

African tunic - DASHIKI

African village - KRAAL

African wildcat - SERVAL

African witchcraft - OBEAH

Again, in music - BIS

Agaves plant - SISAL

Agaves root - AMOLE

Aging - SENESCENT

Agouti or coypu - CAVY

Agricultural pesticide - LINDANE

Air dwellers of folklore - SYLPHS

Air: pref. - ATMO

Airplane controls - AELERONS

Air sacs in the lungs - ALVEOLI

Airtight - HERMEDIC

Aladdin parrot - IAGO

Alarm bell or signals - TOCSIN

Alaskan or Aleutian isle - ADAK, ATKA orATTU

Alaskan knife - ULUL

Alaskan National Park - DENALI

Alaskan volcano - KATMAI

Alcoholic cakes - BABAS

Ale holder - TUN

Alencon - LACE

Aleutian island - ADAK

Alfonso's queen - ENA

Algerian cavalryman - SPAHI

Algerian port - ORAN

Algonquian chief - SACHEM

Algonquian leaders - SAGAMORES

Alkene - OLEFINE

Alligator shirt maker - IZOD

Allowance for waste - TRET

Alloy of lead & tin - TERNE

Alloy of silver & gold - ELECTRUM

Alluring woman - HORIS

Almond poison - AMARINE

Alms box - ARCA

Aloe fiber - PITA

Alpine peak - EIGER

Alpine region: var. - TIROR

Alpine river - AARE

Altar cloth - DOSSAL

Altar enclosure - BEMA

Altar of stars - ARA

Altar screen - REREDOS

Aluminum coin of Israel - AGORA

Amateur newsletter - FANZINE

Amazon bird - HOATZIN

Amazon dolphin - INIA

Amazon estuary - PARA

Amazon feeder - NEGRO

Amazon port - BELEM

Amazon rain forest - SELVA

Amazon valley people - TUPI

Ambrosia of immortality - AMRITA

American chameleon - ANOLE

American dogwood - OSIER

American hog - DUROC

American Indian grouping - TUPI

American larch - TAMARACK

American lizard - AMOLE

American saint - SETON

Amerind - ERIE or OTOE

Ammonia compound - AMIDE or AMINE

Ammonia derivative - IMIME

Among other things - INTERALIA

Amorous glance - OEILLADE

Amulet - MOJO

An amino acid - ARGININE, LYSINE or SERINE

An archangel - URIE

Anatomical cavity - FOSSA

Anatomical duct - VAS

Anatomical intersection - CHIASMA

Anatomical network - RETE

Ancient - HOARY

Ancient: Pref. - PALEO

Ancient African city - UTICA

Ancient African kingdom - NUMIDIA

Ancient ally of Sparta - ELIS

Ancient alphabetic character - RUNE

Ancient Arabian kingdom - SHEBA

Ancient ascetic - ESSENE

Ancient assemblies - FORA

Ancient Balkan region - THRACE

Ancient Biblical country - ARAM

Ancient Biblical land - ELAM

Ancient box - CIST

Ancient British Celts - ICENI

Ancient capital of Lydia - SARDIS

Ancient catapult - ONAGER

Ancient Caucasian - OSSET

Ancient Celtic tribe - ICENI

Ancient chariot - ESSED

Ancient Chinese capital - XIAN

Ancient Chinese poet - LIPO

Ancient Chinese money - TAEL

Ancient city of Edom - PETRA

Ancient city of Mesopotamia - EDESSA

Ancient city on the Nile - MEROE

Ancient country in Africa - NUMIDIA

Ancient country in the Peloponnesus - ELIS

Ancient Dead Sea country - MOAB

Ancient Egyptian city - TANIS

Ancient Egyptian diety - PTAH or SHU

Ancient Egyptian gold - AMENRA

Ancient Egyptian papers - PAPYRI

Ancient Ethiopian capital - MEROE

Ancient fertility god - BAAL

Ancient fertility goddess - ASTARTE

Ancient fiddle - REBEC

Ancient German - GEAT

Ancient gold coin - AUREUS

Ancient Greece - HELLAS

Ancient Greek belts - CESTI

Ancient Greek city or state - ELEA or POLIS

Ancient Greek coin - OBOL or STATER

Ancient Greek colony - IONIA

Ancient Greek courtesan - HETAERA

Ancient Greek covered walks - STOAS

Ancient Greek dialect - EOLIC or IONIC

Ancient Greek district or region - IONIA or LACONIA

Ancient Greek Geographer - STRABO

Ancient Greek goddess - ENYO

Ancient Greek marketplace - AGORA

Ancient Greek Mystic - ORACLE

Ancient Greek Physician - GALEN

Ancient Greek Poet - SAPPHO

Ancient Greek portico - STOA

Ancient Greek region - AEOLIA

Ancient Greek sage - SOLON

Ancient Greek sculptor - SCOPAS

Ancient Greek serf - HELOT

Ancient Greek soldier - HOPLITE

Ancient Greek tunic - CHITON

Ancient Greek weight - MINA

Ancient hall of music - ODEA

Ancient Hebrew coin – GERAH

Ancient Hebrew lyre - ASOR

Ancient Hebrew kingdom – SAMARIA

Ancient Hewbrew stringed instrument - NABLA

Ancient Hebrew prophet - ELIAS

Ancient Hebrew vestment - EPHOD

Ancient idol - BAAL

Ancient Incan capital - CUZCO

Ancient inscription - RUNE

Ancient Irani - MEDE

Ancient Irish god - LUG

Ancient Italian area - ETRUSCAN

Ancient Italian deity - FAUN

Ancient Italian town - ELEA

Ancient Italic people - SABINES

Ancient Jewish sect member - PHARISEE

Ancient King of England - HAROLD

Ancient kingdom - EDOM

Ancient kingdom on the Nile - NUBIA

Ancient laborer - ESNE

Ancient letter - RUNE

Ancient lute - REBEC

Ancient marketplace - FORA

Ancient markings - OBELI or RUNE

Ancient metal collar - TORC

Ancient Mexican resident - OLMEC

Ancient mid east kingdom - MOAB

Ancient Nile kingdom - NUBIA

Ancient ointment - NARD

Ancient oracle site - DELPHI

Ancient Palestinian - ESSENE

Ancient paper - PAPYRUS

Ancient part of Iran - MEDIA

Ancient people - OSSET

Ancient Persian - MEDE or ELEAMITE

Ancient Phoenician city - SIDON

Ancient Phoenician seaport - TYRE

Ancient rabbi - HILLEL

Ancient region of France - ALSATIA

Ancient Roman historian - LIVY

Ancient Roman port - OSTIA

Ancient Roman province - RAETIA

Ancient sage - SOLON

Ancient Scandinavian poets - SKALDS

Ancient Semitic country - EDOM

Ancient Spanish kingdom - NAVARRE

Ancient stone tool - EOLITH

Ancient stringed instrument - PSALTERY

Ancient strong box - ARCA

Ancient Syrian city - ELBA

Ancient Syrian kingdom - MOAB

Ancient temple - NAOS

Ancient Theban supreme god - AMENRA

Ancient tome - CODEX

Ancient Tuscan nation - ETRURIA

Ancient Turkish city - EDESSA

Ancient Umbrian city - SPOLETO

Ancient warship - TRIEME

Ancient wine flask - OLPE

And others: abbr. - ETAL

Andes plateau - PUNA

Andes tuber - OCA

Andean shrub - COCA

Andorran coin - PESETA

Angel - SERAPH

Angel of the highest order - SERAPH

Angle measurer - ALIDADE

Angle symbol - THETA

Angler's bars - HERLS

Anglo-Saxon coin - ORA

Anglo-Saxon laborer - ESNE

Anglo-Saxon spear - GAR

Anglo-Saxon tax - DANEGELD

Anglo-Saxon Theologian - BEDE

Animal fat - ADIPOSE

Animal's backbone - CHINE

Animal's breadbasket - MAW

Anise liqueur - PERNOD

Ankle bone - TALUS

Ankle bones - TALI or TARSI

Annealing oven - LEHR

Annuity scheme - FONTANE

Ant - EMMET

Antarctic penguin - ADELIE

Antarctic predators - SKUAS

Antelope of Tibet - GOA

Anticlimax - BATHOS

Antigone's uncle - CREON

Antilles Island - SABA

Antipathy - ODIUM

Antiquated - FUSTY

Antique coin - ACU

Antiquity - ELD

Antitoxins - SERA

Ants, old style - EMMETS

Anvil - INCUS or OSSICLE

Apertures - STOMATA

Apathy - ACEDIA

Apparition - EIDOLON or WRAITH

Appetite - EDACITY

Apple, e.g. - POME

Apple acid - MALIC

Apollo's birth place - DELOS

Apollo's twin sister - ARTEMIS

Apse dome - CONCHA

Apteryx - KIWI

Aquatic nymph - NAIAD

Aquatic rodent - COYPU

Aqualung inventor - COUSTEAU

Aquarium bottom feeder - LOACH

Aquarium fish - DANIO, GOURAMI, NEON, TETRA or WRASSE

Arab boat - DHOW

Arab chieftain - EMEER

Arab commandoes - FEDAYEEN

Arab garment - HAIK

Arab headdress - KAFFIYEH

Arab land - OMAN

Arab market place - SOUK

Arab robes - ABAS

Arab Satan - EBLLS

Arabian cloak - BURNOOSE

Arabian coast vessel - DHOW

Arabian gazelle - ARIEL

Arabian port - ADEN

Arabian Sea feeder - INDUS

Arabic father - ABOU

Arabic letter - ALIF

Arbitrary penalty - AMERCE

Arbor - PERGOLA

Arboreal lemur - INDRI

Archaic bidding - HEST

Archangel - URIEL

Archetype - PARADIGM

Architectural pier - ANTA

Arctic bird - SKUA

Arctic goose - BRANT

Arctic gull - XEMA

Arctic jacket - ANORAK

Arctic whale - NARWHAL

Area of expertise - METIER

Arenas - STADIA

Argentine grassland - LLANO

Argentina port - PARANA

Argo captain - AENEAS

Argonne forest river - AISNE

Argue frivolously - CAVIL

Arguments - POLEMICS

Arikara - REE

Arizona Indian - PIMA

Arm bones - RADII or ULNAE

Arm of the Amazon - PARA

Arm pit - AXILLA

Armadillo - APAR

Armadillo armor - SCUTE

Armless, backless seat - TABORET

Armor piece - TASSE

Armor plate - TUILLE

Armored breastplate - CUIRASS

Armpit - AXILLA

Army victuals - MRES

Aromatic herb - HYSSOP

Aromatic herb - HYSSOP

Aromatic plant - CHIA or NARD

Aromatic resin - MYRRH

Arrange in threes - TERNATE

Arrogance - HUBRIS

Arrow poison - CURARE, INEE or UPAS

Arsenic sulphide - REALGAR

Art deco Artist - ARTE

Art medium - GESSO

Art of the absurd - DADA

Artemis's twin - APOLLO

Article of food - VIAND

Artificial Intl language - ESPERANTO

Artificial rubber - BUNA

Artist's studio - ATELIER

Artist's surface - GESSO

Artistic movement - DADA

Artistic prayer - ORANT

Arrow smith's wife - LEORA

Artistic taste - VIRTU

Arum plants - AROIDS

As - QUA

As above - ADEM

As written - SIC

As written musically - STA

Ascetic - ESSENE

Ashy substance - CALX

Asia Minor - ANATOLIA

Asia Minor region - AEOLIA

Asian ass - ONANGER

Asian boat - SAMPAN

Asian citrus - POMELO

Asian deer - SIKAS

Asian fish - LOACH

Asian gazelle - GOA

Asian goat - TAHR

Asian holiday - TET

Asian language - LAO or SHAN

Asian legume - SOYA

Asian long horned sheep - ARGALI

Asian mountain goat - TAHR

Asian mushroom - SHIITAKE

Asian mustard plant - MASABI

Asian noodles - RAMEN

Asian nurse or nursemaid - AMAH

Asian ox - GAUR or ZEBU

Asian palm - ARECA or BETEL

Asian range - ALAI

Asian River between China & Russia -

AMUR or LENA

Asian sea - ARAL

Asian snake - KRAIT

Asian soy product - MISO

Asian starlings - MYNAS

Asian tree - ASAK

Asian weight - TAEL

Asiatic herb - ORACH

Assail persistently - BELABOR

Assam or Oolong - TEA

Assam silkworm - ERIA

Assembly place of old - AGORA

Assert - POSIT

Assyrian city - ARBELA

Assyrian god - ASHUR

Assyrian god of war - ASUR

Astringent - ACERB

Astrinent compound - TANNIN

Astronomer's light ratio - ALBEDO

Astronomical unit - PARSEC

At full speed - AMAIN

At last: Fr. - ENFIN

Athenian hangout - STOA

Athenian law giver - DRACO

Athenian lawmaker or sage - SOLON

Athenian magistrate - ARCHON

Athenian solon - DRACO

Atlantic clam - QUAHOG

Atlantic fish - LING, MENHAGEN or SCUP

Atlantic food fishes - PORGIES

Atlantic mackerel - CERO

Atlas' seven daughters - PLEIADES

Atmospheric pressure unit - TORR

Atomic number 1 - HYDROGEN

Atomic number 5 - BORON

Atomic number 10 - NEON

Atomic number 16 - SULFER

Atomic number 23 - ARSENIC

Atomic number 26 - IRON

Atomic thirty - ZINC

Atomic number 45 - RHODIUM

Atomic number 50 - TIN

Atomic number 54 - XENON

Atomic number 55 - CESIUM

Atomic number 56 - BARIUM

Atomic number 68 - ERGIUM

Atomic number 74 - TUNGSTON

Atomic number 86 - RADON

Atomic number 96 - CURIUM

Atomic particle - MESON or NEUTRON

Attachment to a fishing line - SNELL

Aunt, Sp. - TIA

Auricular - OTIC

Aurora's Greek counterpart - EOS

Austerlitz name change - ASTAIRE

Australian Alps - TIROL

Australian bird - ARARA

Australian cockatoo - GALAH

Australian cuckoo - KOEL

Australian horse - WALER

Australian lizard - MOLOCH

Australian sheep dog - KELPIE

Authorative edict - UKASE

Avatar of Vishnu - RAMA

Avifauna - ORNIS

Away - FRO

Away from one's mouth - ABORAL

Awkward - SPLAY

Awns - ARISTAS

Ax handle - HELVE

Axiom - TENET

Ayla's creator - JEAN AUEL

BC/Alaska River - STIKINE

Baby barracuda - SPET

Baby beaver - KIT

Baby bird - EYAS

Baby food - PAP

Baby oyster - SPAT

Babylonian goddess - ISHTAR

Babylonian numeral - SAROS

Babylonian sky god - ANU

Babylonian sun god - SHAMASH

Babylonian tower - ZIGGURAT

Baccarat variation - CHEMIN DE FER

Bacchanalian cry - EVOE

Bacchante - MAENAD

Backs - DORSA

Bacterium - AEROBE

Bactrian beast - CAMEL

Bad blood - ANIMUS

Bad: pref. - MAL

Bad imitation - ERSATZ

Bad luck - HOODOO

Bad taste in art - KITSCH

Bad Tempered - WASPISH

Bad tempered old woman - HARRIDAN

Badger kin - RATEL

Bagpipe kin - MUSETTE

Baja seaport - ENSENADA

Bake eggs - SHIRR

Balance - STASIS

Balcony - MIRADO

Balderdash - FLUMMERY

Baldness - ALOPECIA

Balearic Island - IBIZA

Balkan capital - TIRANA

Ball of yarn - CLEW

Ball point pen inventor - BIRO

Ballerina - DANSEUSE

Ballerina step - PAS

Ballerina's rail - BARRE

Ballet jump - ENTRECHAT or PAS DE CHAT

Ballet leap - JETE

Ballet movement or pose - CHASSE, ELANCE or PLIE

Ballet position - ECARTE

Ballet stars - ETOILES

Ballet step - PAS

Balloon probe - SONDE

Ballroom dance - SALSA

Balm for aches & pains - ARNICA

Balsam burner - CENSER

Baltic Sea barge - PRAM

Baltic Sea port - RIGA

Bamako's land - MALI

Bambi's aunt - ENA

Banana kin - ABACA

Bank of France - RIVE

Bantu language - XHOSA

Bantu native - ILA

Barbary ape - MAGOT

Barbary sheep - AOUDAD

Barbed-wire barricade - ABATIS

Barge - HOY

Bark cloth - TAPA

Barley beards - ARISTAS or AWNS

Barracuda - SPET

Barrel maker - COOPER or STAVER

Barrio grocery - BODEGA

Based on the number six - SENARY

Basic sugar - SUCROSE

Basket fiber or material - RAFFIA

Basket making need - ISTLE

Basketry willow - OSIER

Basswood - LINDEN

Bast fiber - RAMIE

Basutoland - LESOTHO

Bat-eared fox - ASSE

Bat haven - ANTRE

Bat wood - ASH

Bathsheba's husband - EURIAH

Battery inventor - VOLTA

Battery type - NICAD

Battlefield fence - ABATIS

Battlement opening - CRENEL

Battleship nickname - BIGMO

Bauble - GEWGAW

Bauxite component - ALUMINA

Bavarian leatherwear - LEDERHOSEN

Bay - LAGUNA

Bay of the White Sea – ONEGA

Bay window - ORIEL

Beak - NEB

Bean, for sprouting - MUNG

Bear young - YEAN

Beard of rye - AWN

Bearded - BARBATE

Beat - ICTUS

Beatify - BLESS

Beautiful woman of paradise - HOURI

Beaver hat - CASTOR

Become rigid - OSSIFY

Bed canopy - TESTER

Bed covering - DUVET

Beehive - SKEP

Beethoven dedicatee - ELISE

Beethoven opus - EROICA

Beetle - CHAFER

Beetle wings - ELYRA

Before: pref. - ANTE

Before birth - INUTERO

Begum's spouse - AGHA

Behold, to Caesar - ECCE

Beige - ECRU

Beijing coin - YUAN

Being - ESSE

Belgian port city - GHENT or OSTEND

Belgian princess - ASTRID

Belgian waterway - OISE

Belgium River - YSER

Believer in God - DEIST

Belladonna lily - AMARYLLIS

Bellflower - LOBELIA

Bell like instrument - CELSTRA

Bell shaped hat - CLOCHE

Bell tower - CAMPANILE

Bell town - ATRI

Bellini opera - NORME

Belly - WAME

Belly button - AMPHALOS

Belly muscles - RECTI

Below: Pre. - INFRA

Bend in a ships timber - SNY

Benedictine title - DOM

Benefactor Yale - ELIHU

Benign tumor of the skin - WEN

Berber nomads - TUAREG

Bern's river - AARE

Berry parts - ACINI

Best vision spot - FOVEA

Bet to lose every trick in cards - MISERE

Betel palm - ARECA

Beyond: Prefix - META

Bible prophet - JOEL

Biblical book - HOSEA, JONAH or PROVERBS

Biblical bushel - EPHA

Biblical herdsman - AMOS

Biblical incense - MYRRH

Biblical judge - ELI

Biblical king - ELAH

Biblical kingdom - ELAM or MOAB

Biblical land - OPHIR

Biblical liar - ANANIANS

Biblical lion - ARI

Biblical mount - HOREB, NEBO or SINAI

Biblical name of Syria - ARAM

Biblical place of exile - HARA

Biblical prophet - AMOS, HOSEA, PESGAH or ISAIAH

Biblical queen - ESTHER

Biblical spy - CALEB

Biblical twin - ESAU

Biblical weed - TARE

Biblical witch's home - ENDOR

Big baboon - MANDRILL

Big bird - RHEA

Big bug - CICADA

Billiard table cloth - BAIZE

Binary compound - OXIDE

Binary star in Perseus - ALGOL

Biochemical catalyst - OXIDASE

Biological bristle - SETA

Biology classes - GENERA

Birch family tree - HORNBEAM

Bird beak - NEB

Bird bill part - CERE

Bird droppings - GUANO

Bird of Greenland - ERNE

Bird of prey - ELANET

Bird with a crest - HOOPOE

Birds - ORNIS

Bird's wing - PINION

Birth a lamb - YEAN

Birth sack - CAUL

Birthmark - NEVUS

Birthplace of Apollo - DELOS

Birthplace of Buddha - NEPAL

Birthplace of CAMUS - ALGERIA

Birthplace of Jules Verne - NANTES

Bishop of Rome - POPE

Bishoprics - SEERS

Bishop's headdress - MITRE

Bishop's permission - EXEAT

Bishop's staff - CROSIER

Bit of mosaic - TESSERA

Bitter - ACERB

Bitter vetch - ERS

Bitter vetches - TARES

Bizarre - OUTRE

Black and white diving bird - MURRE

Blackbird - MERLE or OUSEL

Black cuckoo - ANI

Black- current liqueur - CASSIS

Black fish - TAUTOGS

Black footed albatross - GOONEY

Black forest tree - BAUM

Black gibbon of Asia - SIAMANG

Black grape - ZINFANDEL

Black gum tree - TUPELO

Blackjack - COSH

Black sea arm - AZOY

Black sea port - ODESSA, ORDU or VARNA

Black tailed gazelle - GOA

Black tea - BOHEA

Black vulture - URUBU

Blacksheep - ROUE

Blackstone - ONYX

Black-tailed gazelle - GOA

Blackthorn fruit - SLOE

Bleach - ETIOLATE

Bless - SAIN

Blessing - BENISON

Blindfold a falcon - SEELS

Blissful - ELYSIAN

Blissful state - NIRVANA

Blister - BLEB

Blithe - JOCUND

Bloated - TUMID

Block of Earth's crust - MASSIF

Blood: Pref. - HEMA

Blood clots - EMBOLI

Blood of the gods - ICHOR

Blood pigment - HEMA

Blood sucking fly - TABANID

Blood vessel network - RETE

Blood vessels - VENAE

Bloodstone - HELIOTROPE

Blossom-bearing stems - SCAPES

Blue dye - ANIL, ANILIN or WOAD

Blue grass genus - POA

Blue-gray - BLAY

Blue myrtle - LILACS

Blue Nile source - TSANA

Blue sky - WELKIN

Blue-violet - PERSE

Blue wildflower - GENTIAN

Boadicea's people - ICENI

Boatman on the river Styx - CHARON

Bobby's blackjack - COSH

Bobolink - ORTOLAN

Body - SOMA

Body cavities - ANTRA

Body duct - VAS

Body of beliefs - ETHOS

Body of poetry - EPOS

Body of work - OEUVRE

Body sacs - BURSA

Bog plant - SUNDEW

Boil down - DECOCT

Bolero composer - RAVEL

Boletus mushroom - CEPE

Bollard - KEVEL

Bombastic - OROTUND

Bombay suburb - THANA

Bon mot - EPIGRAM

Bone cavities or chambers - ANTRA

Bone cavity - FOSSA

Bone: Fr. - OSTE

Bone inflammation - OSTEITIS

Bone material - APATITE

Bone: Pref. - OSTE

Bones - OSSA

Bony - OSTEAL

Book after Daniel - HOSEA

Book after Ezekiel - HOSEA

Book after Ezra - NEH or NEHEMIAH

Book after Gal. - EPH

Book after Hosea - JOEL

Book after Joel - AMOS

Book after Jonah -MICAH

Book after Judges - RUTH

Bppk after Leviticus - NUM

Book after Mark - ST.LUKE

Book after Micah - NAHUM

Book after Neh - ESTH

Book after Num. - DEUT

Book before Amos - JOEL

Book before Daniel - EZEKIEL

Book before Habakkuk - NAHUM

Book before Jeremiah -ISAIAH

Book before Jobe - ESTHER

Book before Joel - HOSEA

Book before Nehemiah - EZRA

Book before Nehum - MICAH

Book before Philemon - TITUS

Book before Romans - ACTS

Book before Titus - TIM

Book of Hymns - PSALYER

Book of prophecies - HOSEA

Book of reprints - OMNIBUS

Book of Sayings - ANA

Book size - OCTAVO

Bookbinder's leather - ROAN

Bookbinding leather - ROAN

Bookplate - EXLIBRIS

Books with eight pages - OCTAVOS

Boorish person - CHURL

Boot wheel - ROWEL

Bordered by a ridge - VALATE

Borden's spokes cow - ELSIE

Boredom - ENNUI

Boring oration - SCREED

Boring tool - WIMBLE

Borneo Sea - SULU

Borodin prince - IGOR

Botanic structure - OVULE

Botanical bristle - SETA

Botanical cell - CYST

Botanical opening - STOMA

Botanical sac - ASCUS

Both: pref. - AMBI

Bothered - ATE

Bottle holding 3 magnums of Champagne - REHOBOAM

Bottle in wickerwork - DEMIJOHN

Bounce over water - DAP

Bounce playfully - DANDLE

Bound bundle of sticks - FAGOT

Bovine hybrid - CATALO

Bovine stomachs - OMASA

Bowed, in music - ARCO

Boxlike sled - PUNG

Braided bread - CHALLAH

Brain membrane - DURA or DURAMATER

Brain passage - ITER

Branch of the Amazon - PARA

Branches - RAMI

Branch training trellises - ESPELIER

Brazilian airline – VARIG

Brazilian macaw - ARA

Brazilian palm - ASSAI

Brazilian rattler - MARACA

Brazilian river - TIETE

Brazilian rubber tree - ULE

Brazilian seaport - BAHIA, BELEM, NATAL, or SANTOS

Brazilian state - BAHIA

Brazilian timber tree - SATINE

Breakfast cereal - MUESLI

Breakfast roll - BIALY

Breastbones - STERNA

Breastplate - AEGIS, CUIRASS or EGIS

Breathing affliction - APNEA

Breed of sheep - CHEVIOT

Brew - DECROCT

Bribe - SOP or SUBORN

Bric-a-brac shelves - ETAGERE

Brief insight or summary - APERCU

Bright star - ALGOL

Brightly colored fish - OPAH

Brightly colored parrot - LORY

Brilliance - ECLAT

Brindled cat - TABBY

Bring forth sheep or young - YEAN

Bring forward as proof - ADDUCE

Bristle: Prefix - SETI

Bristle like appendage - AWN

Bristle like part - SETAE

Bristly - SETOSE

British farm structure - BYRE

British medical journal - LANCET

British sonar - ASDIC

Brit's morning break - ELEVENSES

Brittany seaport - BREST

Brittle resin - COPAL

Broad bean - FAVA

Broken down horse - JADE

Brood of pheasants - NIDE

Brook trout - SALTER

Broom of twigs - BESOM

Brother of Castor - POLLUX

Brother of Electra - ORESTES

Brother of Ethan Allen - IRA

Brother of Esau - JACOB

Brother of Fidel - RAUL

Brother of Hector - PARIS

Brother of Iphigenia - ORESTES

Brother of Jacob - EDOM

Brother of Miriam - AARON

Brother of Moses - AARON

Brother of Ophelia - LAERTES

Brother of Osiris - SET

Brother of Polynices - ETEOCLES

Brother of Prometheus - ATLAS

Brother of Saud - FAISAL

Brother of Seth - ABEL

Brother of Tamar - ABSALOM

Brother of Van Gogh - THEO

Brown bear - URSID

Brown ermine - STOAT

Brown fur - NUTRIA or STOAT

Brown pigment - SIENNA

Brown tint - SEPIA

Brownish songbird - LINNET

Brunei coin - SEN

Brunei's locale - BORNEO

Brynhild's beloved - SIGURD

Buckthorn - CASCARA

Buckwheat porridge - KASHA

Buddhist angels - DEVAS

Buddhist enlightenment - SATORI

Buddhist holy city - LHASA

Buddhist language - PALI

Buddhist monk - BONZE

Buddhist movement - CHAN

Buddhist people - LAO

Buddhist religious center in Japan - NIKKO

Buddhist sacred mountain - OMEI

Buddhist Satan - MARA

Buddhist Shrine - STUPA

Buddhist teachings - DHARMA

Buddhist temple - WAT

Buddhist tower - PAGODA

Buckwheat porridge - KASHA

Buffalo, for one - BOVID

Buffalo of the Celebes - ANOA

Bug group - HETEROPTERA

Bug repellent - DEET

Build a nest - NIDIFY

Bulgarian coin - LEV

Bulgarian seaport - VARNA

Bulletin board runners - SYSOPS

Bullfighter's cloak - CAPA

Bullfighter's march - PASEO

Bulrush - TULE

Bundle of nerves - RETE

Bundle of twigs - BESOM or FAGOT

Bung - SPILE

Bunny tail - SCUT

Burgundy wine - MACON

Burial urn - OSSUARY

Burmese rice dish - SELA

Burmese tribesman - SHAN

Burn balm - ALOE

Burn suddenly - DEFLAGRATE

Burn with a ray - LASE

Burp - ERUCT

Burrowing rodent - PACA

Bur sera resin - ELEMI

Burst open - DEHISCE

Bush baby - GALAGO

Bush cricket - KATYDID

Buster Brown's dog - TIGE

Butcher bird - SHRIKE

Butcher's scraps - OFFAL

Butterfly - SATYR

Cabot's ship - MATHEW

Cacophony - DIN

Cactus - SAGUARO

Cactus features - AREOLAE

Cactus plant - OPUNTIA

Cadmus' daughter - INO

Caesar's dog - CANIS

Caesar's horse - EQUUS

Caesar's wife - UXOR

Cain's brother - ABEL or SETH

Cake - GATEAU

Calla - ARUM

Calcareous rock deposit - TUFFA

Calculating machine inventor - PASCAL

Calcutta cloth - DHOTI

California bulrush - TULE

California oaks - ROBLES

California resort city - OJAI

California town - APTOS

California volcano - LASSEN

Calligraphy line - SERIF

Caliph - IMAM

Called - YCLEPT

Calvary - GOLGOTHA

Calyx part - SEPAL

Cambodia (once) - KHMER

Camel - BACTRIAN

Camel kin - GUANACO

Camel's hair fabric - ABA

Cameo stone - SARDONYX

Camping place for troupes - ETAPE

Campus life - ACADEME

Canaanite commander - SISERA

Canaanite deity - BAAL

Canal to the Baltic - KIEL

Canary Island - TENERIFE

Canary's cousin - SERIN

Canary's nose - CERE

Candies fruit - GLACES

Candle ingredient - STEARIN

Cannabis - BHANG

Canonical hour - MATIN or NONES

Canopy - TESTER

Canopy for a boat - TILT

Cant - ARGOT

Cantina tidbit - TAPA

Canvas coating - GESSO

Capacitance unit - FARAD

Cape fox - ASSE

Capek play - RUR

Caper - DIDO

Capillary's cousin - TABULE

Capital of Afghanistan - KABUL

Capital of Albania - TIRANA

Capital of American Samoa - PAGO PAGO

Capital of ancient Elam - SUSA

Capital of ancient Laconia - SPARTA

Capital of ancient Syria - ANTIOCH

Capital of Angola - LUANDA

Capital of Antigua - ST. JOHN

Capital of Armenia - YEREVAN

Capital of Aruba - ORANJESTAD

Capital of Assyria - NINEVEH

Capital of Azerbaijan- BAKU

Capital of Bahrain - MANAMA

Capital of Bali - DENPASAR

Capital of Bangladesh - DACCA or DHAKA

Capital of Belarus - MINSK

Capital of Belgium - BRUSSELS

Capital of Benin - PORTO-NOVO

Capital of Bihar - PATNA

Capital of Boeotia - BETA

Capital of Bolivia - LA PAZ and SUCRE

Capital of Bosnia - SARAJEVO

Capital of Botswana - GABORONE

Capital of Brittany - RENNES

Capital of Bulgaria - SOPHIA

Capital of Burundi - BUJUMBURA

Capital of Cambodia - RIEL

Capital of Cameroon -YEOUNDE

Capital of Chad - N'DJAMENA

Capital of Chile - SANTIAGO

Capital of Colombia - BOGOTA

Capital of Congo - KINISHASA

Capital of Costa Rica - SAN JOSE

Capital of Crete - CANEA

Capital of Croatia - ZAGREB

Capital of Cyprus - NICOSIA

Capital of Delaware - DOVER

Capital of Dominica - ROSEAU

Capital of Drome - VALENCE

Capital of East Flanders - GHENT

Capital of Egypt - CAIRO

Capital of Ecuador - QUITO

Capital of Eritrea - ASMARA

Capital of Estonia - TALLINN

Capital of Ethiopia - ADDIS ABABA

Capital of Fiji - SUVA

Capital of Georgia - TBILISI

Capital of Ghana - ACCRA

Capital of Guam - AGANA

Capital of Guyana - GEORGETOWN

Capital of Haiti - PORT-AU-PRINCE

Capital of Hejaz - MECCA

Capital of Honduras - TEGUCIGALPA

Capital of Hungary - BUDAPEST

Capital of Iceland -REYKJAVIK

Capital of Idaho - BOISE

Capital of India - NEW DELHI

Capital of Indonesia - JAKARTA

Capital of Iraq - BAGHDAD

Capital of Isere - GRENOBLE

Capital of Jamaica - Kingston

Capital of Jordan - AMMAN

Capital of Kansas - TOPEKA

Capital of Kazakhstan - AQMOLA or ALMAATA

Capital of Kenya - NAIROBI

Capital of Korea - SEOUL

Capital of Laconia - SPARTA

Capital of La Manche - STLO

Capital of Laos - VIENTIANE

Capital of Latvia - RIGA

Capital of Lesotho - MASERU

Capital of Libya - TRIPOLI

Capital of Liechtenstein - VADUZ

Capital of Lithuania - VILNUS

Capital of Lorraine - METZ

Capital of Lydia - SARDIS

Capital of Macedonia - SKOPJE

Capital of Majorca - PALMA

Capital of Maldives - MALE

Capital of Mali - BAMAKO

Capital of Malta - VALLETTA

Capital of Manche -ST LO

Capital of Mauritius - PORT LOUIS

Capital of Mongolia - ULAN BATOR

Capital of Montana - HELENA

Capital of Morocco - RABAT

Capital of Mozambique - MAPUTO

Capital of Muscat - OMAN

Capital of Nepal - KATHMANDU

Capital of New Jersey - TRENTON

Capital of New South Wales - SYDNEY

Capital of New Mexico - SANTA FE

Capital of Niger - NIAMEY

Capital of Nigeria - ABUJA or LAGOS

Capital of North Carolina - RALEIGH

Capital of North Dakota - BISMARK

Capital of Okinawa - NAHA

Capital of Oman - MUSCAT

Capital of Oregon - SALEM

Capital of Pakistan - ISLAMABAD

Capital of Phoenicia - TYRE

Capital of Portugal - LISBON

Capital of Qatar - DOHA

Capital of Queensland - BRISBANE

Capital of Roman Britain - YORK

Capital of Rwanda - KIGALI

Capital of Samoa - APIA

Capital of Saskatchewan -REGINA

Capital of Saudi Arabia - RIYADH

Capital of Schleswi-Holstein - KIEL

Capital of Senegal - DAKAR

Capital of Shensi - SIAN

Capital of Sicily - PALERMO

Capital of Slovakia - BRATISLAVA

Capital of South Dakota - PIERRE

Capital of Spain - MADRID

Capital of St. Kitts - BASSETERRE

Capital of Suriname - PARAMARIBO

Capital of Swaziland - MBABANE

Capital of Switzerland - BERN

Capital of Syria - DAMASCUS

Capital of Thailand - BANKOCK

Capital of Taiwan - TAIPEI

Capital of Tanzania - DAR ESSALAAM,

Capital of Tasmania - HOBART

Capital of Texas - AUSTIN

Capital of Tibet - LHASA

Capital of Timor - DILI

Capital of Togo - LOME

Capital of Transfer - UMTATA

Capital of Tunisia - TUNIS

Capital of Turkey - ANKARA

Capital of the Bahamas - NASSAU

Capital of the Crimea - SIMFEROPOL

Capital of the Dominican Republic - SANTO DOMINGO

Capital of the Netherlands Antilles - WILLEMSTAD

Capital of the Punjab - LAHORE

Capital of the Ukraine - KIEV

Capital of Uganda - KAMPALA

Capital of Uruguay - MONTEVIDEO

Capital Uzbekistan - TASHKENT

Capital of Valise - SION

Capital of Vanuatu - VILA

Capital of Venezuela - CARACUS

Capital of Vermont - MONTPELIER

Capital of Vietnam - HANOI

Capital of Western Samoa - APIA

Capital of Xizang - LHASA

Capital of Yemen - ADEN or SANA

Capital of Zimbabwe - HARRARE

Capital on the AAR - BERN

Capital on the Casouab - BAKU

Capital on the Songka River - HANOI

Capital on the Vltava - PRAGUE

Capital once know as Salisbury - HARARE

Capri or Elba - ISOLA

Captive of Hercules - IOLA

Capuchin monkey - SAI

Caravansary - SERAI

Car amide - UREA

Carbon compound - ENOL or KETONE

Card game - ECARTE

Cardiac contraction - SYSTOLE

Cardinal flower - LOBELIA

Cardinal's cap - BIRETTA

Carefree - BLYTHE

Carefree episode - IDYLL

Cargo derrick - STEEVE

Caribbean dance music or style - SOCA

Caribbean island - ARUBA or SABA

Carmen composer - BIZET

Carnelian - SARD

Carnivorous mammal - RATEL

Carnivorous plant - SUNDEW

Carpathian range - TATRA

Carpet fiber - ISTLE

Carried by the wind - EOLIAN

Carrion - OFFEL

Carthaginian queen - DIDO

Cartilage disc - MENISCI

Cascade of ruffles - JABOT

Case for a small article - ETUI

Caspian feeder - URAL

Caspian sturgeon - BELUGA

Cassava root - MANIOC

Cassia plant - SENNA

Castle's back gate - POSTERN

Castle's stronghold - KEEP

Castor's mom - LEDA

Castorum - BEAVER URINE

Cat genus - FELIS

Cat nip - NEPETA

Cat's monogram - TSE

Categorized groups - TAXA

Catamount - PUMA

Cataplasm - POULTICE

Catapult - BALLISTA

Caterpillar hairs - SETAE

Cathedral city - ELY

Catholic calendar - ORDO

Catkin - AMENT

Catlike - FELID

Catlike mammal - CIVET

Cato's course - ITER

Cattle genus - BOS

Cattle, old style - KINE

Cattle plague - MURRAIN

Caucho-ule - RUBBER TREE

Cautious - CHARY

Cave or cavern - ANTRE

Caveman's flint - EOLITH

Cavern on the way to Hades -
    EREBUS

Cavity - FOSSA

Cedar of the Himalayas -
    DEODAR

Ceiling feature - TRAVE

Celebes buffalo or ox - ANOA

Celestial being with three pairs
    of wings- SERAPH

Celestial dog - CANIS

Celestial shadow - UMBRA

Cell body - SOMA

Cell constituent - RNA

Cell division process - MITOSIS

Celtic Mayday - BELTANE

Celtic Neptune or sea god - LER

Celtic spirit - BANSHEE

Center of activity - LOCI

Central American tree - EBO

Central Asian mountains - ALTA

Central point - NODE

Century plant - AGAVE,
    ALOE or MAGUEYS

Cereal fungus - ERGOT

Ceremonial chamber - KIVA

Ceremonial Feast - POTLATCH

Cereal grass - RAGI

Certain alloy - TERNE

Certain Asian soldier - ROK

Certain bacterium - AEROBE

Certain bird - TRILLER

Certain church calendar day -
    FERIA

Certain cleaner - SALSODA

Certain consonant - LABIAL or
    LENIS

Certain cotton - PIMA

Certain cue used in singing -
    PRESA

Certain electronic tubes -
    TRIODES

Certain epoch - EOCENE

Certain fruit - POME

Certain gemstones - SPINELS

Certain group - NONET

Certain Indian - CADDO

Certain Japanese American -
    SANSEI

Certain muscle - TENSOR

Certain rabbits - LAPINS

Certainly - IWIS

Cete or cetacean - ORC or
    WHALE

Chair back - SPLAT

Chalcedony - SARD

Chalice - CALIX

Chalice veil - AER

Chalk or marble - CALCITE

Chameleon - ANOLE

Chan portrayer - OLAND or TOLER

Chancel - BEMA

Change: Pref. - META

Chanted hymn - CANTICLE

Charging policy - PRIX FIXE

Channel - GAT

Channel Island - SARK

Chanticleer - ROOSTER

Chantilly's river - OISE

Chapter of the Koran - SURA

Characteristic spirit - ETHOS

Charged lepton - MUON

Charged particle - ANION, ION or PROTON

Charlemagne's capital - AACHEN

Chat idly - PRATE

Chattering bird - DAW

Chauvinistic patriot - JINGO

Cheekbone - MALAR

Cheep wine - PLONK

Cheerful - JOCUND

Cheese variety - STILTON

Chef's hat - TOUQUE

Chef's thickening agent - ROUX

Chemical compound - ALKALI, AMINE, ENOL, ESTER, HALIDE, ISOMER, OXIDE or STEROLChemical nuclide - ISOMER

Chemical salt - CITRATE or ARSENAT

Chemical suffix - ENE or ENOL

Cherub superior - SERAPH

Chest for valuables - ARCA

Chestnut coating - BUR

Chewing-gum ingredient - CHICLE

Chicken - TREPID

Chicken breed - WYANDOTTE

Chickle source - SAPODILLA

Chickpea - GRAM

Chief Vedic god - INDRA

Child of Ra - SHU

Childbirth - PARTURITION

Childish - PUERILE

Chilian deset - ATACAMA

Chilean seaport - ARICA

Chills & fever - AGUE

Chilly - ALGID

China/Russia border River - AMUR

Chinawood oil - TUNG

Chinese coin - TAEL

Chinese coins - YUANS

Chinese cuisine - HUNAN

Chinese deer - SIKA

Chinese division - MIAO

Chinese dynasty - CHI, CHOU, HSIA or LIAO

Chinese fruits - LITCHIS

Chinese gooseberry - KIWI

Chinese house idol - JOSS

Chinese ideal or "way" - TAO

Chinese industrial area - WUHAN

Chinese isinglass - AGAR

Chinese money – YUAN

Chinese noodle dish - LOMEIN

Chinese official residence - YEMAN

Chinese pagoda - TAA

Chines pasta - LOWEMIN

Chinese philosopher - LAOTSE

Chinese poet - LIPO

Chinese port - AMOY or LUDA

Chinese pottery - CHUN

Chinese puzzle - TANGRAM

Chinese seaport - AMOY or LUDA

Chinese secret society -TONG

Chinese tea - CHA, LAPSANG or SOUCHONG

Chinese weight unit - LIANG or TAEL

Chipped stone - EOLITH

Chiromancer - PALMIST

Chitinous body - CARAPACE

Chivalrous undertaking - EMPRISE

Choise dish - VIAND

Choise tea - HYSON

Choler - ANGER

Chopin piece - ETUDE or MAZURKA

Choral composition - ARIOSA

Chorus girl - CHORINE

Christ stopped at - EBOLI

Chronic liar - ANANIAS

Church book - PSALTER

Church calender - ORDO

Church council - SYNOD

Church cup - CALIX

Church desk - AMBO

Church music - MOTET

Church oil - CHRISM

Church part - APSE or NAVE

Church passageway - NARTHEX

Church roster or tribunal - ROTA

Church screen - RERADOS

Church yearbook - ORDO

Circle - COTERIE

Circle dance - HORA

Circuit - AMBIT

Circuit courts - EYRES

Circular - GYRAL

Circular window - ROUNDEL

Circumference - AMBIT

Citrus garden - ORANGERY

City in Afghanistan - HERAT

City in Africa - MOMBASA

City in Alabama - SELMA

City in Alaska - SITKA

City in Asia - MANILA

City in Belgium - AALST, LIEGE or YPRES

City in Bolivia - LA PAZ or ORURO

City in Brittany - BREST

City in China - XIANGTAN

City in Denmark - ARHUS

City in Egypt - ZAGAZIG

City in Ethiopia - HARAR

City in Finland - ABO or ESPOD

City in France - METZ or STLO

City in Germany - BREMAN, KIEL or TRIER

City in Greenland - THULE

City in Hokkaido - SAPPORO

City in India - POONA

City in Iran - QOM or TABRIZ

City in Israel - LOD

City in Italy - MANTUA, TORINO or UDINE

City in Japan - OSAKA or OTARU

City in Judah - ADAR

City in Kansas - IOLA

City in Kirghizia - OSH

City in Korea - TAEGU

City in Kyrgyzstan - OSH

City in Macedonia - EDESSA

City in Magdeburg - ELBE

City in Maine - SACO

City in Mexico - OAXACA

City in Moravia - BRNO

City in Morocco - CEUTA or FE

City in Nebraska - LINCOLN

City in New York - ORLEAN

City in Nigeria - EDE, IWO, IFE, KANO or LAGOS

City in Northern Italy - MANTUA

City in Norway - BERGAN

City in Ohio - ELYRIA

City in Oregon - SALEM

City in Pakistan - LAHOR

City in Portugal - OPORTO

City in Provence - ARLES

City in Romania - ARAD

City in Russia - KIROV or TULA

City in RWANDA - KIGALI

City in Siberia - OMSK

City in Sicily - ENNA

City in South Korea - TAEGU

City in Spain - LEON

City in Sweden - UPPSALA

City in Switzerland - BASEL

City in Syria - ALEPPO

City in Texas - PAMPA, ODESSA or WACO

City in Transylvania - CLUV

City in the Ukraine - LVOV

City in Transylvania - DEVA

City in Tuscany - LUCCA or SIENNA

City in Utah - OREM

City in Vietnam - HAIPHONG

City in Wisconsin - EAUCLAIRE or NEENAH

City in Yorkshire - LEEDS

City near Amsterdam - HAALEM

City near Bremen - EMDEN

City near Dallas - DENTON

City near Lake Nassar - ASWAN

City near Moscow - KIROV

City near Padua - ESTE

City near Provo - OREM

City near San Marino - RIMINI

City near the Caspian Sea - AMUL

City near Venice - UDINE

City north of Leon - OVIEDO

City north of Triest - UDINE

City of ancient Ionia - SMYRNA

City of ancient Palestine - SAMARIA

City of ancient Rome - OSTIA

City of Ishikar Bay - OTARU

City of Moravia - BRNO

City of Panama - COLON

City of Spain - GRENADA or ORENSE

City of the Mudhens - TOLEDO

City of the Philistines - GATH

City of Yemen - ADEN

City on Crow Creek - CHEYENNE

City on Great South Bay - ISLIP

City on Lac Leman - GENEVA

City on Lake Michigan - GARY

City on Lake Winnebago - NEENAH or OSHKOSH

City on Long Island - RYE

City on Minorca - MAHON

City on Puget Sound -TACOMA

City on Seneca Lake - GENEVA

City on the Aare - BERNE

City on the Adige - TRENT

City on the Aire - LEEDS

City on the Aker - OSLO

City on the Alabama - SELMA

City on the Allegheny - GENEVA

City on the Amazon delta - BELEM

City on the Arkansas - TULSA

City on the Arno - PISA

City of the Bay of Biscay - LaRochelle

City on the Bay of Haifa - ACRE

City on the Black sea - YALTA

City on the Bosporus - ISTANBUL

City on the Brazos - WACO

City on the Clyde - GLASGOW

City on the Colorado - YUMA

City on the Columbia - ASTORIA

City on the Cuyahoga - AKRON

City on the Danube - BUDAPEST, LINZ, NOVI, SAD, ULM or VIENNA

City on the Delaware -CAMDEN, EASSTON or TRENTON

City on the Dnieper - KIEV

City on the Douro - OPORTO

City on the Dvina - RIGA

City on the Ebro - LOGRONO or SARAGOSSA

City on the Erie canal - ITHICA

City on the Euphrates - BABYLON

City on the Fox - ELGIN

City on the Ganges - AGRA, ALLAHABAD, BENARES or PATNA

City on the Guadalquivir - CORDOBA

City on the Han - SEOUL

City on the Hari Rud - HERAT

City on the Hudson - ALBANY, NYACK, TROY or YONKERS

City on the Humboldt - ELKO

City on the Ij - AMERSTAM

City on the Ijsslemeer - EDAM

City on the Illinois - PEORIA

City on the Inn - St.MORITZ

City on the Irtysh - OMSK

City on the Isere - GENOBLE

City on the Jumna - AGRA or DELHI

City on the Ligurian Sea - GENOA

City on the Loire - BLOIS, NANTES, NEVERS, ORLEANS or TOURS

City on the Merrimack - NASHUA

City on the Meuse - LIEGE, NAMUR or SEDAN

City on the Mississippi - MEMPHIS, MOLIN MOLINE or ST. PAUL

City on the Missouri - OMAHA or PIERRE

City on the Mohawk - UTICA

City on the Moselle - METZ or TRIER

City on the Mures - ARAD or MURESUL

City on the Nile - THEBES

City on the Oder - BRESLAU or WROCLAW

City on the Ohio - CINCINATI

City on the Oka - OREL

City on the Orne - CAEN

City on the ORSK - URAL

City on the Penobscot - BANGOR or ORONO

City on the Potomac - ARLINGTON

City on the Po - CREMONA or TURIN

City on the Raccoon - DES MOINES

City on the Red - HANOI

City on the Red Cedar - LANSING

City on the Rhine - ARNHEM, BASLE, BERN, BONN, COLOGNE, MAINZ or WEISBADEN

City on the Rhone - ARLES, AVIGNON GENEVA or LYONS

City on the Rio Grande – EL PASO or LAREDO

City on the Roaring Fork - ASPEN

City on the Ruhr - ESSEN

City on the Saone - LYON

City on the Salt - MESA

City on the Savannah - AUGUSTA

City on the Seine - PARIS or ROUEN

City on the Shannon - LIMERICK

City on the Skunk - AMES

City on the Smokey Hills - ABILENE or SALINA

City on the Somme - AMIENS

City on the Songka - HANOI

City on the Squamscott - EXETER

City on the Styr - LUTSK

City on the Susquehanna - ONEONTA

City on the Tanaro - ASTI

City on the Tanshui - TAIPAI

City on the Thames - ETON

City on the Tiber - ROME or OSTIA

City on the Tigris - AMARA or BAGHDAD

City on the Trinity - DALLAS

City on the Truckee - RENO or TAHOE

City on the Ural - ORSK

City on the Vardar - SKOPJE

City on the Vire - ST LO

City on the Vistula - WARSAW

City on the Vltava - PRAGUE

City on the Volga - SAMARA

City on the Willamette - EUGENE or SALEM

City on the Yamuna - AGRA

City on the Yangtze - CHUNG KING

City on the YODO - OSAKA

City on the Yonne - SENS

City Southwest of Frunze -OSH

Civet cousin - GENET or RASSE

Civilian clothes - MUFTI

Clairvoyant - FEY

Clan - GENS or SEPT

Clan chief - THANE

Clarion call - TANTARA

Clarified butter - GHEE

Classes - GENERA

Classical theaters - ODEA

Clavier - PIANO

Claw - CHELA

Clay-rich soil - MARL

Cleaving tool - FROE

Cleopatra's eye makeup - KOHL

Cleopatra's maid - IRAS

Cleric's vestment - AMICE

Clerical cap - BIRETTA

Clerical garment - RABAT

Clerical wear - ORALES

Clever prank - DIDO

Click beetle - ELATER

Cliff-base pile - SCREE

Climber's gear - CRAMPON

Climber's spike - PITON

Climbing palm - RATTAN

Climbing plant - CLEMATIS or LIANA

Clinging mollusk - LIMPET

Clinging vine - CIPO

Clinophobe's fear – SLEEP

Clique - COTERIE

Clone part - RAMET

Clot - COAGULUM

Cloth fibre - RAMIE

Cloth made from bark - TAPA

Cloth ridge - WALE

Clothe - ENDUE

Clown fish - ANEMONES

Cloy - PALL

Clump of wool - TOD

Coachman - JEHU

Coal dust - CULM

Coarse clothes - STAMMEL

Coarse fern - BRACKEN

Coarse hominy - SAMP

Coarse round basket - SKEP

Coarse rug - DRUGGET

Coarse, twilled cotton fabric - CHINO

Coarse woolen fabric - CADDIS

Coastal dune - DENE

Coatings - PATINAE

Coat of fur - PELAGE

Coat-of-Arms border - ORLE

Cobra's cousin - MAMBA

Cockeyed - AGEE

Cocktail flavoring - ORGEAT

Coconut fibre - COIR

Coconut flesh - COPRA

Cod's cousin - HAKE

Code of the Samurai - BUSHIDO

Coerse - DRAGOON

Coffeecake - KUCHEN

Coin - SPECIE

Coin of ancient Rome - SESTERCE

Coin of Cairo - PIASTER

Coin of Helsinki - EURO

Coin of Pakistan - PAISA

Coined money - SPECIE

Coins of Iceland - AURAR

Coins of old Italy - SOLDI

Cold - ALGID

Cold confection - BOMBE

Cold-weather gear - ANORAK

Cold winds - SARSARS

Collected sayings or Anecdotes - ANA

Collection - COTERIE or OMNIBUS

Collection of poems - DIVAN

Collection of primative poetry - EPOS

Collection of writings - ENOCH

College teacher - DOCENT

Colonial blackbirds or cuckoos - ANIS

Colorado peak - LAPLATA

Colorado River feeder - GILA

Colorful chalcedony - AGATE

Colorful fish - OPAH or TETRA

Colorful lizard - AGAMA

Colorful moth - LUNA

Colorful parrot - KORIKEET

Colorful perch - DARTER

Colorful pullover - DASHIKI

Coloring process - BATIK

Colorless liquid - ALDOL

Columbian conifer - PINO

Columbine - AQUILEGIA

Column base - PLINTH

Column support - ORLO or SOCLE

Column type - ANTA

Come forth - DEBOUCH

Comet's head - COMA

Comic verse - DOGGEREL

Command - BEHEST

Commemorative vase - AMPHORA

Common - VULGATE

Common mineral - BLENDE

Common people - PLEBS

Commonplace - PROSAIC or PROSSY

Communal cuckoo - ANI

Communion cup - AMA

Compacted coal - CANNEL

Complication - NODUS

Complications - NODI

Component of fertilizer -UREA

Compound containing Element 5 - BORATE or BORIDE

Computer code - EBCDIC

Computer language - ALGOL

Computer Screen - VDU

Concave arches - TORIC

Concealed - PERDU

Concerning - ANENT

Concert hall - ODEON or ODEUM

Concerto solo - CADENZA

Concise summary - PRESCIS

Conflicting drama - AGON

Conger - EEL

Congo River - EBOLA or UELE

Conic section - PARABOLA

Coniferous forest - TAIGA

Connection - NEXUS

Connective tissue - FACIA

Connoisseur - EPICURE

Consort of Opps - SATURN

Consorty of shiva - SHAKTI

Consort of Siva - SATI

Conspicuous success - ECLAT

Constriction of the pupil - MIOSIS

Construe - EDUCE

Constituent of DNA - ADENINE

Constituent of living cells - RNA

Container for bones - OSSCIARY

Containing copper - CUPRIC

Containing gold - AURIC

Containing iron - FERRIC

Contemporary - COEVAL

Control freak - SVENGALI

Controversial - ERISTIC

Convent - PRIOY

Converging points - FOCI

Convert into soap - SAPONIFY

Convex at both edges - GIBBOUS

Convex moulding - OVOLO orTORI

Convincing - COGENT

Convocation of witches - ESBAT

Cooked cereal - KASHA

Cooked pheasant - SALMI

Cooked salad - SALMAGUNDI

Coot - SCOTER

Copper film - PATINA

Copycat - EPIGONE

Coral, e.g. - POLYP

Coral reef - CAY

Cordage fibre - ISTLE, JUTE, RAMIE or SISAL

Corday's victim - MARAT

Corduroy feature - WALE

Core group - CADRE

Cormorant - SHAG

Corn lily - IXIA

Cornea's companion - SCLERA

Corner of the eye - CANTHUS

Corner stone - QUOIN

Corner stone tablets - STELAE

Cornmeal bread - TORTILLA

Cornmeal mush - SAMP

Cornmeal patty - HOECAKE

Corduroy rib - WALE

Cornice bracket - CORBEL

Corpulent - OBESE

Correct text - EMEND

Corrigenda - ERRATA

Corsican patriot - PAOLI

Corymb - CYME

Cosmetic material - ORRIS

Cote d'azur menu - SCAD

Coterie - SET

Cotton cloth - CHINO

Cotton fabric - KHADDAR, LENO or PEMA

Cotton fiber - NOIL

Cotton thread - LISLE

Cotton type - PIMA

Cottonwood tree - ALAMO

Counsel - REDE

Counter stroke - REPOSTE

Country between France & Spain - ANDORRA

Couple - DYAD

Course rug - DRUGGET

Court call - ADIN

Court decree - ARRET

Courtyard - QUAD

Cover an enbankment - REVET

Covered walk - STOA

Covered with hair - PILAR

Cow barn - BYRE

Cow corn - SILAGE

Cow genus - BOS

Cow's first stomach - RUMEN

Cows - KINE

Coxcomb - FOP

Coypu fur - NUTRIA

Crab claw - CHELA

Crane's kin - BUSTARD

Cranial nerve - VEGUS

Creative movement of the 60's - OPART

Creattor god of the Incas - VIRACOCHA

Crenshaws - MELONS

Creolized English - GULLAH

Crescent on a fingernail - LUNULA

Crescent-shaped - BICORN

Crescent shaped outline - LUNETTE

Cretan port - CANEA

Crevasse pinnacle - SERAC

Cricket sound - CHIRR

Crime against the ruler - LESE MAJESTE

Criminal intent - MENSREA

Critical explanation - EXEGESIS

Critical study - EXAMEN

Crocodile kin - GAVIAL

Crocus part - CORM

Cromosome blueprint - GENOME

Crone - BELDAME

Cronic liar - ANANIAS

Cross - ROOD

Cross or crucifix letters - INRI

Cross threads - WOOF

Cross with a circular loop - ANKH

Crossbow - ARBALEST

Crossbeam - TRAVE

Crosshairs - RETICLE

Crosswise - ATHWART

Croud together - SERRY

Crow family member - DAW

Crow's cousin - ROOK

Crucifix - ROOD

Crude bed - DOS

Crude zinc - SPELTER

Crudely chipped flints - EOLITHS

Crushed sugarcane - BAGASSE

Crustacean - ISOPOD

Cry of the Bacchanals - EVOE

Crypic letter - RUNE

Crystal lined stone - GEODE

Crystaline material - DOLOMITE

Crystaline mineral - EPIDOTE

Crystalline rock - SCHIST

Cub Scout leader - AKELA

Cuban dance - HABANERA

Cubic meter - ARE or STERE

Cuckoo - ANI

Cuckoopint, e.g. - AROID or ARUM

Cuckoopint & flamingo lily - ARUMS

Cucumber, e.g. - PEPO

Culex cousin - AEDES

Cultivated land - TILLAGE

Cultural values - ETHOS

Cultured gel or culture medium - AGAR

Cup - CALIX

Cup bearer to the gods - HEBE

Cupboard - AMBRY

Cupid - EROS or AMOR

Cupids - AMORETTI

Curling broom - BESOM

Curly pasta - ROTINI

Currant-flavored liqueur - CASSIS

Currency of Afghanistan - PUL

Currency of Albania - LEK

Currency of Algeria - DINAR

Currency of Andorra - PESETA

Currency of Angola - LWEI

Currency of Austria - SCHILLING

Currency of Belarus - RUBLE

Currency of Bolivia - CENTAVO or PESO

Currency of Bulgaria - LEV or STOTINKA

Currency of Burma - PYA

Currency of Cairo - POUND

Currency of Cambodia - RIEL

Currency of Cameroon - FRANC

Currency of Cape Verde - ESCUDO

Currency of Capetown - RAND

Currency of Chile - PESO

Currency of China - YUAN

Currency of Czecholslovakia - HALERS or KORUNAS

Currency of Denmark - KRONER

Currency of Ecuador - SUCRE

Currency of Egypt - PIASTRE

Currancy of Ethiopia - BIRR

Currency of Finland - PENNI

Currency of Georgia - LARI

Currency of Ghana - CEDI

Currency of Greece - DRACHMA

Currency of Haiti - GOURDE

Currency of Iceland - KRONA

Currency of Iran - RIAL

Currency of Japan - SEN

Currency of Jordan - FILS

Currency of Kuwait - DINAR

Currency of Laos - KIP

Currancy of Lesotho - LOTI

Currency of Libya - RIAL

Currency of Malta - LIRE

Currency of Mauritania - OUGUIYA

Currency of Morocco - DIRHAM

Currency of Nepal - RUPEE

Currency of Nicaragua - CORDOBA

Currency of Nigeria - NAIRA

Currancy of Norway - KRONA

Currency of Panama - BALBOA or CENTESIMO

Currency of Pakhistan - PAISA

Currancy of Paraguay - GUARAN

Currency of Peru - INTI or SOL

Currency of Poland - ZLOTY

Currency of Portugal - ESCUDO

Currency of Romania - LEU

Currency of Samoa - SENE or TALA

Currency of Saudi Arabia - RIYAL

Currency of Sierra Leone - RIAL or LEONE

Currency of Sri Lanka - RUPEE

Currency of Sweden - KRONE

Currency of Thailand - BAHT

Currency of Tonga - PAANGA

Currency of Turkey - LIRA

Currency of Venezuela - BOLIVAR

Currency of Vietnam - DONG

Currency of Western Samoa - TALA

Currency of Yemen - RIAL

Currency of Yugoslavia - PARA

Curse - ANATHEMA or WANION

Curtain fabric - NINON, SCRIM or VOIL

Curtain material - CRETONNE or SCRIM

Curved molding - OGEE

Curved sword - SCIMITAR

Curved timber - FUTTOCK

Cuttlefish ink - SEPIA

Cyclades Island - DELOS

Cylindrical - TOROSE

Cylindrical and tapering - TERETE

Cylindrical larva - REDIA

Cymbeline's daughter - IMOGEN

Cyst - HYDATID

Czar's decree - UKASE

Czarist council - ZEMSTVO

Czech region - MORAVIA

Czech river - ELBE or ODER

DNA component - ADENINE

Dadismpioneer - ARP

Daffodil - NARCISSUS

Dagger - DIRK, PONIARD or STYLET

Dagger, in printing - OBELUS

Dagger with a wavy blade - CREESE

Daisies - ROSTRA

Dakoda dialect - OGLALA

Dakoda Indian - ARIKARA or REE

Dam - WEIR

Dance step - PAS

Dancer's handrail - BARRE

Dandruff - SCALL or SCURF

Dangerous atmosphere - MIAS MA

Dangerous mosquito - AEDES

Danish coin - ORA

Danish King - CNUTE

Danish port - ODENSE

Danube feeder - DRAVA, SAVA or SIRET

Daphni's love - CHLOE

Dark area of the moon - MARE

Dark eyed beauty - HOURI

Dark green mineral - AUGITE

Dark igneous rock - DIABAS

Dark redwood tree - TOON

Darnel - RYE GRASS

Dash - ELAN

Dassie - HYRAX

Daughter of Agamemnon - ELECTRA

Daughter of Amonasro - AIDA

Daughter of Anakin - LEIA

Daughter of Atlas - HYADES

Daughter of Cadmus - INO

Daughter of Cronus - HERA

Daughter of Dieppe - FILLE

Daughter of Geb - ISIS

Daughter of Helios - CIRCE

Daughter of Homer - LISA

Daughter of Hyperion - EOS or SELENE

Daughter of Jacob - DINAH

Daughter of Juan Carlos - ELENA

Daughter of Jupiter - DIANA

Daughter of King David - TAMAR

Daughter of King Juan Carlos - ELENA

Daughter of King Lear - GONERIL or REGAN

Daughter of King Minos - ARIADNE

Daughter of King Pelles - ALAINE

Daughter of Laban - LEAH

Daughter of Leda - HELEN

Daughter of Loki - HEL or HELA

Daughter of Mnemosyne - ERATO

Daughter of Muhammed - FATIMA

Daughter of Oceanus - DIONNE

Daughter of Oedipus - ANTIGONE

Daughter of Ops - CERES

Daughter of Poloneus - LAERTES or OPHILIA

Daughter of Poseidon - EVADNE or RHODE

Daughter of Prospero - MIRAND

Daughter of Rhea - HERA

Daughter of Satan - CERES

Daughter of Saturn - JUNO

Daughter of Tantalus - NIOBE

Daughter of Themis - IRENE

Daughter of Zeus - ATE, ATHENA, ERATO, HEBE, HELEN or IRENE

Dawn diety - AURORA

Dawn goddess - EOS

Dawn song - AUBADE

Day of wrath: Lat. - DIES IRAE

Daybreak song - AUBADE

Days of yore - ELD

Dazzling display - ECLAT

Dead Sea kingdom - EDOM

Deaden - OBTUND

Deadly poison - BANE or URARI

Deadly snake - MAMBA

Dear (Italy) - CARA

Death: pref. - NECRO

Death blow - CORP DE GRACE

Decadent - EFFETE

Deceive - COZEN or GULL

Decendant - SCION

Deciduous conifer - LARCH

Deck post - BITT

Decorate the edge - ENGRAIL

Decorative metalwork - NIELLO

Decorative ribbon - RIBAND

Decorative tinware - TOLLE

Decortive wall basin - LAVABO

Decree - UKASE

Deductive - APRIORI

Deep blue - ANIL or PERSE

Deep dry gulch - COULEE

Deep orange chalcedony - SARD

Deep secrets - ARCANA

Deep sleep - SOPOR

Deer - HART

Deer tail - SCUT

Defeat badly - LARRUP

Delhi stuffed pastry - SAMOSA

Delphinium - LARKSPUR

Demanding attention - CLAMANT

Demon - DJINN

Denmark's largest island - ZEALAND

Denpasar is its capiital - BALI

Deodar - CEDAR

Depict - LIMN

Depression in a bone - FOVEA

Descendants - SCIONS

Describe - LIMN

Desert garment - ABA

Desert or grassland - BIOME

Desert plant - AGAVE or EPHEDRA

Desicated - SERE

Desiduous conifer - LARCH

Designer's studio - ATELIER

Despot - SATRAP

Destiny goddesses - FATES

Detested person - ANATHEMA

Developing - NASCENT

Devil fish - MANTA

Devotee - VOTARY

Dexterous - HABILE

Diacritical mark - MACRON, TILDE or UMLAUT

Diacritical opposite - ANTIPODE

Diagram - SCHEMA

Dictator of ancient Rome - SULLA

Dido's love - AENEAS

Die-shaped - CUBOID

Digestive juice - PEPSIN

Digit - DACTYL

Digitalis sourse - FOXGLOVES

Dijon dance - GAJOT

Dijon donkey - ANE

Dilapidated tenaments - ROOKERIES

Dill, old style - ANET

Dill seed - ANIS

Dionysus follower - MAENAD

Diplomatic protest - DEMARCHE

Direction, in music - SAGUE

Directly - SPANG

Disciples - ACOLYTES

Disciplinarian - MARTINET

Discomfit - ABASH

Discriminate - SACERN

Disease carrying mosquito - AEDES

Disgrace - ODIUM

Disgusting - UGSOME

Dish stewed in wine - SALMI

Disparaging comment - HUMPH

Dispatch boat - AVISO

Distainful pout - MOUE

Distribution curves - OGIVES

Divine spirit - NUMEN

Diving bird - AUK, GANNET, GREBE,LOON, MURRE, MURRELET, SCOTER or SKUA

Diving duck - SCAUP or SCOTER

Diving sea bird - PETREL

Division of a long poem - CANTO

Division into fractions - SCHISM

Do all assistant - FACTOTEM

Doctor's replacement - LOCUM

Dog family - CANID

Dog in the sky - CANIS

Dog salmon - KETA

Dogstar - SIRIUS

Dogmas - ISM

Dolphin genus - INIA

Domesticated ox - ZEBU

Domination - HEGEMONY

Don Juan's mother - INEZ

Donkey - MOKE

Donut shape - TORUS

Donut shaped - TORIC

Doodad - GEEGAW

Doorkeeper of a lodge - TILER

Doormouse - LEROT

Doorway curtain - PORTIERE

Doosie - ONER

Doric dress - CHLAMYS

Dormant volcano in Peru - ELMISTI

Dorsal - NOTAL

Dorsal plate - NOTUM

Dos y dos - SUATRO

Dottering - ANILE

Double - BINAL

Double curve - OGEE

Double dagger - DIESIS

Double star in Auriga - CAPELLA

Dovekies - AUKS

Down under G.I. - ANZAC

Downhill challenge - MOGEL

Downhill run - PISTE

Downhiller's run - SCHUSS

Draft Org. - SSS

Dragon of puppetry - OLLIE

Dragonfly larva - NYMPH

Drain of color - ETIOLATE

Dramatic conflict - AGON

Drapery material - NINON

Draw a picture - LIMN

Drawstring handbag -
RETICULE

Dreaded mosquito - AEDES

Dream: Fr. - REVE

Dreamer - FANTAST

Dregs - LEES

Dresden duck - ENTE

Dress material - NINON

Dress shape - ALINE

Dried - SERE

Dried plants - HERBERIA

Drink deeply - BIRLE

Drink of forgetfulness -
NEPENTHE

Drivel - PAP

Dropsy - EDEMA

Dross - SCORIA

Drudge - DOGSBODY

Drudgery - MOIL

Drum set - TIMPANI

Drunkard - TOPER

Dry gully - WADI

Dry lakes - PLAYAS

Dry plaster painting - SECCO

Dry red wine - RIOJA

Drying frame - TENTER

Duck - SMEW

Duck genus - ANAS

Duct - VAS

Dugout: Fr. - ABRI

Dugout shelter - ABRI

Duke's domain - DUCHY

Dumplings - GNOCCHI

Dung - ORDURE

Dust particle - MOTE

Dutch cheese - LEYDEN

Dutch city - LEIDEN

Dutch city or commune - EDE

Dutch eathenware - DELFT

Dutch island - AROE

Dutch painting - STEEN

Dutch province - ZEELAND

Dutch river - IJSSEL

Dwarf buffalo - ANOA

Dwarf fish - PYGMEAN

Dying method - BATIC

Dying vat - KIER

Dynamite inventor - NOBEL

Dynasty of French Kings -
CAPET

Eagle in the night sky - AQUILA

Eagle's home - AERIE

Ear: pre. - OTO

Earache - OTALGIA

Ear bone - INCUS

Ear drum - TYMPANUM

Eared seal - OTARY

Earlier form of a word - ETYNOM

Early adder - ABACUS

Early Bible - ITALA

Early computer - ENIAC or UNIVAC

Early English coin - ORA

Early Irish alphabet - OGHAM

Early Jewish ascetic - ESSENE

Early Mexican inhabitant - OLMEC

Early podium - AMBO

Early radar - ASDIC

Early stage seed - OVULE

Earth goddess - GAEA

Earth: pre. - GEO

Earth quake - SEIS

Earth wolf - AARDWOLF

Earthenware crock - OLLA

Earthenware decorated with Opaqueglazes - FAIENCE

Earthenware from Holland - DELFT

Earthenware jar - CRUSE

Earthly - TERRENE

Earth's crust - HORST

Earth's crust layer - SIMA

Earthtone - OCHER

Earthworm and leech - ANNELIDS

Earthy pigment - OCHER

Earthy substance - SIENNA

Earthy tone - OCHER

East Indian boat - DONI

East Indian gum tree - DHAVA

East Indian heartwood - SAPAN

East Indian herb - SOLA

East Indian sailor - LASCAR

East Indian swine - BABIRUSA

Easter - PASCH

Easter Island - RAPA

Eastern Church member - UNIATE

Eastern eye makeup - KOHL

Eastern floor covering -TATAMI

Eastern Siberian - YAKUT

Eastern tip - BAKSHEESH

Eastern VIP - AGA

Easy lope - DOGTROT

Eccentric - FEY

Ecclesiastical caps - BIRETTAS

Ecclesiastical council - SYNOD

Ecclesiastical court - ROTA

Ecclesiastical residence - DEANERY

Edging loop - PICOT

Edible - ESCULENT

Edible clam - QUAHOG

Edible corkscrews - ROTINI

Edible root - PARSNIP

Edible roots - OCAS

Edible rootstock - EDDO

Edible seaweed - ARAME, DULSE or IRISH MOSS

Edible starchy root - JICAMA

Edible tuber - OCA, SALEP or TARO

Edict - FIAT or UKASE

Edit - REDACT

Eelworm - NEMA

Eerie - ELDRITCH

Effeminate - EPICENE

Egg - OOCYTE

Egg, for one - GAMETE

Egg: pref. - OVI

Egg shaped - OVOID

Egg shaped ornaments - OVA

Egg white - GLAIR

Egg-laying mammal - ECHIDNA

Eggplant salad - BABAGHANOUJ

Eggs, fish & rice dish - KEDGEREE

Eggy bread - CHALLAH

Egyptian amulet or beatle - SCARAB

Egyptian Christian - COPT

Egyptian corn - DURRA

Egyptian cross - ANKH

Egyptian diety or god - AMENRA, AMON, AMONRA, ATEN, HORUS, OSIRIS, PTAH, SEB or SHU

Egyptian god of evil - SET

Egyptian god of music - BES

Egyptian god of the Underground - OSIRIS

Egyptian god of tombs - ANUBIS

Egyptian god of the universe - AMENRA

Egypian goddess of magic - ISIS

Egyptian king of the dead - OSIRIS

Egyptian pharaoh - RAMSES

Egyptian sacred bull - APIS

Egyptian solar disk - ATEN

Egyptian sun god - AMENRA, ATEN or HORUS

Egyptian symbol of life - ANKH

Egyptian temple site - LUXOR

Egyptian underworld god - OSIRIS

Egyptian underworld queen - ISIS

Egyptian weight - ARDEB or KANTAR

Eight: Fr. - HUIT

Eight: (Italy) - OTTO

Eight: pref. - OCTA

Eight on the mohs scale - TOPAZ

Elaborate decoration - FROU FROU

Elaborate operetic solo - SCENA

Elaborate tapestry - ARRAS

Elbe feeder - EGER

Eldritch - EERIE

Electric battery inventor - VOLTA

Electric cat fish - RAAD

Electric horn - KLAXON

Electric measure - VOLT

Electrical unit - FARAD, GAUSS or TESLA

Electrical unit of conductance - MHO

Electrified particle - ION

Electron tube - TRIODE

Electronic control system -SERVO

Elegently designed - SOIGNE

Element #1 - HYDROGEN

Element #5 - BORON

Element #10 - NEON

Element #24 - CHROMIUM

Element #26 - IRON

Element #27 - COBALT

Element #29 - COPPER

Element #30 - ZINC

Element #34 - SELENIUM

Element#39 - ATTRIUM

Element #45 - RHODIUM

Element #50 - TIN

Element #53 - IODINE

Element #54 - XENON

Element #56 - BARIUM

Element #68 - ERBIUM

Element #72 - HAFNIUM

Element #75 - RHENIUM

Element #76 - OSMIUM

Element #77 - IRIDIUM

Element #79 - GOLD

Element #80 - MERC

Element #83 - BISMUTH

Element #86 - RADON

Element #99 - EINSTEINIUM

Element used in alloys - YTTRIUM

Elementary particle - BOSON, LEPTON or MUON

Elephant man - MAHOUT

Elevated tract of open country - WOLD

Elicit - EDUCE

Emancipate - MANUMIT

Embarrass - DISCOMFIT

Embropmoc sac - AMNION

Embroidery frame - TAMBOUR

Embroidery edging or loop - PICOT

Embroidery yarn - CREWEL

Emerald - BERYL

Emetic agent - IPECAC

Empedolcles last stand - AETNA

Emperor after Kaligula - CLAUDIUS

Emperor after Galba - OTHO

Emperor after Trajan - HADRIAN

Emperor of China - YAO

Empress of Byzantium - IRENE

Emu or rhea - RATITE

Enamalware - TOLE

Encampment - LAAGER

Enchanted - FEY

Encircles - GIRTS

Enclosed areas - VERGES

Enclosed part of a blimp - NACELLE

Enclosed passage in a church - NARTHEX

Enclosed within walls - IMMURE

Encore - BIS

Endangered antelope - ORYX

Endangered buffalo - ANOA

End of small intestine - ILEUM

Endive - ESCAROLE

Endure - DREE

Ends - OMEGAS

England, in poems - ALBION

English bard - SCOP

English cathedral city - ELY

English Channel Island - SARK

English cheese - STILTON

English dishboard - FACIA

English horn - COR

English monk - BEDE

English river - EXE

English seaport - DOVER

Entity's manifestation - AVATAR

Entomb - INTER or INURN

Entrance gallery - LOGGIA

Entrance to Hades - AVERNO

Entreat - OBTEST

Enzyme ending - ASE

Envoy - LEGATE

Enzyme stimulent - COFACTOR

Epic poem - ILIAD

Epoch - ERA

Equatorial's opposite - AXIAL

Equilateral parallelograms - RHOMBI

Equivocate - PALTER

Ermine - STOAT

Eros' love - PSYCHE

Eskimo craft - UMIAK

Eskimo knife - ULU

Eskimo settlement - ETAH

Esau's grandson - OMAR

Esau's twin - JACOB

Essayist - ELIA

Essential constituent of both RNA & DNA - GUANINE

Essential oil - ATTAR

Ethiopian prince or title - RAS

Eucharistic vessel - PYX

Eucharistic vestment - MANIPLE

Eurasian crows - DAWS

Eurasian deer - ROES

Eurasian duck - SMEW

Eurasian falcons- SAKERS

Eurasian fish - LOACH

Eurasian forest - TAIGA

Eurasian grass - REDTOP

Euroasian mountains - URAL

Eurasian primrose - OXLIP

Euransian ruminant - ROEDEER

Eurasian sandpiper - REE

Eurasian tree - OLEANSTER

Europe's largest lake - BALATON

European barracuda - SPEC

European blackbird - MERL or OUZEL

European canary - SERIN

European card game - OMBRE

European ciema - KINO

European cows - DAWS

European crow - CHOUGH

European doormouse - LEROT

European eagle - ERN

European ermine - STOAT

European finch - SERIN

European flowering tree - OLEASTER

European gull - MEW

European lake - ONEGA

European mint - HYSSOP

European plantain - FLEAWORT

European polecat - FERRET

European shore bird - DOTTEREL

European songbird - WOODLARK

European thrush - MERLE or MISTLE

European tree - SORB

European water bird - OUSEL

European weed - GOAT'S BEARD

European wheat - SPELT

Evening bell or star - VESPER

Evergreen - YEW

Evergreen oak - HOLM

Evergreen of the Pacific Northwest - MADRONO

Evergreen shrub - ILEX or TOYON

Evolutionary theory - COSMISM

Ewe's-milk cheese - PECORINA

Exact opposites - ANTIPODES

Exaggerated pride - HUBRIS

Examine by touch - PALPATE

Excessive flow of saliva - PTYALISM

Exchange premium - AGIO

Excretes - EGESES

Exodys figure - AARON

Exodus hero - ARI

Expert - MAVEN

Expert hunter - NIMROD

Exploit - GESTE

Explosive - TONITE

Explosive compound - AMATOL

Explosive gas - FIREDAMP

Explosive ingredient - TOLUENE

Expressively, in music - RUBATO

External boundary - AMBIT

Extinct bird - DODO or MOA

Extract - ELUTE

Extremely dry - XERIC

Eye annoyances - MOTES

Eye lashes – CILIA

Eyelike spots - OCELLI

Eye makeup - KOHLS

Eye membrane - SCLERA

Eye part - CORNIA, IRIS, RETINA or UVEA

Eyeball covering - SCLERA

Eyelike spots - OCELLI

Eyes - OCULI

Fabled bird - ROC

Fabric dyeing technique - BATIC

Fabric finish - PLISSE

Facade part - CEDILLA

Facing a glacier - STOSS

Fading away - EVANESCING

Fairylike creature - PERI

Fairy king - OBERON

Fairy queen - MAB or TITANIA

Fake pearl - OLIVET

Falconry strap - JESS

False argument - SOPHISM

False god - BAAL

False report - CANARD

Falsely blamed - TRADUCED

Famed hostess - MESTA

Fancy cakes - GATEAUX

Fancy marbles - TAWS

Fancy timepiece - HOROLOGE

Far East weight - TAEL

Farewell - VALE

Far flying seabird - PETREL

Farm cart - WAIN

Fast, in music - MOSSO

Fast and exciting, in music - AGITATO

Fast vibreto, in music - TREMOLO

Fat - ADIPOSE or LIPO

Fat component - OLEIN

Fatal bacteria - ANTHRAX

Father of Abraham - TERAH

Father of Achiles - PELEUS

Father of Agamemnon - ATREUS

Father of Ahab - OM

Father of Ajax - TELAMON

Father of Antigone - OEDIPUS

Father of Aaron - AMRAN

Father of Balder - ODIN

Father of Cainan - ENOS

Father of Cassandra - PRIAM

Father of Dauphin - ROI

Father of Diomedes - ARES

Father of Electra - AGAMEMNON

Father of Eliphax - ENOS

Father of Enos - SETH

Father of Esau - ISAAC

Father of Fauvism - MATISSE

Father of Hannibal - AGAMEMNON

Father of Harmonia - ARES

Father of Hector - PRIAM

Father of Horus - OSIRIS

Father of Icarus - DAEDALUS

Father of Isaac - ABRAHAM

Father of Jacob - ISAAC

Father of Japheth - NOAH

Father of John the Baptist - ZACHARIAS

Father of Joseph - JACOB

Father of Junipero - TERRA

Father of King Arthur - UTHER

Father of King David - JESSE

Father of King Harald - OLAV

Father of Leah - LABAN

Father of Menelaus - ATREUS

Father of Methuselah - ENOCH

Father of Moab - LOT

Father of Moses - AMRAN

Father of Niobe - TANTALUS

Father of Odysseus - LAERTES

Father of Paris - PRIAM

Father of Phobos - ARES

Father of Rachel - LABAN

Father of Regan - LEER

Father of Reuel - ENOS

Father of Romulus - MARS

Father of Seth - ADAM

Father of Teucer - TELAMON

Father of Theseus - AEGEUS

Father of Thor - ODIN

Father of Zeus - CRONUS

Father of the gods - AMENRA

Father of the Muses - ZEUS

Father of the Titans - URANUS

Fatty - ADIPOSE

Fatty acid - OLEIC or
    STEARATE

Fatty compound - LIPID

Faultfinder of Olympus -
    MOMUS

Faux pas - GAFFE

FDR's dog - FALA

Fe - IRON

Fear of foreigners -
    XENOPHOBIA

Feared mosquito - AEDES

Feast of lots - PURIM

Feathered head ornament -
    AIGRETTE

Febrile condition - AGUE

Felt sunhat - TERAI

Felt-like fabric - BAIZE

Female advisor - EGERIA

Female demon - LAMIA

Female donkey - JENNET

Female fox - VIXEN

Female gamete - OVUM

Female lovers - INAMORATES

Female prophet - SIBYL

Female red deer - HIND

Female ruff - REE or REEVE

Female sandpiper - REE

Female surfer - WAHINE

Female swan - PEN

Female swimmer - NAIAD

Female vampire - LAMI

Female water sprite - UNDINE

Fence pickets - PILING

Fencing dummy - PEL

Fencing feint - APPEL

Fencing foil - EPEE or FLEURET

Fermented foam - BARM

Fern-like plant - CYCAD

Fertile earth - MARL

Fertile loam - LOESS

Fertility god - BAAL

Fertilizer compound or ingredient
    - UREA or BONEASH

Fertilizer sourse - GUANO

Fertilizer sype - MARL

Fettering - GYVING

Feudal estate - FIEFDOM

Feudal land - FIEF

Feudal lord - LIEGE, MESNE or THANE

Feudal serf or worker - ESNE

Feverish - FEBRILE

Fiber - NEP or RAFFIA

Fiber palm - RAFFIA

Fiber plant - ABACA, ALOE, HEMP or THANEX

Fictional ring bearer - FRODO

Field mouse - VOLE

Fiery root - WASABI

Fifth canonical hour - NONES

Fifth pillar of Islam - HAJ

Fig genus - FICUS

Figure eight scale on a globe - ANALEMMA

Figure of speach - TROPE

Film - PATINA

Film fan - CINEAST

Filthy lucre - PELF

Finales - CODAS

Finch - SERIN

Find fault - CAVIL

Fine - AMERSE

Fine cigar - CLARO

Fine cotton - PIMA

Fine grained rock - TRAP

Fine twilled linen - DAMASK

Fine violin - AMATI

Finely ground gypsum - TERRAALBA

Finger or toe - DACTYL

Finger pressure - SHIATSU

Fingernail crescent - LUNULA

Finial - EPI

Finsh seaport - TURKU

Firecracker - PETARD

Fireopal - GIRASOL

Fireplace - INGLE

Fireplace projection or shelf - HOB

First book of prophets - HOSEA

First Chinese capitol - NARA

First computer - ENIAC

First canonical hour - MATIN

First family of Florence - MEDICI

First Hebrew king - SAUL

First King of Egypt - MENES

Firth of Clyde Island - ARRAN

Fish genus - AMIA

Fish hawk - OSPREY

Fish-eating duck - SMEW

Fish serving - SASHIMI

Fishing line - SNELL

Fishing net - SEINE

Fistic Muslim - ALI

Flaky pastry - FILO or PHYLLO

Flanders River - YSER

Flask - DEWAR

Flat bread of India - NAN

Flat fish - DAB, PLAICE or
SKATE

Flat plinth - ORLO

Flavored wine - KIR or NEGUS

Flavorful - SAPID

Flaw - WART

Flax filament - HARL

Flax-like fiber - RAMIE

Flea genus - TUNGA

Fleet of ships - ARGOSY

Flemish capital - GHENT

Flemish River - YSER

Fleshy fruit - PEPO

Fleshy stone fruit - DRUPE

Fleur-de-lis - IRIS

Fleuret - EPEE

Flight of Mohammed -
HEGIRA

Flightless bird - RHEA

Flintlock musket - FUSIL

Flint-like rock - CHERT

Flip over - OBVERT

Flock of geese - SKEIN

Flora and fauna - BIOTA

Floral specialist - ROSARIAN

Florence fennel -
FINOCCHIO

Florentine palace - PITTI

Florid musical passage -
BRAVURA

Flower arrangement - UMBEL

Flower cluster - AMENT,
CATKIN, RACEME or
UMBEL

Flower of the southwest -
PENOLE

Flower part - CALYX,
NECTARY or SEPAL

Flower polyp - ANEMONE

Flowing moss - PYXIE

Flower spike - AMENT

Flowering tree - CATALPA

Fluid carrier - VENA

Fly - AVIATE

Fly before the wind - SCUD

Fly catcher - PHOEBE

Fly catching bird - PEWEE

Flying flock of geese - SKEIN

Foam - SPUME

Focal point - NODE

Fodder grass - MILLET or
SORGO

Folk medicine plant - BONESET

Follow without interruption - SEGUE

Follower of Zeno - STOIC

Fondle - COSSET

Food - ALIMENT

Food-coloring plant - SAFFRON

Food fish - BASS, CERO, HADDOCK, HAKE, IDE, LING, PERCH, PIKE, SCUP, SHAD, SMELT, SNAPPER, SOLE or TUNA

Food of forgetfulness - LOTUS

Food of the gods - AMBROSIA

Food scrap - ORT

Food stuf from orchids - SALEP

Fool, of yore - MOME

Foolish - GLAIKIT

Foolish talk - BOSH

Foot bones - TARSI

Footless - APODAL

Footlike part - PES

Footnote abbr. - ETSEQ or IBID

Footnote word - IBIDEM

For both sexes - EPICENE

Forage crop - SOYA

Forage legume - GUAR

Forbidden City - LHASA

Force - DINT

Forcefully - AMAIN

Forcible seizure of property - RAPINE

Foreboding atmosphere - MIASMA

Foreigner to Honolulu - HAOLE

Foreigner: pref. - XENO

Forerunner of the KGB - OGPU

Forest diety - PA

Forest of evergreens - PINERY

Forested area - SILVA

Foretell - AUGUR or SPAE

Foreword - PROEM

Forgetfulness - LETHE

Fork-tailed flier - KITE

Form of boxing - SAVATE

Form of sugar - HEXXOS

Formal assumption - LEMMA

Formal pronouncements - DICTA

Formally, once - ERST

Formative seed - OVULE

Former African kingdom - ASHANTI

Former African rulers - DEYS

Former capital of Spain - TOLEDO

Former British coin - FARTHING

Former capital of Japan - EDO, KYOTO or NARA

Former capital of Kazakhstan - ALMAATA

Former coin of Iran - KRAN

Former French coin - ECU

Former Hungarian coin - PENGO

Former Latvian coins - LATI

Former part of USSR - KAZAKHSTAN, KYRGYZSTAN, TAJIKISTAN or UZBEKISTAN

Former Puruvian currency - INTL

Former Queen of Jordan - ALIA

Former Queen of Spain - ENA

Former Spanish coin - DOBLA, DURO or REAL

Former weight for wool - TOD

Formerly, formerly - ERST or WHILOM

Forskers of the Faith - APOSTATES

Fort parts - REDOUCTS

Forte - METIER

Fortification - REDAN

Fossil resin - AMBER or COPAL

Foul smelling - OLID

Found in lakes - LACUSTRINE

Founder of Babylon - SEMIRAMIS

Founder of Stoicism - ZENO

Four fluid ounces - GILL

Four pence - GROAT

Foursome - TETRAD

Fourteen line poem - RONDEL

Fourth caliph - ALI

Fragrant, of old - OLENT

Fragrant gum - TOLU

Fragrant ointment - NARD

Fragrant oleoresin - ELEMI

Fragrant resin - ELEMI or TOLU

Fragrant rootstock - ORRIS

Framework - CADRE or SCHEMA

Frankish - SALIC

Fraulein's frock - DIRNDL

Freckle - LENTIGO

Freezing - GELID

French apartment payments - RENTES

French brandy - ARMAGNAC

French card game - ECARTE

French cathedral city - NIMES

French cavalryman - SPAHI

French city - STLO

French clergyman - ABBE

French coins - ECUS

French comune - CAEN

French corp. - CIE

French department - ISERE or ORNE

French earl - COMPE

French eye - OEIL

French goose - OIE

French help - AMOI

French inn - AUBERGE

French lace - VAL

French landscape painter - COROT

French lawmaking group - SENAT

French leather - CUIR

French military leader - NEY

French noble - COMTE or VICOMTE

French patron saint - DENIS

French port - CALAIS

French possessive pronoun - SES

French queen - REINE

French river - AISNE, ISERE, LOIRE, OISE or ORNE

French seaport - BREST

French smell - ODEUR

French soldier - POILU

French soldiers - ARMEE

French soldier's hats - KEPIS

French stew - RATATOUILLE

French story - ETAGE

French textile city LILLE

French vineyard - CRU

French wine region - ALSACE

Frenchman's income - RENTE

Frenchmen - GAULS

Frenzied female - MAENAD

Frequency distributions - OGIVES

Freshwater crustacean - ISOPOD

Freshwater fish - DACE, PLATY or ROACH

Freshwater green algae - DESMID

Freshwater mussel - UNIO

Freshwater polyps - NYDRAE

Friend of Job - ELIHU

Friction match - FUSEE or LOCOFOCO

Friend of Hamlet's - HORATIO

Frilly hat - MOBCAP

Frog genus - RANA

From oil - OLEIC

Froth - SPUME

Frozen desert - BOMBE

Fruit cakes - SIMNELS

Fruit decay - BLET

Fruit of the maple tree - SAMARA

Fruit of the rowan - SORB

Fruit salt - CITRATE

Fruit type - UVA

Fuji footwear - ZORI

Fulda river feeder - EDER

Full of cracks - RIMOSE

Full of froth - SPUMY

Full of wisdom - SAPIENT

Full skirt - DIRNDL

Fullness - PLENUM

Fulmar - PETREL

Funeral music - DIRGE

Fungi reproduction - ISOGAMY

Fur trader - FELLMONGER

Furies, in Greek myth - ERINYES

Furry - PILOSE

Fur-trimmed cloak - PELISSE

Future ovum - OOCYTE

Gabled window - DORMER

Gaea, for one - GODDESS

Gaelic - ERSE

Gaelic sea god - LER

Galatea's beloved - ACIS

Gallic goose - AIE

Gambling expert - SCARNE

Game fish - CERO

Game point, in tennis - ADIN

Game ragout - SALMI

Gamets - OVA

Gaming table cover - BAIZE

Gannet goose - SOLAN

Gap - LACUNA

Gaping grin - RICTUS

Garden pest genus - APHI

Garden rocket - ARUGULA

Garden tool - DIBBLE

Garden trumpet - DATURA

Gargantua creator - RABELAIS

Garland, old style - ANADEM

Garland for the head - ANADEM
  or CHAPLET

Garlic mayonnaise or sauce -
  AIOLI

Gauzy fabric - LENO

Gazelle hound - SALUKI

Geisha's instrument - SAMISEN

Gelded male pigs - GALTS

Gelling agent - AGAR

Gem faces - CULETS

Gemlike stone - SARD

Gemsbok - ORYX

Gemstone - LAPIS

Genetic enzyme - RNASE

Geneva's lake - LEMAN

Genre - SORT

Gentle slope - GLACIS

Genuine - PUKKA

Genuine: Ger. - ECHT

Genus of birds - PITTA

Genus of dogs - CANIS

Genus of frogs - AHURA

Genus of furs - ABIES

Genus of geese - ANSER

Genus of grass - AVENA

Genus of herbs - GILIA

Genus of heather – ERICA

Genus of lizards - AGAMA

Genus of olives - OLEA

Genus of palms - ARENGA

Genus of sheep - OVIS

Genus of showy plants - SCABIOSA

Genus of shrubs - BERBERIS

Genus of species - TAXON

Geological epoch - EOCENE or MIOCENE

Geological period - AXOIC or NEOCENE

Geological ridge - ESKER

Geometric Buddhist designs - MANDELAS

Geometric curve - PARABOLA

Geometric figure - RHOMBUS

Geometric structure - FRACTAL

Geraint'slady - ENID

German article - DER

German basin - SAAR

German city - HALLE

German coal region - SAAR

German folk songs - LIEDER

German for Germans - DEUTSCH

German fruit bread - STOLLEN

German industrial region - SAAR

German porcelain - MEISSEN

German river - EDER, EGER or EMS

German seaport - EMDEN

German wine - RHENISH

Germanic god of thunder - DONAR

Germanic god of war - TIU

Germanic water spirit - NIXIE

Getup and go - BRIO

Giant in Norse mythology - YMIR

Giant with a hundred eyes - ARGUS

Ginger plants - CURCUMAS

Giraffe relative - OKAPI

Girasol - OPAL

Give off - EGEST

Glacial deposit - MORAINE

Glacial groove - STRIA

Glacial mass - SERAC

Glacial pinnacle or ridges - ESKER, OSAR or SERAC

Glacial snow - NEVE

Gladly - LIEF

Glass: Fr. - VERRE

Glass component - SILICA

Glassmaker's oven - LEHR

Glass-polishing powder - CERIA

Gliding dance step - CHASSE

Gloomy - STYGIAN

Gloomy and obscure - TENEBROUS

Goat antelope - SEROW

Goat of Asia - SEROW

Goat cheese - CHEVRE or FETA

Goat legged diety - FAUN

Goatlike antelope - SAIGA

God of Agriculture - SATURN

God of commerse or cunning - HERMES

God of discord - LOKI

God of doorways - JANUS

God of fertility - BAAL

God of fire - AGNI or LOGI

God of Hades - ORCUS

God of India - KRISHNA

God of love - CUPIOD, EROS or KAMA

God of marriage - HYMAN

God of Memphis - PTAH

God of mischief - LOKI

God of music - APOLLO

God of old Memphis - PTAH

God of passion - EROS

God of pleasure - BES

God of ridicule - MOMUS

God of sleep - HYPNOS

God of Spain - DIOS

God of Strife - TYR

God the ancients - DAEMON

God of the east wind - EURUS

God of the heavens - ZEUS

God of the Incas - VIRACOCHA

God of the lower world - DIS

God of the north wind - BOREAS

God of Thebes - AMON

God of the sea - AEGIR, NEPTUNE or POSEIDEN

God of the sun - ATEN or HELIOS

Godof the underworld - DIS or PLUTO

God of the universe - AMENRA

God of the winds - AEOLUS

God of wisdom - THOTH

God of thunder - DONAR or THOR

God of war - ARES, TIU or TYR

God of war, magic & poetry - ODIN

God's blood - ICHOR

Goddess of abundance - OPS

Goddess of agriculture - CERES

Goddess of beauty - VENUS

Goddess of chance - TYCHE

Goddess of child bearing - HERA

Goddess of childbirth - HERA

Goddess of criminal folly - ATE

Goddess of dawn - AURORA or EOS

Goddess of destiny - FATES, FORTUNA, ORN or URD

Goddess of discord - ATE or ERIS

Goddess of divine retribution - NEMESIS

Goddess of earth - GAEA

Goddess of fate - NORN

Goddess of fertility - ASTARTE or ISIS

Goddess of folly - ATE

Goddess of fortune - TYCHE

Goddess of fruit trees - POMONA

Goddess of hades - HECATE

Goddess of healing - EIR

Goddess of hope - SPES

Goddess of justice - ASTRAEA

Goddess of love - APHRODITE, ASTART or VENUS

Goddess of love poetry - ERATO

Goddess of magic - ISIS

Goddess of marriage - JUNO

Goddess of mischief - ERIN

Goddess of nature - ISIS

Goddess of night - NOX

Goddess of Norse myth - NURN

Goddess of peace - IRENE or PAX

Goddess of plenty - OPS

Goddess of recklessness - ATE

Goddess of sorcery - HECATE

Goddess of strife - DISCORDIA or ERIS

Goddess of the earth - GAEA or RHEA

Goddess of the harvest - CERES or OPS

Goddess of the hearth - HESTIA or VESTA

Goddess of the hunt - ARTEMIS or DIANA

Goddess of the moon - ARTEMIS, DIANA, HECATE or SELENE

Goddess of the Nile - ISIS

Goddess of the rainbow - IRIS

Goddess of the seasons - HORAE

Goddess of the underworld - HECATE

Goddess of vengance - NEMESIS

Goddess of victory - NIKE

Goddess of war - ATHENA, ENYO or SELLONA

Goddess who loved Odysseus - CIRCE

Goddess of wisdom - ATHENA

Goddess of witchcraft - HECATE

Goddess of Youth - HEBE

Goddess with an owl - ATHENA

Goddess with cow horns - ISIS

Gods of ancient Rome - DEI

Gold braid - ORRIS

Gold coin of ancient Rome - SOLIDUS

Gold coin of old - DUCAT

Gold: Sp. - ORO

Gold/Silver alloy - ELECTRUM

Golden - AURIC

Golden tin alloy - ORMOLU

Golf ball covering - BALATA

Golf term - DORMIE

Gong - TAMTAM

Goose - BRANT

Goosefoot plant - ORACH

Goose genus - ANSER

Gorge - ARROYO

Gormet delight - VIAND

Gothic arch - OGIVE

Gourd-like plant - CUCURBIT

Government by a few - OLIGARCHY

Govt. org. - USIA

Graceful girl - SYLPH

Grafting shoot - SCION

Grain awn - ARISTA

Grain beard - AWN

Grain blight - ERGOT

Grain bristles - ARISTAE

Grain diety - SERES

Grain sorghum - KAFIR

Granada governess - DUENNA

Granada greeting - HOLA

Grand - HOMERIC

Grand dame - DOYEN

Grand slam - VOLE

Grandchild of Japanese Immigrants - SANSEI

Grandfather of Abraham - NAHOR

Grandfather of Saul - NER

Grandma Moses first name - ANNA

Grandmother to Caesar - AVIA

Grandson of Abraham - JACOB

Grandson of Jacob - ERI

Grandson of Methuselah - NOAH

Granitelike rock - GNEISS

Grape, e.g. - UVA

Grapefruit hybrid - UGLI

Grapefruit kin - POMELO

Graph line - YAXIS

Grass or sedge stem - CULM

Grassland - LEA

Grassland area - PAMPA

Grasslike plant - SEDGE

Grassy area - SWARD

Grassy plain - LLANO

Gravelly ridges - OSAR

Gravid - PREGNANT

Gray haired - HOARY

Gray horse - DUN

Gray mineral - TRONA

Grayish green - RESEDA

Grayish blend of colors - LOVAT

Grayish brown duck - GADWALL

Graylags - GEESE

Greaseproof paper - GLASSINE

Great barrier island - OTEA

Great helmsman follower - MAOIST

Great: Lat. - MAGNA

Great lakes whitefish - CISCO

Great mosque site - ALEPPO

Greater Omenta - CAULS

Grecian Theater - ODEA

Greedy - ESURIENT or RAPACIOUS

Greek - ARGIVE or HELLENE

Greek adviser - NESTOR

Greek aurora - EOS

Greek cafe - TAVERNERA

Greek cheese - FETA

Greek city/state - POLIS

Greek colonade - STOA

Greek colony - IONIA

Greek community - DEME

Greek concert site - ODEA

Greek concubines - HETAERAE

Greek contest - AGON

Greek cross - TAU

Greek demigod - SATYR

Greek dessert - BAKLAVA

Greek diety - HERMES

Greek drink - RETSINA

Greek earth goddess - HECATE

Greek flask - OLPE

Greek goat god - PAN

Greek goddess - ATHENA, HERA or ORNYX

Greek goddess of the moon - SELENE

Greek harp - TRIGON

Greek heaven - URANUS

Greek horseshoe - OMEGA

Greek island - CRETE, DELOS KITHERA, SAMOS or TINOS

Greek lasagna - MOUSSAKA

Greek letter - ALPHA(1), BETA(2), CHI(22), DELTA(4), EPSILON(5), ETA(7), GAMMA(3), IOTA(9), KAPPA(10), LAMBDA(11), MU(12), NU(13), OMEGA(24), OMICRON(15), PHI(21), PI(16), PSI(23), SIGMA(18), RHO(17), TAU(19), THETA(8), UPSILON(20), XI(14), or ZETA(6)

Greek legislature - BOULE

Greek lyric poem - EPODE

Greek lyric poet - SAPPHO

Greek marketplace - AGORA

Greek monster - LAMIA

Greek monument - SELA

Greek mount - ATHOS

Greek peak - OSSA

Greek philospher DIOGENES, TIMON or ZENO

Greek Physician - GALEN

Greek portico - STOA

Greek resistance movement- ELAS

Greek/Roman god - APOLLO

Greek sculptor - PHIDIAS

Greek sorceress - MEDEA

Greek temple - NAOS

Greek under ground river - LETHE

Greek war god - ARES

Greek warrior - AJAX

Greek weeper - NIOBE

Greek weight units - OBOLI

Greek wind god - AEOLUS

Greek wine - RETSINA

Greek wine flask - OLPE

Greek woods god - PAN

Green - VERDANT or VIRID

Green fly - APHID

Green gem - BERYL or PERIDOT

Green, in heraldy - VERT

Green parrots - KEAS

Green turtles - CHELONIA

Greenbrier - SMILAX

Greenhorn - NAIF

Greenish sloths - STIKINE

Gribble - ISOPOD

Grimace - MOUE

Groom: var. - OSTLER

Groove - STRIA

Group fund - TONTINE

Group of badgers - CETE

Group of eight - OCTAD or OCTIVE

Group of five - PENTAD

Group of four - TETRAD

Group of frogs - ARMY

Group of geese - GAGGLE or SKEIN

Group of larks - BEVY

Group of nine - NONET or ENNEAD

Group of one hundred - SENATE

Group of pheasants - NIDE

Group of poems - EPOS

Group of quail - BEVY

Group of seven -HEPTAD or SEPTET

Group of six - HEXAD

Group of three - TRIAD or TRINE

Group of toads - KNOT

Group of turtles - BALE

Group of twenty - SCORE

Group of two - DYAD

Grow together - ACCRETE

Growing around rocks - SAXATILE

Growing old - SENESCENT

Growl - GNAR

Guardian spirits - LARES

Guest bungalow - CASITA

Guidonian note - ELA

Guilded - AUREATE

Guinea pig - CAVY

Guitar cousin - SAMISEN

Guitar device - CAPO

Guitar solo - RIFF

Gulch - COULEE

Gulf of Aden vessel - DHOW

Gullet - MAW

Gullible one - NAIF

Gulliver's first name - LEMUEL

Gully - NULLAH

Gum Arabic tree - ACACIA

Gum base - CHICKLE

Gum resin - ELEMI

Gum-producing plant - GUAR

Gunundrum's husband or victim - ATLI

Gunwale pin - THOLE

Guru's community or retreat - ASHRAM

Gutta-Percha alternative - BALATA

Guttersnipe - GAMIN

Gypsy - CALO or ROMANY

Gypsy males - ROMS

Gyro compass inventor - SPERRY

Habit - WONT

Hacienda room - SALA

Haggis ingredient - OATS

Hair covering - MANTILLA

Hair protein - KERATIN

Hairlike structure - PILUS

Hairy - HIRSUTE or PILOSE

Hairy ox - YAK

Half - MOIETY

Half a cone - NAPP

Half a decade - LUSTRUM

Half a Zwei - EINS

Half brother of Athena - ARES

Half-goat man - FAUN or
   SATYR

Half eagle, half lion creature -
   GRIFFIN

Half note - MINIM

Hallux - TOE

Halogen compound - HALIDE

Halogen salt - IODATE

Hamite - AGAO

Hamlet - DORP or THORP

Hamlet's home - ELSINORE

Ham's relative - CBER

Hand died fabric - BATIK

Hand operated mill - QUERN

Hand tied fly - HERL

Hand woven rugs - RYAS

Handel opera - SEMELE

Handrail post - NEWEL

Hands: Sp. - MANO

Hang fire - PEND

Hanging basket plant -
   VERBENA

Hanoi dress - AODAI

Happiness - EUDAEMONIA

Hard, crisp bread - RUSK

Hard, crumbly cheese - ASIAGO

Hard money - SPECIE

Hard liquor - ARAK or ARRACK

Hard resin - COPAL

Hard rubber - EBONITE

Hardy wheat - SPELT

Hare constelation - LEPUS

Harem - SERAGLIO, SERAI
   or ZENANA

Harem room - ODA

Harness part - HAME

Harness ring - TERRET

Harpsicor - CEMBALO

Harridan - SHREW

Harshness - ASPERITY

Hartebeest - TORA

Harvest blubbler - FLENSE

Hat ornament - TORSADE

Hatred - ANIMUS

Haul with tackle - BOUSE or
   BOWSE

Hautboy - OBOE

Having a ragged edge - EROSE

Having handles - ANSATE

Having no key - ATONAL

Having wings - ALAR

Hawaiian acacia - JOA

Hawaiian beverage - KAVA

Hawaiian carving - TIKI

Hawaiian chant - MELE

Hawaiian cloth - TAPA

Hawaiian coffee - KONA

Hawaiian cooking pit - IMU

Hawaiian goose - NENE

Hawaiian grass - HILO

Hawaiian hawk - IOS

Hawaiian island - KAUAI, LANAI or OAHU

Hawaiian non-native - HAOLE

Hawaiian song - MELE

Hawaiian thrush - OMAO or SHAMA

Hawaiian tree - KOA

Hawaiian tuber - TARO

Hawaiian tuna - AHI

Hawaian VIP - KAHUNA

Hawaiian wind - KONA

Hawk cage - MEW

Hawk-headed god - HORUS

Hawk parrot - HIA

Hay wagon - WAIN

Headache remedy - APC

Head band - BANDEAU

Head wreath - ANADEM

Headland - NESS

Healthful - SALUTARY

Healthy: Fr. - SAIN

Healing herb - COMFREY

Heart chamber - ATRIA

Hearth - INGLE

Heat resistant material - CERMET

Heather - LING

Heather genus - ERICA

Heaven: comb.form or prefix - URANO

Heavenly - SUPERNAL

Heavenly altar - ARA

Heaviest metal - OSMIUM

Heavy barge - HOY

Heavy drapery fabric - MOREEN

Heavy mallet - MAUL

Heavy material - LODEN

Heavy metric weight - TONNE

Heavy particle - BARYON

Heavy reading - TOME

Heavy silk fabric - SAMITE

Heavy twillied fabric - PRUNELLA

Nebdomad - WEEK

Hebrew ascetic - ESSENE

Hebrew dry measure - OMER

Hebrew eve - EREB

Hebrew dry measure - EPHAH

Hebrew fathers - ABBAS

Hebrew holiday - PURIM

Hebrew judge - ELI

Hebrew leader: var. - ALEF

Hebrew letter - ALEPH (1), BETH (2), AYIN (16), DALETH (4), GIMEL (3), HEH (5), HETH (8), KAPH (11), LAMED (12), MEM (13), NUN(14), PEH(17), QOPH(19), RESH(20), SADHE(18), SAMEKH(15), SHIN(21), SIN(22), TAV(23), TETH(9), TSADE(18), WAW(6), YOD(10) or ZAYIN (7)

Hebrew letter: var. - ALEF

Hebrew lyre - ASOR

Hebrew measure - EPHAH, KOR or OMER

Hebrew monastic brotherhood - ESSENAS

Hebrew month - ADAR (6), AV (11), ELUL (12), HESHVAN (2), YAR (8), KISLEV (3), NISAN (7), OMER, SHEBAT (5), SIVAN (9), TAMMUZ (10), TEVET (4) or TISHRI (1)

Hebrew patroarch - ABRAHAM

Hebrew priest - ELI

Hebrew prophet - AMOS, ELISHA, EZEKIEL, HOSEA, ISAIAH, JEREMIAH, MICAH or NAHUM

Hebrew school - YESHIVA

Hebrew ten - ESER

Hewbrew toast - LCHAIM

Hebrew underworld - SHEOL

Hebrew weight - OMER or REBA

Hebrew zither - ASOR

Hebrides Island - IONA or SKYE

Heir - SCION

Helen of Troy's mother - LEDA

Heliotrope - BLOODSTONE

Hellenic: pref. - GRECO

Hellenic letter - PHI or ETA

Helmet - CASQUE

Helmet with a visor - BASINET

Helmet shaped - GALEATE

Helmet wreath - ORLE

Hemp fibre for caulking - OAKUM

Hemp for rope - SISAL

Heraldic - ARMORIAL

Heraldic band border or filets - ORLE

Heraldic cross - SALTIRE

Heraldic dragon - WYVERN

Heraldic fur - VAIR

Heraldic design - SEME

Heraaldic silver - ARGENT

Herald's tunic - TABARDS

Heraldry wreath - TORSE

Herbal beverage - INFUSION or TISANE

Herbal drink - SAGE TEA

Herculon's fiber - OLEFIN

Here: Sp. - ACA

Heretofore - ERENOW

Hermit - ERMITE

Heroic champion - PALADIN

Heroic tale - EPOS

Heroin - SCAG

Heroine of "The Last Days of Pompeii - IONE

Heron colony - SIEGE

Herring - SPRAT

Herring kin - SHAD

Herringlike fish - MOONEYE

Hic-Hoc link - HAEC

Hidden - PERDU

High altitude probe - SONDE

High dudgeon - IRE

High energy snack - GORP

High explosive - TONITE

High grade cotton - PIMA

High plateau - PUNA

High protein stuff - MISO

High society - BON TON

Highland hillside - BRAE

Highland plant - GORSE

Highland tongue - ERSE

Highly seasoned stew - BURGOO

Hillock – KNOLL

Hillside Dugout or shelter - ABRI

Him in Italy - LUI

Himalayan antelope - SEROW

Himalayan Buddhist language - PALI

Himalayan cedars - DEODARS

Himalayan monkhood - ATIS

Himalayan River - GANGES

Himalayan wild goat - TAHR

Hindu ascetic - FAKIR, SADHU or YOGI

Hindu creator - BRAHMA

Hindu diety - DEVA, RAMA, SIVA or VISHNU

Hindu disipline - YOGA

Hindu doctorine - TANTRA

Hindu garment - SARI

Hindu gateway - TORAN

Hindu gentleman - BABU

Hindu god - DEVA, MARA, RAMA or SIVA

Hindu god of desire - KAMA

Hindu god of destruction - SHEVA or SIVA

Hindu god of fire - AGNI

Hindu god of love - KAMA

Hindu goddess - DEVA, DEVI, KALI or VAC

Hindu gods - DEVAS

Hindu holy man - SADHU

Hindu honorific - SWAMI

Hindu incarnation - AVATAR

Hindu law giver - MANU

Hindu loincloth - DHOTI

Hindu master - SWAMI

Hindu maxim - SUTRA

Hindu music - RAGA

Hindu mystic - YOGI

Hindu peasand - RYOT

Hindu philosophy - VEDANTA

Hindu prince or ruler - RAJA

Hindu queen - ASURA or RANEE

Hindu rain god - INDRA

Hindu retreat - ASHRAM

Hindu sacred text or scripture - VEDA

Hindu sage - RISHI

Hindu scripture - VEDA

Hindu slave girl - DASI

Hindu spirit - AHURA

Hindu teacher - GURU or SWAMI

Hindu title of respect - SHRI or SRI

Hindu truths - SUTRA

Hindu weight - SER

Hindu writings - TANTRA

Hinged tongue - PAWL

Hip bones - COXAE or ILIA

Historical record - ACTA

Histrionic - STAGY

Hives - UREDO

Hodgepodge - FERRANGO, MELANGE, PASTICHE or OLIO

Hogfish - WRASSE

Hokkaido City - SAPPORO

Hokkaido people - AINU

Hokkaido port - OTARU

Hold forth - OPINE

Holiday - FETE

Holiday time - EVE

Holing device - TREPAN

Hollow rocks - GEODES

Holly or Holm oak or genus - ILEX

Holy places - SANCTA

Holy Roman emperor - OTTO or OTTOII

Holy water basin - STOUP

Home of Odysseus - ITHACA

Home of the Muses - HELICON

Home of the Norse gods - ASGARD

Home of the sirens - CAPRI

HOMES - GREAT LAKES (Huron, Ontario, Michigan, Erie, Superior)

Homo sapiens - HOMINID

Hondurian River - ULUA

Honey badger - RATEL

Honorary deg. - LLD

Honshu mat - TATAMI

Honshu seaport - KOBE, NAGOYA or OSAKA

Hoofed mammal - UNGALATE

Hooked anatomical part - UNCUS

Hooded clock - CAPOTE

Hooded jacket - ANORAK

Hoopster - CAGER

Hopi doll - KACHINA

Hops oven - OAST

Hops stems - BINES

Horizontal threads - WEFT

Hormone - ACTH

Horned antelope - BONGO

Horned goddess - ISIS

Horned shaped bone or structure - CORNU

Horned viper - ASP or CERASTES

Hornless - MULEY

Horny - CORNEOUS

Horny: pref. CERATO

Horse bit - SNAFFLE

Horse-donkey offspring - HINNY

Horse foot part - PASTERN

Horse handler - OSTLER

Horsehue - DUN

Horse pill - BOLUS

Horse shoe part - CALK

Horsemint genus - MONARDA

Hot compress - STUPE

Hot milk curdled with ale - POSSET

Hot wind - SAMIEL

Hot wine drink - GLOGG or NEGUS

Household - MENAGE

Household gods - LARES or PENATES

Household spirit - LAR

Hovering falcon - KESTREL

Howling - ULULANT

Hub - NAVE

Hubris - PRIDE

Hudson tributary - MOHAWK

Hulled grain - GROATS

Humman cpu's - SENSORIA

Hummus ingredient - TAHINI

Humpback's kin - SEI

Humped bovine - ZEBU

Hungarian - MAGYAR

Hungarian coin - ENGO

Hungarian language e.g. -
   UGRAIN

Hungarian river - EGER

Hungarian sheep dog - PULI

Hungarian wine - TOKAY

Hung-wu's dynasty - MING

Hunter's cap - MONTERO

Hunting call - TANTARA

Huntress of myth - ATALANTA
   or ARTEMIS

Husband of Amiens - MARI

Husband of Bathsheba - URIAH

Husband of Desdemona -
   OTHELLO

Husband of Fatima - ALI

Husband of Frigg - ODIN

Husband of Gundrun - ATLI

Husband of Helen - MENELAUS

Husband of Isis - OSIRIS

Husband of Jezabel - AHAB

Husband of Judith - ESAU

Husbandof Kali - AGNI

Husband of Octavia - NERO

Husband of Ops - SATURN

Husband of Persephone - HADES

Husband of Pocahontas -
   ROLPHE

Husband of Rebekah - ISAAC

Husband of Ruth - BOAZ

Husband of Sarah - ABRAHAM

Husband of SITA - RAMA

Husband of Titania - OBERON

Hyalite - OPAL

Hybrid citrus - UGLI

Hybrid meat - CATTALO

Hybrid primrose - OXLIP

Hydroxyl compound - ENOL

Hymn of praise - PAEAN

Hymn of Thanksgiving -
   TEDEUM

Iberian sheep - MERINO

Icecream creation - BOMBE

Icelandic coin - EYRIR

Icelandic work - EDDA

Ice mass or pinnacle - SERAC

Icy - GELID

Icy pinnacles - OSAR

Idle - FAINEANT

Igneous rock - BASALT or
   OBSIDIAN

Iguana relative - ANOLE

Ike's command - ETO

Ilicitly distilled whiskey - POTEEN

Ilium - TROY

Ill gotten gains - PELF

Image: pre. - ICONO

Imaginary moster - CHIMERA

Imaginary substance - ETHER

Imitation - ERSATZ

Imitation of gold - ORMOLU

Immature cucumber - GHERKIN

Implied - TACIT

Imported cheese - HAVARTI

Imported porcelain - IMARI

Impressive display - PANOPLY

Improve - AMELIORATE

Impudent - MALAPERT

Impulse conductor - AXON

Impute - ASCRIBE

In hiding - DOGGO

In name only - TITULAR

In the same place: Lat. - IBIB or IBIDEM

Inability to read - ALEXIA

Inability to smell - ANOSMIA

Inactive state - TORPOR

Incan capital - CUZCO

Incarnation of Vishnu - AVATAR, KRISHNA or RAMA

Incised carving - INTAGLIO

Incisive - MORDANT

Inclination from vertical - HADE

Inconsistent - ANOMALOUS

Indehiscent fruit - ACHENE

Indian - CREE, OTOE or UTE

Indian address - SAHIB

Indian beans - CATALPAS

Indian bigwig - NAWAB

Indian bread - NAN or NANN

Indian butter - GHEE

Indian cave temple sote - ELLORA

Indian chief - SACHEM

Indian diety - KRISHNA

Indian dish - DAL

Indian dog - DHOLE

Indian drum - MRINDANGAM or TABLA

Indian evergreen - NEEM or SANDALWOOD

Indian fabric - MADRAS

Indian fig tree - PEEPUL or PIPAL

Indian flour - ATTA

Indian grass - KANS

Indian groom - SYCE

Indian instruments - TABLAS

Indian kettle - TABLA

Indian language - ORIYA

Indian lentil dish - DAL

Indian lute - SAROD, SITAR or TAMBURA

Indian nurse - AMAH

Indian musical form - RAGA

Indian nanny - AMAH

Indian ox - GAUR or ZEBU

Indian pastry - SAMOSA

Indian peasant - RYOT

Indian port - CALCUTTA

Indian prince - MAHARAJA or RANI

Indian queen - RANEE

Indian rug - DHURRIE

Indian sage - MAHATMA

Indian sailor - LASCAR

Indian seaport - MADRAS

Indian soldier - SEPOY

Indian sovereign - MAHARANI

Indian spice - CARDAMON

Indian state or tea - ASSAM

Indian stork - ARGALA

Indian title - NAWAB

Indian turban - PATA

Indian VIP - SIDAR

Indian water vessel -LOTA

Indian weight - SER or TOLA

Indiana's flower - PEONY

Indic language - URDU

Indiginous Japanese AINU

Indigo dye or plant - ANIL

Individual clone member - RAMET

Indo-European - ARYAN

Indo-Malayan evergreens - BETELS

Indonesian island - BALI, BORNEO, CERAM, SUMATRA, SUMBA or TIMOR

Indonesian island group - ANU

Indonesian ox - ANOA

Indonesian sailboat - PROA

Indonesian soybean cake - TEMPEH

Indonesian volcano - KRAKATAU

Inedible orange - OSAGE

Indoor pool - NATATORIUM

Inert gas - ARGON or ZENON

Inert gaseous element - KRYPTON

Infant - NEONATE

Infantry campsite - ETAPE

Infantry officer's half pike - SPONTOON

Infernal abyss - TARTARUS

Infidel in Islam - KAFIR

Inflammmatory swelling - BLAIN

Ingenuous - NAIF

In honor of, or in the manner of - ALA

Ink ingredient - EOSIN

Inland sea - ARAL

Inlay material - NIELLO

Inlet - RIA

Inn, in the east - CARAVANSARY

Inner Hebrides island - IONA

Inner part of a Greek temple - NAOS

Inner self - ANIMA

Innkeeper - BONIFACE

Innocent - NAIF

Inscribed pillar - STELE

Insect adult stage - IMAGO

Insect appendage or feeler - PALP

Insect repellent - CITRONELLA

Insect stage - IMAGO or PUPA

Insectivorous bird - VIREO

Insense spice - STACTE

Insense stick - JOSS

Insertion mark - CARET

Insincere person - POSEUR

Insincere speech - CANT

Insolublle protein - KERATIN

Insulating material - PERLITE

Intermediate, in law - MESNE

Intermission - CAESURA or ENTRACTE

Interrobang - QUESTIONMARK

Intersection point - NODE

Interstices - AREOLAE

Intestinal divisions - ILIA

Intro - PROEM

Intuit knife - ULU

Intuitive apprehension of spiritual truth - CORRIGENDA

Invaders of Kent - JUTES

Invaders of Rome - VANDELS

Inward - ENTAD

Ionian island - CORFU, ZAKINTHOS or ZANT

Ionian Sea gulf - ARTA

Iota - WHIT

Iowa commune - AMANA

IQ test developer - BINET

Iranian coin - RIAL

Iranian faith - BAHAI

Irational number - SURD

Ireland's De Valera - EAMON

Irish county - LAOIS or SLIGO

Iris part - UVEA

Irish lad - BOYO

Irish lake - LOUGH

Irish money - PUNT

Irish moonshine - POTEEN

Irish river - SHANNON

Irish Sea god - LER

Irish seaport - SLIGO or TRALEE

Irish toast - SLAINTE

Iron - FE

Iron ore - HERMATITE, OCHER or SIDERITE

Ironic - WRY

Iron rich mountain range - MESABI

Iroquois Indian - SENECA

Iroquoian language - ERIE or WYANDOT

Irregular edge - DECKLE

Irregularly notched - EROSE

Isaac's mother - SARAH

Isinglass - MICA

Islam follower - SUNNI

Islam holy month - RAMADAN

Islamic call to prayer - AZAN

Islamic decrees - FATMAS

Islamic devil - WHAITAN

Islamic diety - ALLAH

Islamic divorse - TALAK

Islamic doctor - ULEMA

Islamic holy war - JIHAD

Islamic infidel - KAFIR

Islamic leader or ruler - CALIPH, EMIR or IMAM

Islamic patriarch - SHEIK

Islamic salutation - SALAAM

Islamic scholars - IMAMS

Islamic spirit - DJINN

Islamic spiritual leader - CALIPH

Islamic temple - MOSQUE

Islamic title - EMIR

Islamic tower - MINARET

Island - AIT

Island country in the Pacific - PALAU

Island goose - NENE

Island in Galway - ARAM

Island in the Antilles - SABA

Island in the Saronic - SALAMIS

Island off Donegal - ARAN

Island off Greenland - ELLESMERE

Island off Scotland - IONA

Island resort IBIZA

Islands near New Guinea - AROE

Islet - AITor HOLM

Isolated hill - BUTTE

Isolated mountain - MASSIF

Isotope of Thorium - IONIUM

Israeli airline - ELAL

Israeli city - ACRE

Israeli coin - AGORA

Israeli dance - HORA

Israeli native - SABRA

Israeli port - ACRE

Israeli port city - EILAT or ELATH

Israeli seaport - ACRE

Italian brandy - GRAPPA or SREGA

Italian cathedral - DUOMO

Italian cheese - ASIAGO or DOLCELATTE

Italian city - ASTI

Italian colony, once - ERITREA

Italian commune - ATR, AOSTA, ASOLO, CASERTA, or ESTE

Italian dessert - TIRAMISU

Italian dumplings - GNOCHI

Italian friends - AMICI

Italian ice cream - CASSATA or GELATO

Italian industrial center - PADUA

Italian innkeeper - OSTE or PADRONE

Italian instrument - ARPA

Italian isle - ISOLA

Italian magistrate - PODESTA

Italian marble city - MASSA

Italian noble family - ORSINI

Italian nobleman - CONTE

Italian noblewoman - MARCHESA

Italian port - ANCONA, GENOA, SALERNO or TRIETE

Italian range - APENNINES

Italian resort - LIDO

Italian seaport - ANCONA, BARI or SALERNO

Italian staircase - SCALA

Italian stringed instrument - ARPA

Italian river - ARNO

Italian title of respect -SIGNOR

Italian violin - AMATI

Italian white wine - SOAVE

Italy's largest lake - GARDA

Itchy - PRURIENT

Itchy problem - TINEA

Ivied stand - PERGOLA

Jack-in-the-pulpit plant - ARUM

Jacob's brother - ESAU

Jacob's father - ISAAC

Jacob's father-in-law - LABAN

Jacob's son - ASHER, LEVI or REUBEN

Jacob's twin - ESAU

Jacob's wife - LEAH

Jagged - EROSE

Jamaican citrus - UGLI

Jamaican dish - ACKEE

Jamaican music - SKA

Jamaican rum - TAFIA

Japan's first capital - NARA

Japanese aborigine or native - AINU

Japanese American - ISSEI or NISEI or SANSAI

Japanese art form - ORIGAMI

Japanese apricot - UME

Japanese bathtub - FURO

Japanese bedroll - FUTON

Japanese box - INRO

Japanese brew - KIRIN

Japanese caldera - ASO

Japanese carp - KOI

Japanese cartoons - ANIME

Japanese carved ivory items - NETSUKES

Japanese city - OTARU

Japanese commander - SHOGUN

Japanese divine being - KAMI

Japanese dog - AKITA

Japanese drama or drum - NOH

Japanese dressing gown - YUKATA

Japanese elder - GENRO

Japanese emperor - AKIHITO

Japanese fencing - KENDO

Japanese feudalnobleman - DAIMYO

Japanese fish delicacy - FUGU

Japanese food fish - TAI

Japanese gateway - TORII

Japanese home divider - SHOJI

Japanese honorific - SAN

Japanes horse radish - WASABI

Japanese imigrant - ISSEI

Japanese ink - SUMI

Japanese instrument - SAMISEN

Japanese isinglass - AGAR

Japanese island - OKI

Japanese knife - GINSU

Japanes legislature - DIET

Japanese martial art - AIKIDO or KENDO

Japanese mat - TATAMI

Japanese metalware - TOLE

Japanese money - RIN

Japanese mushroom - ENOKI or SHIITAKE

Japanese nobleman - DAIMYO

Japanese noodle - SOBA

Japanese noodle soup - RAMEN

Japanese paper art - ORIGAMI

Japanese paper folding - KIRIGAMI

Japanese parliament - DIET

Japanese pearl diver - AMAS

Japanese people - SINU

Japanese pill box - INRO

Japanese plum - LOQUOT

Japanese poem - HAIKU or TANKA

Japanese porcelain - IMARI

Japanese porgy - TAI

Japanese portal - TORII

Japanese pottery - IMARI or RAKU

Japanese primitve - AINU

Japanese radish - WASABI

Japanese receptacle - INRO

Japanese salad ingredient - UDO

Japanese sandal - ZORI

Japanese sash - OBI

Japanese seaport - KOBE, OSAKA, OTARU or SASEBO

Japanese seaweed - NORI

Japanese script - KANA

Japanese ship - MARU

Japanese shrine gateway - TORII

Japanese sliding door - SHOJI

Japanese soup - MISO

Japanese statesman - ITO

Japanese stringed instument - KOTO

Japanese style arbor - PERGOLA

Japanese tourist center - NARA

Japanese vegetables - UDOS

Japanese verse - HAIKU

Japanese volcano - ASO

Japances waist pouch - INRO

Japanese wooden clog - GETA

Japanese working dog - AKITA

Japanese wrestling - JUJISU

Japanese writing - KANA or KANJI

Japanese zither - KOTO

Japan's first capital - NARA

Jar - OLLA

Jargon - CANT

Jason's wife - MEDIA

Java seaport - SEMARANG

Javanese carriages - SADOS

Javanese ruler - RAJA

Jawbone - MAXILLA

Jelly for germs - AGAR

Jersey genus - BOS

Jester's cap - COXCOMB

Jewel - BIJOU

Jewelery stone - JET

Jewish festival - HANUKKAH

Jewish harvest festival -
    SUKKOTH

Jewish holiday - PURIM

Jewish Jehovah - ELOHIM

Jewish month - ADAR (6),
    AV(11), ELUL(12),
    HESHVAN(2),IYAR(8),
    KISLEV(3), NISAN(7),
    SHEVAT(5), SIVAN(9),
    TAMUZ(10), TEVET(4) or
    TISHRI (1)

Jewish mystic of old -ESSENE

Jewish mystics - HASIDIM

Jewish noodle pudding -
    KUGEL

Jewish occult phiosophy -
    CABALA

Jewish religious cap -
    YARMULKE

Jewish sage - HILLEL

Jewish shawl - TALLITH

Jewish teacher REBBE

Jews not in Israel - DIAPORA

Jezebel's husband - AHAB

Jiao - MAO

Jipajapa hat - PANAMA

Johnny cakes - PONES

Joie de vivre - ELAN

Joker - WAG

Jordan queen - NOOR

Jot - ATOM or WHIT

Joule fraction - ERG

Judah's son - ONAN

Judeo-Spanish language -
    LADINO

Judges bench - BANC

Judge's chamber - CAMERA

Judicial proceedings - ACTA

Juliet's family name - CAPULET

July birthstone - CORNELIAN

Jump on skates - LUTZ

Jungfrau, e.g. - ALP

Jungian self - ANIME

Jungle cat - CIVET

Jungle cuckoo - ANI

Jungle ivy - LIANNA

Juniper tree - CADE

Junk copper - NARC

Jupiter - JOVE

Jury pool - VENIRE

Justification for existing -
    RAISON D'ETRA

KGB forerunner - OGPU

Kapok tree - CEIBA

Karate school - DOJO

Karate teacher - SENSEI

Kazakhstan range - ALTAI

Keellike structure - CARINA

Keepers of sacred fire -
    VESTALS

Kenyan oxan - ZEBU

Kernel's coat - TESTA

Kettle drum - NAKER

Kettle drums - PIMPANI

Key - AIT

Keyboard instrument - CELESTA

Kid around - JAPE

Kidney bean - HARICOT

Kidney enzyme - RENIN

Kidney related - RENAL

Killer of a god - DEICIDE

Kimono sash - OBI

Kind of acid - OLEIC

Kind of algebra - LINEER

Kind of antenna - DIPOLE

Kind of bean - SIEVA

Kind of bulrush - TULE

Kind of butterfly - SATYR

Kind of canto - BEL

Kind of cap - COIF

Kind of charm - TOADSTONE

Kind of cherry - GEAN

Kind of engine - CARNOT

Kind of fibre - BAST

Kind of gazelle - DORCAS

Kind of hut - NISSEN

Kind of jay - SCRUB

Kind of lily - SEGO

Kind of moth - LUNA

Kind of Mushroom - MOREL

Kind of orange - SEVILLE

Kind of palm - SAGO

Kind of terrier - CAIRN

Kind of thread - LISLE

Kind of tide - AGGER

King mackerel - CERO

King of Crete - MINOS

King of Denmark - CANUTE

King of Egypt - FUAUD

King of France - CAPET, LEROI
or ROI

King of Israel - JEHU or OMRI

King of Judea - AMON, ASA
or HEROD

King of legend - MIDAS

King of Phrygia - MIDAS

King of Pylos - NESTOR

King of Scotland - BALIOL

King of the fairies - OBERON

King of the Visigoths - ALARIC

King of the Huns - ATLI

King of Thebes - CREON

King of Troy - PRIAM

King of Tyre - HIRAM

Kingdom east of Babylonia -
ELAM

Kingdom in the Himalayas -
BHUTAN

Kingdom of Tereus - THRACE

Kingly - BASILIC

Kings Peak range - UINTA

Kirghiz Mtn range - ALAI

Kirsch, for one - SCHNAPS

Kishke covering - DERMA

Kissed - OSCULATED

Knave - VARLET

Kneeling bench for prayer - PRIEDIEU

Knife, of old - SNEE

Knight's tunic - TABARD

Knit fabric -TRICOT

Knobby - NODAL

Knot at the nape - CHIGNON

Knot in wool - BURL

Knowledge gained through Meditation - JNANA

Knowledge of spiritual truth - GNOSIS

Koeon - RIDDLE

Korean apricot - ANSU

Koran chapter - SURA

Korea/China separator - YELLOW SEA

Korean soldier - ROK

Kyushu volcano - ASO

Lab gel - AGAR

Lab heaters - ETNAS

Lab straw - PIPETTE

Lab tube - PIPET

Labratory tube - BURET

Lace end - AGLET

Lace maker's thread - GIMP

Lachrymose - TEARFUL

Lacquer - JAPAN

Lacquered metalware - TOLE

Lacquer resin - ELEM

Lacy frills - PICOTS

Lacy openwork - TRACERY

Ladder like - SCALAR

Ladder step - RUNDLE or STAVE

Lady friend in Italy - AMICA

Ladylove - INAMORATA

Lady oracle - SIBYL

Lady's maid in Indian - AYAH

Lake: Fr. - LAC

Lake in Ireland - ERNE

Lake in Italy - COMO or GARDA

Lake in Scotland - KATRINE

Lake near Rome - ALBANO

Lake of Geneva - LAMAN

Lake or pond - MERE

Lamb or kid - YEANLING

Lambs: Lat. - AGNI

Land of hope - RURITANIA

Lament - ELEGY

Lament loudly - ULULATE

Laments loudly - KEENS

Land locked country - UGANDA

Language Jesus spoke -
    ARAMAIC

Language of India - TAMIL

Language of Iran - FARSI

Language of Provence -
    OCCITAN

Language of South China -
    KOBO

Language of Sri Lanka - TAMIL

Language of the Gypsies -
    ROMANY

Lanos - WOOLY

Lapland nomad - SAMI

Lapwing - PEEWIT

Large African stork - MARABOU

Large antelope - BONGO or
    ORYX

Large awk - MURRE

Large basket - PANNIER

Large Brazilian parrot -
    HYACINTH or MACAW

Large cacti - SAGUROS

Large center piece - EPERGNE

Large clam - PISMO

Large eyed primate - LORIS

Large duck - PEKIN

Large fern - BRACKEN

Large fish - CERO

Large green moth - LUNA

Large nocturnal animal - PACA

Large parrot - KEA

Large pill - BOLUS

Large raptor - GOS HAWK

Large red hog - DUROC

Large sea bird - SKUA or SOLAN

Large statues - COLOSSI

Large tuna - ALBACORE

Large umbrella - GAMP

Large wine bottle -
    METHUSELAH

Large whale - LEVIATHAN

Large wooden goblet - MAZER

Largess - ALMS

Largest asteroid - CERES

Largest domesticated cattle -
    GAURS

Largest lake in central Europe -
    BALATON

Largest Lake in Europe -
    LADOGA

Last book of the Torah - DEUT

Last month - ULTIMO

Last of the Minor Prophets -
    MALACHI

Last six lines of a sonnet -
    SESTET

Last supper room - CENACLE

Late sleeper - SLUGABED

Latin American Christmas Festival - PASADA

Latin being - ESSE

Latin case - DATIVE

Latine north wind - BOREAS

Latin I word - EST

Latin farewell - VALE

Latin law - LEX

Latin Mass - MISSA

Latin poet - OVID

Latino grocery - BODEGA

Latvian port - RIGA

Latino beliefs - FES

Laugh in contempt - FLEER

Laughing - RIANT

Laughing jackass - KOOKABURRA

Laurel wreath - CORONAL

Lawn bowling - BOCCE

Lawyer's group - ABA

Laxative from aloe - ALOIN

Layer - LAMINA

Layer of skin - DERMA

Layers of tissue - TELAE

Layman at the monastery - OBLATE

Lazy - OTIOSE

Lead ore or sourse - GALENA

Lead-tin alloy - TERNE

Leaf pore - STOMA

Leaflike part - BRACT

Leaf-stem angle - AXIL

Leafstock - PETIOLE

Leander's love - HERO

Leap - CAPRIOLE

Learned scholar - SAVANT

Lear's daughter - REGAN

Leather flask - OLPE

Leather whip - TAWS

Leatherwood - TITI

Lebanese malitia - DRUSE

Lebanese port - Beirut

Lecherous man - ROUE

Lector - OSTIARY

Lecture hall - LYCEUM

Lecturer - DOCENT

Lecturn - AMBO or PODIUM

Leeward Island - NEVIS

Left hand page - VERSO

Left handed - SINISTRAL

Leftover food - ORT

Leg covering - PUTTEE

Leg of lamb - GIGOT

Legal copy - ESTREAT

Legal matter - RES

Legal right - DROIT

Legendary tales - MYTHI

Legislators - SOLONS

Leguminous plant of India - DAL

Lei man - HAOLE

Leisurely stroll - PASEO

Leporid - HARE

Lethargy - HEBETUDE or TOPOR

Let stand - STET

Letter embellishment - SERIF

Lettuce alternative - ESCAROLE

Libertine - ROUE

Library cubicle - CARREL

Lice and ticks - EPIZOA

Lie - TARRADIDDLE

Light beige - ECRU

Light carriage - GIG

Light cotton - ETAMINE

Light four-wheeled carriage - PHAETON

Light granite rock - SIAL

Light helmet - ARMET

Light measure - PHOT

Light trianngular scarf - FISH

Light unit - PHOT

Light turban - PUGREE

Light yellow cheese - TILSIT

Lighthouse - PHAROS

Lightweight cotton - ETAMINE

Lightweight cotton cloth - JACONET

Lightweight fabric - ETAMINE, NINON, PLISSE or VOILE

Lightweight material - FOULARD

Like a goose - ANSERINE

Like a soothsayer - VATIC

Like a wolf - LUPINE

Like an old woman - ANILE

Like some victories - PYRRHIC

Lily: Fr. - LIS

Lily family plant - CAMAS

Lily like plant - HOSTA orYUCCA

Lily plant - ALOE, CALLA, HOSTA or MARIPOSA

Limbless genus - APODA

Lime tree - TEIL

Limestone rock formation - KARST

Lingo - ARGOT or PATOIS

Link - NEXUS

Link together - CONCATENATE

Linking verb - COPULA

List extender - ETC

List of errors - CORRIGENDA

List of lapses - ERRATA

Listen - HIST

Literary collection - ANA or ANALETS

Literary conflict - AGON

Literary connection - SEGUE

Literary devise - TROPE

Litter of pigs - FARROW

Little bits of land - AITS

Little cupids - AMORETTI

Little gray birds - VIREOS

Liturgical language - SYRIAC

Liturgical vestment - AMICE

Lively - TARE

Lively, in music - ANIM

Lively dance - GIGUE

Lively old dance - GALOP

Lively wit - ESPRIT

Liverleaf - HEPATICA

Living in still waters - LENTIC

Lizard - AGAMA, ANOLE or SAURIAN

Lizardlike - SAURIAN

Llama relative - VICUNA

Loamy deposit - LOESS

Loamy fertilizer - MARL

Lobster claw - CHELA

Lobsters & crabs - DECAPODS

Local theater - NABE

Local trees - SILVAN

Location of ancient Samos - IONIA

Location of the Great Mosque - HERAT

Locking lever - DETENT

Locust bean - CAROB

Lodge doorkeeper - TILER

Lohengrin's love - ELSA

Log-birling contest - ROLEO

Loincloth - DHOTI

Long bodied cat - EYRA

Long legged bird - AVOCET

Longest river - NILE

Long-leaved lettuce - COS

Long poem- EPOEE

Long stole - TIPPET

Long tailed African monkey - GUENON

Long tailed finch - TOWHEE

Long tailed lizard - AGAMA

Long tailed monkey - TITI

Long tunic - CAFTAN

Long winded - PROLIX

Long wooden bench - SETTLE

Loom attachment - DOBBY

Loom bar - ERASER

Loom reed - SLEY

Looped handle - ANSA

Loose cloak - RELISSE

Loose rock debris- SCREE

Loose tunic - CAFTAN

Lop eared hog - DUROC

Lord's lands - FIEFS or
DEMESNE

Loss-of-hair condition -
ALOPECIA

Loss of sense of smell -
ANOSMIA

Loss of volition - ABULIA

Loud firecrackers - PETARDS

Loudness measure - PHON

Loudness units - BELS

Louisiana tribe - CADDO

Louvre Pyramid designer - PEI

Love: Sp. AMOR

Love of fine art - VIRTU

Love poem for singing -
MADRIGAL

Lover of Aeneas - DIDO

Lover of Aphrodite - ARES

Lover of Daphnis - CHLOE

Lover of Eros - PSYCHE

Lover of Narcissus - ECHO

Lover of Radames - AIDA

Low stool - TABORET

Lower - NETHER

Lower Niger River people -
EBOS

Lowest deck on a ship -
ORLOP

Lowly freeman - CEORL

Lozenge - TROCHE or
PASTIL

Luau baking pits - IMUS

Lucerne - ALFALFA

Lugubrious - MOURNFUL

Luke's father - DARTH

Lulaby - BERCEUSE

Lulu - ONER

Luminous eminations - AURAE

Lunar plain - MARE

Lunar valley - RILLE

Luncheon, in London -
TIFFIN

Lustrus velvet - PANNE

Lute of India - SARODE or
SITAR

Luzon port - MANILA

Lyons River - SAONE

Lyric poem - EPODE

Lysergic acid sourse - ERGOT

M1 - GARAND

\M. Hulot creator - TATI

Macadamize - PAVE

Macao money - AVO

Macaw - ARA or ARARA

Macbeth witch - HECATE

Mace bearer - BEADLE

Macedonian mall - AGORA

Mackerel's kin - CERO

Madagascar primate - INDRI or LEMUR

Mafioso's code of silence - OMERTA

Magic amulet - MOJO

Magic image - SIGIL

Magic showplace - ORENA

Magical goddess - CIRCE

Magical symbol - SIGIL

Magnetic accelerators - BETATRONS

Magnetic alloy - ALNICO

Magnetic induction unit - HAUSS or TESLA

Magnetic mineral magnetite - LODESTONE

Mah-jong suit - BAM

Maiden loved by Hercules - IOLE

Maiden turned into a spider - ARACHNE

Maine seaport - BATH

Majestic shield - AEGIS or EGIS

Major or Minor - CANIS

Make a mosaic - TESSELATE

Make better - AMELIORATE

Make cloth gathers - SHIRR

Make inconspicuous - EFFACE

Make slender - ATTENUATE

Make undrinkable - DENATURE

Make unnecessary - OBVIATE

Makeshift conveyance - TRAVOIS

Malay boat - PROA

Malay coin - TRA

Malay gibbon - LAR

Malay ismus - KRA

Malayan dagger - CREESE or KRIS

Malayan outrigger - PROA or PRAU

Malayan palms - SAGOS

Malaysian knife - PARANG

Malasian seaport - MALACCA

Malasian state - PERAK or SARAWAK

Male badger - BOAR

Male ballet dancer - DANSEUR

Male cat - GIB

Male demon - INCUBUS

Male eagle or hawk - TIERCEL

Male gypsy - ROM

Male hawk - TERCEL or TIERCEL

Male reddeer - HARTS or SPAYS

Male swan - COB

Maligne - TRADUCE

Malt kiln - OAST

Malt liquor yeast - BARM

Mammal's coat - PELALGE

Man of prominence - NABOB

Manatee's cousin - DUGONG

Mandarin residence - YAMEN

Mandela org. - ANC

Maneuverable, nautically - YARE

Manorial land - DEMESNE

Manuscript gap - LACUNA

Manuscript marks - OBELI

Maori canoe - WAKA

Map in a map - INSET

Maple genus - ACER

Marabou - STORK

Marat's assassin - CORDAY

Marble mount of Greece - PENTELICUS

Marshy - PALUDIC

Mariana Island - GUAM or ROTA

Marine mollusk - SEAHARE

Marine snail - WHELK

Mark of insertion - CARET

Mark used in part singing - PRE

Market town - BOURG

Mars moon - DEMOS or PHOBOS

Marsh bird - CRAKE, RAIL, REEVE, SNIPE or SORA

Marsh grass - SEDGE

Marsh hawk - HARRIER

Marsh hen - COOT

Marsh plant - CATKIN, REED or TULE

Martinique volcano - PELEE

Masada defender - ESSENE

Masked buffoon - HARLEQUIN

Masquerade ball - RIDOTTO

Masonary block or stone - ASHLAR

Masonic doorkeeper - TILER

Mass calender - ORDO

Massacre - POGROM

Massage deeply - ROLPH

Massenet opera - THAIS

Massonet opera - THAIS

Matador - TORERO

Material used to make glass - FRIT

Matter Matter - MUON

Mature insect - IMAGO

Maturing egg cell - OOTID

Maui retreat - HANA

Maui tree - KOAQ

Maven - SAVANT

Maxims - DICTA

Mayan gibbon - LAR

Mayan Indian - NAM

Meadow mouse - VOLE

Means of connection - NEXUS

Measure of electric charge - COULOMB

Measure of loudness - SONE

Meat avoider - VEGAN

Meat dross - GRISTTLE

Meat pie - PASTY

Mecca shrine - KAABA

Mecca visitors - HAJIS

Mechanical device - PAWL

Medical staffs - CADUCEI

Medicinal - IATRIC

Medicinal brew - TISANE

Medicinal herb or plant - ARNICA, BONESET, JALAP, SAGE or SENNA

Medicinal shrub - CASSIA or IPECAC

Medicinal tuber - SALEP

Medieval brass horn - CLARION

Medieval capital of Flanders - LILLE

Medieval catapult - ONAGER

Medieval chest - ARCA

Medieval devil - MEPHISTO

Medieval form of trombone - SACKBUT

Medieval French coins - OBOLES

Medieval fluid - HANSA

Medieval helmet - ARMET or BASINET

Medieval instruments - REBECS

Medieval money - ORA

Medieval musical pieces - MADRIGALS

Medieval poem - LAI

Medieval Scottish soldier - KERN

Medieval Sicilian coin - TARI

Medieval sword - ESTOC

Medieval tale - GEST

Medieval weapon - POLEAXE

Mediteranian region - LEVANT

Mediteranian vessel - CAIQUE, FELLUCA or ZEBEC

Mediteranian wind - MISTRAL or SIROCCO

Medium-sweet sherry - OLOROSO

Melodic - ARIOSE

Melodic flourish - CADENZA

Melodies: Sp. - AIRES

Melodious composition or passage - ARIOSO

Melville character - PELEG

Melville opus - OMOO or TYPEE

Member of a convent - CENOBITE

Member of a Jewish sect - ESSENE

Member of a ruling clique - OLIGARTH

Membrane of grasses - PALEA

Membranes - SEPTA

Membranous covering - VELAMEN

Membranous tissue - TELA

Memorial stone - STELE

Memory - ROTE

Memory pathway - ENGRAM

Memphis god - PTAH

Menial worker - DOGSBODY

Mercenary - VENAL

Merchant guild - HANSA

Merchantman - ARGOSY

Mercurous cloride - CALOMEL

Mercury ore - CINNABAR

Mercury, to an Alchemist - AZOTH

Merganser - SMEW

Merry - JOCOSE or RIANT

Mesopotamian earth god - AGAN

Messy munchie - SMORE

Metal alloy - ALNICO

Metal basket - CRESSET

Metal marble - STEELIE

Metal mixture - MATTE

Metal mold - PIG

Metal shaper - SWAGE

Metal used in alloys - BISMUTH

Metal waste - DROSS

Metalic element - NIOBIUM or RHENIUM

Metamorphic rock - GNEISS or SCHIST

Metaphysical concepts - MONISMS

Meteoric fireballs - BOLIDES

Meteorite remains - TEKTITE

Metonymy - TROPE

Metric feet - IAMBS

Metric measure - ARE or STERE

Metric unit of area - ARE

Metric unit of mass - GRAM

Metric unit of volumn - STERE

Metrical foot - ANAPEST, DACTYL or TROCHEE

Metrical unit - IAMBUS

Metrical unit of two feet - DIPODY

Mexicali munchie - TOSTADA

Mexican annuals - CHIAS

Mexican Indian - ZAPOTEC

Mexican Indians - OTOMI

Mexican January - ENERO

Mexican language - NEHUATL

Mexican mountain - ORIZABA

Mexican policeman - RURALES

Mexican raccoon - COATI

Mexican resort - OAXARA

Mexican salamander - AXOLTI

Mexican sandel - HUARACHE

Mezzanine - ENTESOL

Miasma - ODOR

Mica, in thin sheets - ISINGLAS

Microwave generator - MASER

Midmorning prayer - TERSE

Middle East beverage - ARRACK

Mideast appetizer - FALAFEL

Mideast marketplace - SOUK

Mideast Muslim militants - HAMAS

Mideast religion - BAHAI

Mid eastern porters - HAMALS

Middle ear bone - MALLEUS

Middle East chief - AMEER

Middy - CADET

Midianite king - REBA

Midieval chest - ARCA

Midieval fortress - ESTE

Midieval helmet - ARMET

Midnight stroll - PASEO

Mignonette - RESEDA

Migrating Herring - ALEWIFE

Mild breeze - ZEPHYR

Mild cigar - CLARO

Military cap - KEPI or SHAKO

Military dictator - CAUDILLO

Military post office - APO

Military storehouse - ETAPE

Milk cheese - EDAM

Millionth of a meter - MICRON

Mills waterwheel - NORIA

Milne' donkey - EEYORE

Mind: Lat. MENS

Mine entrance - ADIT

Mine excavation - STOPE

Mine: Fr. AMOI

Mine prop - SPRAG

Mineral pigment - OCHER

Mineral residue - CALX

Mineral salt - ALUM

Mini monkey - TITI

Mining nail - SPAD

Mining tool - TREPAN

Minnesota range - MESABI

Minor actor - SUPE

Minor parish official - BEADLE

Minor profit - AMOS

Minstrel's song - LAY

Mint family member - CHIA

Mint family plant - SALVIA

Mint product - SPECIE

Minute amounts (Scottish) - HAETS

Minute aquatic organism - ROTIFER

Mirror backing - TAIN

Miscellany - VARIA

Mischievious girl - GAMINE

Mischievious prank - DIDO

Mishmash - OLIO

Misleading fabrication -CANARD

Mississippi sourse - ITASCA

Missouri feeder - KANSAS, KNIFE or OSAGE

Missouri tribe - ARIKARA

Mist - BRUNE

Mite - ACARUS or ACARID

Moccasin - PAC

Mock - JAPE

Model of the solar system - ORRERY

Moderate in tempo - ANDANTE

Molasses - TREACLE

Molder - ROT

Molly coddle - COSSET

Molting - ECDYSIS

Mom & Pop store group - SBA

Money box, of old - ARCA

Mongolian mountain rang - ALTAI

Mongoose kin - GANET

Monitary unit of Angola - LWEI

Monitary unit of Honduras - LEMPIRA

Money for patronage - PAP

Money in Equador - SUCRE

Money premium - AGIO

Mongol tent - YURT

Mongolian range - ALTAI

Mongolian warrior - TATAR

Mongolian wild sheep - ARGALI

Mongoose - MEERKAT

Monkey bread tree - BAOBAB

Monk's book - PSALTER

Monk's cheese - OKA

Monk's haircut - TONSURE

Monks hood - ACONITE or COWL

Montana peak - BIG ELK

Monteverdi opera - ORFEO

Moon fish - OPAH

Moon goddess - DIANA, LUNA or SELENE

Moon of Jupiter - CALISTA, ELARA,

EUROPA, LEDA or TITAN

Moon of Mars - DEIMOS

Moon of Neptune - TRITON or NEREID

Moon of Saturn - ATLAS, DIONE, HELENE, HYPERION, IAPETUS, JANUS, PHOEBE, RHEA, TETHYS or TITAN

Moon of Uranus - ARIEL, ARIES, OBERON or TITANIA

Moonstone - OPA

Moon valley - RILLE

Moor - HEATH

Moor shrub - GORSE

More, in music - PIU

Mormon: abbr. - LDS

Morph lead in - ENDO

Morrocan port - AGADIR, CEUTA or SAFI

Morrocan tree - ARAR

Mortice insert or mate - TENON

Mosaic piece - SMALTO or TESSERA

Moselle feeder - SAAR

Moses brother - AARON

Moses mount - NEBO

Moslem judge - CADI

Moslem noble - AMIR

Mosque priest - IMAM

Mosquito genus - AEDES

Moth - LUNA

Mother of a holy Hampshire - CREDSOW

Mother of Achilles - THETIS

Mother of Aeneas - VENUS

Mother of Aphrodite - DIONE

Mother of Apollo - LETO

Mother of Ares - ENYO or HERA

Mother of Artimus - LETO

Mother of Brunhilde - ERDA

Mother of Castor - LEDA

Mother of Ceres - OPS

Mother of cities - KIEV

Mother of Clytemnestra - LEDA

Mother of Constantine - HELENA

Mother of Demeter - RHEA

Mother of Dionysus - SEMELE

Mother of Don Juan - ENA or INEZ

Mother of Galatea - DORIS

Mother of Gallahad - ELAINE

Mother of Hades - RHEA

Mother of Hebe - HERA

Mother of Helen - LEDA

Mother of Heleos - THEA

Mother of Hephaestus - HERA

Mother of Hera - RHEA

Mother of Hermes - MAIA

Mother of Horus - ISIS

Mother of Isaac - SARAH

Mother of Ishmael - HAGAR

Mother of Jove - OPS

Mother of Juda or Levi - LEAH

Mother of Jupiter - OPS

Mother of King Minos -
  EUROPA

Mother of Levi - LEAH

Mother of Memnon - EOS

Mother of Maia - PLELONE

Mother of Miletus - ARIA

Mother of Oedipus - JOCASTA

Mother of Paris - HECUBA

Mother of pearl - NACRE

Mother of pearl sourse -
  ABALONE

Mother of Peer Gynt - ASE

Mother of Perseus - DANAE

Mother of Pollux - LEDA

Mother of Poseidon - RHEA

Mother of Promeseus - ASIA

Mother of Proserpine - CERES

Mother of Rajiv - INDIRA

Mother of Reuben - LEAH

Mother of Romulus - RHEA

Mother of Scarlett - ELLEN

Mother of Seth - EVE

Mother of Solomon -
  BATHSHEBA

Mother of Superman - LARA

Mother of the Titans - GAEA

Mother of Uranus - GAIA

Mother of the Valkyries - ERDA

Mother of Venus - DIONE

Mother of Zephyrus - EOS

Mother of Zeus - RHEA

Motherless calf - DOGIE

Mother's kin - ENATE

Motionless - STASIS

Mottled soil - GLEY

Moulding ridge - ARRIS

Mountain ashes - ROWANS

Mountain chain -
  CORDILLERA

Mountain crest - ARETE

Mountain goat - IBEX or TAKIN

Mountain in Geenisis - HOREB

Mountain in Martinique -
  PELEE

Mountain in Thessaly - OSSA

Mountain Lake - TARN

Mountain laurel - KALMIA

Mountain nymph - ECHO or
  OREAD

Mountain of Crete - IDA

Mountain pass - COL

Mountain Pass in India - GHAT

Mountain pool - TARN

Mountain ridge or spur - ARETE, OSAR or TOR

Mountain side debris - SCREE

Mountain spinach - ORACH

Mountain system of Asia - ALTAI

Mountain top fortress in Israel - MASADA

Mountains of Utah - LASAL

Mounted sentry - VEDETTE

Mournful, musically - DOLOROSO

Mourning song - DIRGE

Mouselike mammal - SHREW

Mouth part - UVULA

Mouth: Sp. - BOCA

Mouths - ORA

Movement slower than andante - ADAGIO

Mud fish - AMIA

Mud hut - JACAL

Mug wump - SLAP

Mulberry bark - TAPA

Mulled wine - NEGUS

Multicolored - PIED

Murmer - SUSURRATE

Muscat native - OMANI

Muscular weakness - ATONY

Muse of astonomy - URANIA

Muse of comedy - THALIA

Muse of epic poetry - CALLIOPE

Muse of history - CLIO

Muse of lyric poetry - EUTERPE

Muse of memory - MNEME

Muse of music - EUTERPE

Muse of poetry - ERATO

Muse of sacred poetry - POLYHYMNIA

Muse of song & dance - TERPSICHORE

Muse of tragety - MELPOMENE

Muses - RUMINATES

Museum animal display - DIORAMA

Museum guide - DOCENT

Mushroom - AGARIC

Mushroom cap - PILEUS

Mushroom stem - STIPE

Mushroom variety - ENOKI

Music for nine - NONET

Music halls - ODEA

Music of Indian - RAGA

Musical composition or study - ARIOSO, CANTATA, ETUDE or RONDO

Musical cord - TRIAD

Musical direction - ADUE, ARIOSO, ASSAI, LENTO, POCO, PRESTO, SOPRA or TACET

Musical ending - CODA

Musical florish - GLISSANDO

Musical forms - FUGUES

Musical gourd - MARACA

Musical instrument - OUD

Musical interval - OCTAVE

Musical line - TIMA

Musical medley - OLIO

Musical notation - REST or SECCO

Musical note combinations - TRIOLES

Musical passages - ANDANTE or ARIOSO

Musical postscript - CODA

Musical repeat signs - SEGNI or SEGNOS

Musical tempo - ANDANTINO

Musicly, "Be silent" - TACET

Musicly, from thebeginning - DACAPO

Musicly, not too much - NONTROPPO

Musicly, with the bow - ARCO

Muslim ascetic - DERVISH

Muslim belief - SHIISM

Muslim branch - SUNNI

Muslim caliph - ALI

Muslim call to prayer - ADAN or AZAN

Muslim cap - TAJ

Muslim crusade - JIHAD

Muslim decree - FATWAS or IRADE

Muslim factotum - IMAM

Muslim greeting - SALAAM

Muslim holiday - EED

Muslim holy man - FAKIR

Muslim judge or magistrate - CADI orHAKIM

Muslim months - RABI

Muslim mystics - SUFIS

Muslim pilgrim - HADJI

Muslim pilgrimage - HADJ

Muslim porter - HAMAL

Muslim prayer leader - IMAM

Muslim priest - IMAM

Muslim prince - AMEER

Muslim religious student - SOFTA

Muslim scholers - ULEMA

Muslim shrine - KAABA

Muslim soldier - GHAZI

Muslim spirit - DJIN or DJINNI

Muslim teacher - IMAM or MULLAH

Muslim title - AGA or AGHA

Muslim veil - PURDAH or YASHMAK

Muslim weight - ROTL

Muslim woman's gown - IZAR

Musk sourse - CIVIT

Mustard plants - COLES

Mute swan - OLOR

Myrtle tree - ALLSPICE

Mysterious stuff - ARCANA

Mystic letter - RUNE

Mythical bird - ROC

Mythical dieties - FAUNS

Mythical giant - ANTAEUS

Mythical giantess - URDAR

Mythical goat-man - FAUN

Mythical or obscure - RUNIC

Mythical Greek king - TANTALUS

Mythical horseman - SATYR

Mythical huntress - ATALANTA

Mythical monster - CHIMERA or ORC

Mythical queen of Carthage - DIDO

Mythical son of Helen - XUTHUS

Mythical swan - LEDA

Mythical sorceress - MEDEA

Mythological nymph or swimmer - NAIA

Mythical weaver - ARACHNE

Mythological weeper - NIOBE

NC school - ELON

Nabokov novel - ADA or LOLITA

Nail with a hole - SPAD

Naive girl - INGENUE

Naive person - NAIF

Name - YCLEPT

Name for many a theatre - LYCEUM

Name of God - YAHWEH

Nape - NUCHA

Nape covering style - CHIGNON

Napoleon's Marshall - NEY

Narcotic shrub - KAT or KHAT

Narrative poem - EPOS or IDYL

Narrative tale - CONTE

Narrow channels - STRIAE

Narrow fillet - ORLE

Narrow furrow, groove or ridge - ARETE or STRIA

Narrow inlet - RIA

Narrow minded - ILLIBERAL

Nasal dividers or membranes - SEPTA

Nasal passages - NARES

Nasty rumor - CANARD

Native - INDIGENE

Native African tree - BAOBAB

Native Alaskan language - TLINGIT

Native American rations - PEMMICAN

Native Egyptian - COPT

Native Israeli - SABRA

Native Nigerian - IBO

Native of Patna - BIHARI

Native of the Steppes -TATAR

Natives of Oulu - FINNS

Natterjack - TOAD

Natural gas constituent - ETHAN

Nausea inducing agent - EMETIC

Nautical beginning - AERO

Nautical chain or rope - TYE

Nautical pin - THOLE

Nautical tackles - SWIGS

Navajo dwelling - HOGAN

Navigational system - LORAN or SHORAN

Near east inn - SERAI

Neck of mutton - SCRAG

Neck ruffle - RUCHE

Neclace spacer - RONDEL

Nectar-feeding parrot - LORY

Needle case - ETUI

Negative charged ion or particle - ANION

Negligee - PEIGNOIR

Neighbor of Ethiopia - ERITRIA

Nelumbo-lotus - LILY

Neon fish - TETRA

Neopolitan secret society - CAMORRA

Nepalese peak - ANNAPERNA

Nephrite - JADE

Nero's successor - GALBA

Nerve branches - RAMI

Nerve cell - NEURON or RECEPTOR

Nerve cell extension, fibre or part - AXON

Nerve network - PLEXUS or RETE

Nerve parts - AXONS

Nest - NIDUS or VESPIARY

Nest building fish - GOURAM

Nest of pheasants - NIDE

Nestling - EYAS

Netherland's commune - EDE

Netherlands River - ISSEL

Netlike cap - SNOOD

Netted hat lining - CAUL

Networks of nerves - RETIA

Neural fiber part or transmitter - AXON

Neutral junction - SYNAPSE

Neural network - RETE or RETIA

Never theless - WITHAL

Nevus - BIRTHMARK

New born lamb - EAN

New Guinea port - LAE

New Jersey range - RAMAPCO

New Mexico sky city - ACOMA

New Testament book - TITUS

New world monkey - SAI

New world parrot - MACAW

New Zealand bird - OII

NewZealand Island - NIUE

New Zealand parrot - KAKA,
    KAKAPO or KEA

New Zealand reptile -
    TUATARA

New Zealand tree - RIMU

New Zealand tribe - ATI

Newspaper page - OPED

Newt - EFT

Next-to-last syllable - PENULT

Niamey's land - NIGER

Nicker - NEIGH

Nigerian - IBO

Nigerian ruler - OBA

Nigeria's largest city - LAGOS

Night blooming cactus -
    CEREUS

Night in France - NUIT

Nightclub - BOITE

Nightmare world - DYSTOPIA

Nile valley region - NUBIA

Nimbus - HALO

Nine: pref. - ENNEA

Nine-sider - NONAGON

Nineveh diety - NISROCH

Ninth day before the Ides -
    NONES

Nisei's child - SANSEI

Nit-picker - PEDANT

Nitrogen compound - AMIDE,
    AMINE or AZID

Nitrogen once - AZOTE

Noah's son - HAM or SHEM

Nobby - NODAL

Nocturnal primate - LORIS or
    TARSIER

Noisome - FEDIT

Noisy fight - FRAY

Nonessential amino acid -
    SERINE

None clerics - LAICS

Nordic rugs - RYAS

Norman Neighbors - BRETONS

Norse chieftan - ROLLO

Norse dieties - VANIR

Norse giant - YMER or YMIR

Norse god - AESIR, LOKI,
    ODIN or TYR

Norse god of fate - NORN

Norse god of fire - LOGI

Norse god of peace or good weather - FREY

Norse god of the sea - AEGIR

Norse god of war - ODIN, TIU or TYR

Norse goddess of fate - NORNS

Norse goddess of death - HEL

Norse goddess of destiny - NORN

Norse goddess of love - FREYA

Norse gods - AESIR

Norse literary collection - EDDA

Norse mythological hero - EGIL

Norse pantheon - AESIR

Norse sea god - AEGIR

Norse underwolrd queen - HEL

North African Antelope - ADDAX

North African lizard - ADDA

North African mountains - ATLAS

North African seaport - ALGIERS

North American dogwood - OSIER

North American forest - TAIGA

North Dakota native - MANDAN

North Sea feeder - DEE, ELBE, EMS, MEUSE, ODOR or YSER

North Sea islands - FRISIAN

North Sea monster - KRAKEN

North seaport - AMDEN

North wind or northeast - BORA

Northeast wind - BORA

Northern bird - AUK

Northern constellation - LYRA

Northern forest - TAIGA

Nose & throat problem - CATARRH

Nose feature - ALARE

Nostril - NARES

Not supported by fact - APRIORI

Notch made by a saw - KERF

Notched - EROSE

Not cleric - LAIC

Notable exploit - GEST

Nothing in Tantes - BIEN

Not kosher - TREF

Not spoken - TACIT

Not too much, musically - NONTROPPO

Notch in wood - KERF

Noted fur trader - ASTOR

Noted weeper - NIOBE

Nothing - NIHIL

Notorious - ARRANT

Notty spot - NODUS

Nourishment - ALIMENT

November meteor show - LEONIDS

Now: Sp. AHORA

Noxious - NOISOME

Noxious atmosphere or gases - MIASMA

Noxious weed - TARE

NT book - HEB

Nuclear reactor in PA - TMI

Nucleus element or particle - PION

Number system base - RADIX

Numeric start - OCTO

Nun's cap - COIF

Nurse sharks - GATAS

Nursemaid in India - AMAH or AYAH

Nutgeg's kin - ARIL

Nutria - COYPU

NYC museum - MOMA

NYC subway line - IRT

Nyctalopia - NIGHT BLINDNESS

Nymph - OREAD

Nymph of Greek mythology - CALLISTO

Nymph of the woods - DRYAD

Nymph turned into a laurel tree - DAPHNE

Nymph who loved Apollo - DAPHNE

Nymph who loved Narcissus - ECHO

Oar holder - THOLE

Oatmeal color - ECRU

Oatmeal concoction - POLENTA

Objects d'art - VIRTU

Oblong vestment - AMICE

Observation - ESPIAL

Observation balloon - SONDE

Occasional - ORRA

Occult doctorine - CABALA

Ocean-current vortexes - GYRES

Ocean sunfish - MOLA

Oceanid - NYMPH

Ocular receiver - RETINA

Oder triburary - WARTA

Odin by another name - WOTAN

Odin's home - ASGARD

Odorless, colorless gas - ARGON

Odysseus' dog - ARGUS

"Oedipus" composer - ONESCO

Of a people, pref. - ETHNO

Of an ancient alphabet - RUNIC

Of an epoch - ERAL

Of bears - URSINE

Of blood poisoning - TOXEMIC

Of dreams - ONEIRIC

Of five - PENTA

Of gold - AURIC

Of inferior social statuss - DECLASSE

Of lizards - SAURIAN

Of lyric poems - ODIC

Of sheep - OVINE

Of the breastbone - STERNAL

Of the cheekbone - MALAR

Of the dawn - AUROREAN or EOAN

Of the ear - OTIC or AURAL

Of the farm - AGRI

Of the intestines - ILEAC

Of the liver - HEPATIC

Of the morning - MATUTINAL

Of the soft palate - VELAR

Of the third order - TERTIARY

Of the tongue - GLOSSAL

Officer's badge - COCKADE

Official announcement - RESCRIPT

Official emissary - LEGATE

Official proceedings - ACTA

Official seal - CACHET

Official serving Caesar - AEDILE

Offspring - SCION

Oil free art - TEMPARA

Oil from orange flowers - NEROLI

Oil jar - CRUSE

Oily acid salt - OLEATE

Oily fish - MENHADEN

Oily liquid - OLEIN

Oily resin - ELEMI

Ointment - NARD

Oise feeder - AISNE

Okinawa port - NAHA

Oklahoma Indian - ARAPAHO CHOCTAW

Old adage - SAW

Old alms box - ARCA

Old alphabet script - OGHAM

Old British coin - GROAT

Old card game - OMBER

Old Chinese kingdom - SHU

Old Chinese money - TAEL

Old city in Iran - SUSA

Old Egypian headdress Emblem - URAEUS

Old English bard - SCOP

Old English coin - GROAT or HAPENNY

Old English gold piece - RYAL

Old English letters - EDHS

Old European coin - ECU

Old fool - MOME

Old French coin - ECU, SOU or OBOLE

Old French dance - GAVOTTE

Old Germanic coin - TALER or THALER

Old Germans - TEUTONS

Old gold coin - DUCAT

Old gold coin of Spain - PISTOLE

Old Greek city - ARGOS

Old Greek coins - OBOLI

Old Greek medicine man - GALEN

Old hag - BELDAM

Old Hebrew bushel - EPHA

Old Indian coin - ANNT

Old Irish alphabet - OGHAM

Old Italian coin - SOLDO

Old Jewish village - SHTETLS

Old manuscript sybols - OBELI

Old Italian coins - SCUDI or SOLDI

Old manuscript marks - OBELI

Old Nick - BEELZEBUB

Old Norse character Inscription or poem - RUNE

Old Norse poetry collection - EDDA

Old ointment - NARD

Old person - WIGHT

Old Peruvian currency - INTI

Old Portuguese coin - REI

Old Portuguese currency - ESCUDO

Old quilted garmet - ACTON

Old Roman port - OSTIA

Old sayings - SAWS

Old scratch - SATAN

Old shield - TARGE

Old Spanish coin - DINAR, DURO or REAL

Old stringed instrument - REBEC

Old style poetry - EPODE

Old sweetheart - LEMAN

Old territory in Morocco - IFNI

Old Testament judge - DEBORAH

Old Testament prophet - MICAH

Old Testament scribe - EZRA

Old thrusting sword - ESTOC

Old time dill - ANET

Old Turkish city - EDESSA

Old Turkish coin - ASPER

Old U.S. coin - DESME

Old, ugly woman - BELDAME

Old violin - CREMONA or REBEC

Old wagon - WAIN

Old womanish - ANILE

Old world badger - RATEL

Old world buffalo - ANOA

Old world bunting - ORTOLAN

Old world deer - ROE

Old world doormouuse - LEROT

Old world duck - SMEW

Old world finch - LINNET or SERIN

Old world fruit tree - SORB

Old world grain - RAGI

Old world lily - ASPHODEL

Old world lizard - AGAMA or SEPS

Old world monkey - VERVERT

Old world palm - ARECA

Old world plover - PEEWIT

Old world sandpiper - TEREK

Old world thrush - CHAT

Old world tree - SORB

Olefin - ALKENE

Olive genus - OLEA

Olive-green bird - VIREO

Olivine - PERIDOT

Olla podrida - STEW

Olympic cupbearer - HEBE

Omer, to a ephah - TENTH

Omnium gatherum - OLIO

On ones back - SUPINE

One after another - SERIATIM

One ampere per volt - SIEMENS

One-horse carriage - CARIOLE

One hundred dinars - RIAL

One hundred make a dracma - LEPTA

One hundred square meters - ARE

One-millionth of a meter - MICROD

One name model - IMAN

One name singer - SADE

One of the Archangels - URIEL

One of the Fates - ATROPOS, CLOTHO or LACHESIS

One of the Furies - ALECTO, MEGAERA or TISIPHONE

One of the Hebrides - SKYE or IONA

One of the Maji GASPAR

One of the Muses - EUTERPE

One of the Pleiades - STEROPE

One of the wise men - CASPAR

One piece bathing suit - MAILLOT

One-quarter pint - GILL

One-seat carriage - STANHOPE

One-seeded fruits - AKENES or DRUPES

One square meter - CENTARE

One thousand calories - THERM

One thousand escudos - CONTO

One thousand fils - DINAR

One with a light bodybuild - ECTMORPH

Ones specialty - METIER

Oniony roll - BIALY

On the right - DEXTRAL

Oolong or Assam - TEA

Open air arcade - LOGGIA

Open air swimming pool - LIDO

Open shelter or openwork Trellis - RAMADA

Opera glasses - LORGNETTE

Opera passages - ARIOSOS

Operatic composition - SCENA

Operatic heroine - MIMI

Operatic passage - ARIOSO

Opposite if kosher - TREF

Optical area - UVEA

Optomistic - ROSEATE

Oracle - SIBYL

Oracular - VATIC

Oral statement - PAROL

Orbit point - APSIS

Orchestral gong - TAMTAM

Orchid product - SALEP or TUBER

Ordinary worker - PROLE

Ore of Copper - AZURITE

Ore of iron - SIDERITE

Organ effect - TREMOLO

Organic basis of bone - OSSEIN

Organic compound - ACETAL, AMIDE, AMINE, ENOL, ESTER, HEXANE, IMIDO or PHENOL

Organic fats - LIPIDS

Organized slaughter - POGROM

Oriental inn - SERAI

Oriental lynx - CARACAL

Oriental maid - AMAH

Oriental sailor - LASCAR

Oriental sash - OBI

Oriental tea - CHA

Oriental warehouse - GODOWN

Orifices - ORA

Orinoco feeder - CARONI

Orinoco tributary - ARO

Orion's left foot - RIGEL

Oriole, e.g. - OSENE

Ornamental carp - KOI

Ornamental case - ETUI

Ornamental candlestick - FLAMEAU

Ornamental Chinese tree - GINKGO or GINKO

Ornamental garden - PARTERRE

Ornamental loop - PICOT

Ornamental plant - CANNA or PILEA

Ornamental purse - ETUI

Ornamental shrub - JAPONICA, OLEASTER or SPIREA

Ornamental stud - AGLET

Ornamental tree - CASSIA

Ostiary - LECTOR

Ostrich cousin - RHEA

Orthodox branch of Islam - SUNNI

Ostrich cousin - RHEA

Ostrich relaltive - TINAMOU

Ostrich or emu - RATITE

O T Book - AMOS, DEUT, ECCLES, ESTH, EXOD, EZRA, ESTHER, EZEK, GEN, HAB, HAGGAI, HOSEA, ISA, JONAH, LAM, LEV, MICAH, NEH, NEHUM, NUM, OBAD, OBADIAH, PBAD, PSA, PSALMS or RUTH

Othello's friend - IAGO

Other: Sp. - OTRA

Other: Lat. - ALIA

Otic - AURAL

Ottoma - POUF

Outback instrument - DIGERIDOO

Outcast - PARIAH

Outer boundary - AMBIT

Outer coat of a seed - TESTA

Outer: Pref. - ECTO

Out lying community - EXURB

Oven for drying hops - OAST

Overhead cable car - TELPHER

Ox of India - ZEBU

Oxygen compound - OXIDE

Oxygen dependent creature - AEROBE

Oyster farm: Fr. - PARC

Pacific canoe - BANCA

Pacific island - SAMAR

Pacific plant - TARO

Pacific island country - NAURU

Pack leader - AKELA

Page size of a book - OCTAVO

Pagoda - TAA

Pain unit - DOL

Paint a word picture - LIMN

Painter of ballet dancers - DEGAS

Painter's undercoat - GESSO

Painting genre - OPART

Painting on dry plaster - SECCO

Painting technique - IMPASTO

Pair - DYAD

Pakistan bread - NANS

Pakistan language - ERDU

Pakistan River - INDUS

Pakistan rupee - PRE

Palace in Florence - PITTI

Palace in Istambul - TOPKAPI

Palace in Vatican City - LATERAN

Palatable - SAPID

Pale dry sherry – FINO

Pale yellow - ECRU

Palm cuckatoo - ARA

Palm starch - SAGO

Palm thatch - NIPA

Palm tree - ARECA

Pamper - COSSET

Panamanian coin - CESTESIMO

Pangolin - ANTEATER

Panhandle - CADGE

Papal body - CURIA

Papal cape - FANON or ORALE

Papal court - CURIA

Papal embassador - NUNCIO

Papal garment, veil or Vestment - ORALE

Papal hat - BIRETTE or MITRE

Papal scarf - ORALE

Papal silver coins - PAOLI

Papal tribunal - ROTA

Papaya - PAPAW

Papaya enzyme - PAPAIN

Paper measure - QUIRE

Paper size - DEMY

Papyrus plant - SEDGE

Parade of bullfighters - PASEO

Paradise - ELYSIUM

Paradise dweller - HOURI

Parasidic plant - DODDER

Parched - SERE

Parent of Titan - SATURN

Pariah - LEPER

Paris palace - ELYSEE

Parisian seasons - ETES

Parish official - BEADLE

Parka - ANORAK

Parquet circle - PARTERRE

Parr - SAMLET

Parrot - ECHO, KEA or LORY

Parson bird - TUI

Part of A. D. - ANNO

Part of DOS - SYST.

Part of N.B. - BENE

Part of Q.E.D. - ERAT

Part of RSVP - SIL

Part of TNT - TOLUENE

Part of a T.A.E. - ALVA

Part of a chair - SPLAT

Part of a Krone - ORE

Part of a lariat - HONDO

Part of a meter - IAMB

Part of a nerve cell - AXONE

Part of a neuron - AXON

Part of a ships bow - HAWSE

Part of a sonata - RONDO

Part of a spur - ROWEL

Partial: pref. - SEMI

Particles in electrolysis - ANIONS

Particles in suspension - COLLOIDS

Partner of Charybdis - SCYLLA

Partner of Lares - PENATES

Party to - INON

Passages in the body - ITERS

Passe - DEMODE

Passover - PESACH

Passover feast - SEDER

Pasta variety - ROTINI

Pasta wheat - DURAM

Paste gem - STRASS

Paste made from seseme seeds - TAGINI

Pasternak heroine - LARQA

Pastoral diety - FAUN

Pastoral poem - IDYLL

Pasturage grass - FESCUE

Patched - PIEBALD

Patience - SOLITAIR

Patriotic group - SAR

Patron saint of artists - ELOI

Patron saint of Paris - DENIS

Patron saint of lawyers - IVES

Patronage - AEGIS

Paving block - SETT

Payment to expedite service - BAKSHEESH

Peaceful - IRENIC

Peace pipe - CALUMET

Peaseful - IRENIC

Peach or apricot - DRUPE

Peacock constellation - PAVO

Peacock feather eyes - OCELL I

Peaked cap - KEPI

Pear-shaped fiddle - REBEC

Pear-shaped gem - BOULE

Pear variety - COMISE

Pearl diver - AMA

Pearly muscle - UNIO

Peasant - RYOT

Peasant skirt - DIRNDL

Peculiar: Pre. - IDIO

Pedestal base - PLINTH

Pedestal part - DADO

Peep show - RAREE

PeerGynt's composer - GRIEG

PeerGynt's creator - IBSEN

PeerGynt's dancer - ANITRA

PeerGynt's mother - ASE

Pellet-size pasta - FARFEL

Pelvic bones - ILIA or SACRA

Pennant - FANON

Penquinlike bird - AUK

Pens and needles - STYLI

People of Borneo - DYAKS

People of Eastern Siberia - YAKUT

People of social standing - NOBS

Perceived by the ear - AURAL

Percussion istrument - CELESTA

Perennial herb - ACANTHUS or ARNICA

Perfect expression - MOTJUSTE

Perfidious - PUNIC

Perfume - CENSE

Perfume bottle - FLACON

Perfume ingredient - AMBERGRIS, ORRIS or ROSEOIL

Perfume oil - NEROL

Perfumer's liquid - ACETAL

Perrywinkle genus - VANCA

Persian despot or governors - SATRAP

Persian elves or fairies - PERIS

Perssian profet - ZOROASTER

Persian sun god - MITHRAS

Persian wheel - NORIA

Persians - MEDES

Person with a loud voice - STENTOR

Personal instability - ANOMIE

Perspire - EGEST

Pertaining to dreams - ONEIRIC

Pertaining to hair - PILAR

Pertaining to the ear - OTIC

Pertaining to knowledge - LORAL

Pertinent - ADREM

Peruke - PERIWIG

Peruvian beast - ALPACA

Peruvian city - ICA

Pet peeve - BETA NOIRE

Petrarch's beloved - LAURA

Petty ruler or tyrant - SATRAP

Pharaoh - RED ANT

Pharaonic tomb - MASTABAH

Pheasant brood - NIDE

Philippine banana tree - ABACA

Philippine fibre - ABACA

Philippine fruit - PINA

Philippine island - CEBU, LEYTE, MINDANOA, PANAY or SAMAR

Philippine native - ATI

Philippine palm - NIPA

Philippine people - MOROS

Phiilippine plant - ABACA

Philippine seaport - CEBU, ILOILO, LUZON or MANILA

Philippine termite - ANAI

Philippine tree - IBA

Philippine volcano - TAAL

Philistine city - GATH

Philistine god - DAGON

Philodendron, e.g. - AROID

Phoenician city - SIDON or TYRE

Phoenician diety - BAAL

Phoenician god or goddess - ASTARTE or BAAL

Phoenician port - TYRE

Phoney - POSEUR

Photographic, as memory - EIDETIC

Pianist's challenge - ARPEGGIO

Piano relative - CELESTA

Pickled food - SOUSE

Pictograph - GLYPH

Picture - LIMN

Picture puzzle - REBUS

Pidgeon's nose - CERE

Pie filling - NESSELRODE

Piedmont province - TORENO

Pig: Sp. - GORDO

Piglet - SHOAT

Pigment - OCHER

Pilasters - ANTAE

Pilchard - SARDINE

Pile of hay - MOW

Pile of stones - CAIRN

Pileus - CAUL

Pilgrim to Mecca - MOSLEM

Pillage - RAPINE

Pillow cover - SHAM

Pine tar derivaive - RETENE

Pineapple: Sp. - PINA

Pineapple fiber - ISTLE

Pinguid - OILY

Pintail duck - SMEE

Pions & kaons - MESONS

Pipe - HOOKAH

Pipe residue - DOTTLE

Pipe sealant - LUTE

Piranhas - CARIBES

Pita fiber - ISTLE

Pitcher - EWER or OLLA

Pitcher of beer - GROWLER

Pith helmet - TOPEE or TOPI

Pity - PATHOS

Place: Fr. - LIEU

Place of extreme torment - GEHENNA

Plain weave fabric - BATISTE or REPP

Plains Indians - KIOWA

Plains tribe - DAKOTA

Planetary reflectioms - ABEDOS

Planetary shadow - UMBRA

Plant & animal life - BIOTA

Plant aperture - STOMA

Plant chewed in Arabia - QAT

Plant fluids - SERA

Plant fungus - DRYROT

Plant genus - ALOE

Plant louse - APHID or APHIS

Plant malady - EDEMA

Plant of hot regions - AGAVE

Plant of the arum or lily family - AROID

Plant pest - APHID or PHIS

Plant pore - STOMA

Plant root - RADIX

Plant rust - UREDO

Plant substance - TRAMA

Plant with a fragrant rootstock - ORRIS

Plant with colorful flowers - GENTIAN

Plant with human-like root - MANDRAKE

Plant with sword-shaped leaves - AGAVE or GLADIOLA

Plant with yellow flowers - AVE

Plantain lily - HOSTA

Plaster of Paris - GESSO

Plastics ingredient - UREA

Plate armour - CUIRASS

Plating alloy - TERNE

Playful leap - CAPRIOLE

Playing marble - NIB

Pleasingly plump - ZAFTIG

Pleasure seeker - HEDONIC

Pleated lace edging - RUCHE

Plenty, once - ENOW

Plexus - RETE

Pliable branch - WITHY

Plinth - ORLO or SOCLE

Plot - CABAL

Plow sole - SLADE

Plumb brandy - MIRABELLE

Plumbago - GRAPHITE

Plume of feathers - AIGRETTE

Plumed hat - SHAKO

Plunder - RAPINE or REAVE

Plunderer - RAPPAREE

Plunger for churning butter - DASHER

Pluto - DIS

Pluvious - RAINY

Poem division - CANTO

Poem's final stanza - ENVOI

Poem with 17 syllables - HAIKU

Poet's pause - CAESURA

Poetic feet - PAEONS

Poetic foot - IAMB

Poetic lament - ELEGY

Poetic patchwork - CENTO

Poetic postscript - ENVOI

Poetic Rhythm - METER

Poetic stanza - FESTINA

Poetry collection - EPOS

Poet's feet - ANAPESTS

Poet's Ireland - ERIN

Poet's muse - ERATO

Poinsettia, for one - SPURGE

Point of origin - SITUS

Pointed arch - OGIVE

Pointed window - LANCET

Pointless - OTIOSE

Poi root - TARO

Poison - BANE

Poison oak or shrub - SUMAC

Poison snake - ADDER

Poison tree - UPAS

Poisonous evergreen shrub - OLEANDER

Poisonous evergreens - YEWS

Poisonous mosquito - AEDES

Poisonous mushroom - AMANITA

Poisonous plant - HEMLOCK or HENBANE

Poisonous snake - TAIPAN

Polar wear - ANORAK

Polder - LOWLAND RECLAIMED FROM THE SEA

Polish dance - MAZZURKA

Polish lancer - UHLAN or ULAN

Political falsehood - ROORBACK

Political refugee - EMIGRE

Politically neutral - MUGWUMP

Pollen bearer or produce - ANTHER

Polynesian beverage - KAVA

Polynesian idol - TIKI

Polynesian skirt - PAREU

Polynesian wrap - LAVALAVA

Pompous - OROTUNG

Pond - MERE

Pond dross - SCUM

Pond plant - ALGA

Ponds - SEDGE

Pool table cover - BAIZE

Poor imitation - ERSATZ

Pope's emissary - LEGASE

Pope's fanon ORALE

Popeye's creator Segar - ELZIE

Poplar tree - ALAMO or ABELE

Porous limestone - TUFA

Port in Germany - KIEL

Port in Mexico - TAMPICO

Port in Portugal - TORO

Port near Belfast - LARNE

Port near Haifa - ACRE

Port of Brazil - BELEM

Port of Crete - CANE

Port of Israel - ACRE, EILAT or HAIFA

Port of Italy - BARI

Port of old Rome - OSTIA

Port of Spain - BILBOA or CADIZ

Port of Tunisia - SFAX

Port of Yeman - ADEN

Port on the Gulf of Lion - MARSEILLES

Port on the Seine - ROUEN

Port on the Norweigen Sea - BERGEN

Portable supply cabinet - TABORET

Portents - OMENS or PRESAGES

Portico of old Grease - STOA

Portray - LIMN

Portuguese cape - ROCA

Portuguese colony in India - GOA

Portuguese seaport - SETUBAL

Portuguese statesman - GRANDEE

Portuguese wine - MADEIRA

Positive particle - CATION

Poster paint - TEMPERA

Posterior - CAUDAL

Pot - OLLA

Pot herb - ORACH

Potassium compound - NITER

Potato dumpling - GNOCCI

Potato pancake - LATKE

Potato pastry - KNISH

Potpourri - OLIO

Pouch - BURSE

Pout - MOUE

Pourboire - TIP

Powder from caster oil plant - RICIN

Powdered diamonds - BORT

Powdered, in heraldry - SEME

Powdered volcanic rock - TRASS

Power org. - TV

Powerful - PUISSANT

Powerful explosive - AMATOL

Practice fly ball - FUNGO

Prank - DIDO

Pray in Latin - ORA

Prayer - ORISON

Prayer bench - PRIEDEAU

Praying figure in art - ORANT

Pre-Aztec Indian - TOLTEC

Preamble or preface - PROEM

Predatory bird - KITE or SKUA

Prefix for both - AMBI

Prefix for seven - HEPTA

Prefix meaning "bone" - OSTEO

Prefix meaning "peculiar" - IDIO

Pregnant - ENCIENTE

Prehistoric ax - CELT

Prehistoric stone tool - EOLITH

Prehistoric tomb - CIST

Pre-Mayan people - OLMEC

Prepare into pellets - PRILL

Presidential pooch - FALA

Press to commit perjury - SUBORN

Prestige - CACHET

Pretender - POSEUR

Prickley pear - NOPAL

Prickly plant - TEASEL

Prickley shrub - Briar or GORSE

Priest of Babylon - EZRA

Priestly dress - EPHOD

Priestly vestment - FANO

Priest's cloak - COPO

Priest's robe - ALB

Priestess of Bacchus - MAENAD

Prima ballarina - ETOILE

Primary Roman hill - POLATINE

Prime minister before Gladstone - DISRAELI

Primitive wheat - SPELT

Primrose relative - OXLIP

Prince Valiant's wife - ALETA

Princess of myth - IOLE

Principal ore of lead - GALENA

Principle - TENET

Printer's direction - CARET or STET

Printer's emblem - COLOPHONE

Printer's mark - CARET or DELE

Printer's measure - EM or PICA

Printing ink ingredient - ELEMI

Printing mistakes - ERRATA

Printing term - STET

Prized clam - QUAHOG

Proceedings - ACTA

Process of mountain formation - ORDGENY

Professional retirees - EMERITI

Profet - AUGUR

Profound sleep - SOPOR

Profusion - ARIOT

Progressive emaciation - TABES

Promatory - NESS

Promenade - PASEO

Promise of marriage - AFFIANCE

Promising up-and-comer - PHENOM

Promoting pease - IRENIC

Pronouncements - DICTA

Pronunciation dots - DIAERESIS

Property seller - ALIENOR

Prophet of Delphi - ORACLE

Prophetess of Israel - DEBORAH

Proscribe - BAN

Prosperity - WEAL

Prospero's servant - ARIEL

Prospero's slave - CALIBAN

Protection - AEGIS

Protection: var. - EGIS

Potest angrily - INVEIGH

Protozoan - AMOEBA

Provencal song - SERENA

Provencal verse - SESTINA

Province of China - SHENSI

Prufrock's creator - ELIOT

Prussian lancer - UHLAN

Psychological threshold - LIMEN

Public lecture hall - LYCEUM

Public place for walking - PASEO

Public sentiment - ETHOS

Public warehouse - ETAPE

Publishing # - ISBN

Puccini heroine - MIMI

Puckered fabric finsih - PLISSE

Pueblo ceremonial chamber - KIVA

Pueblo dweller - ZUNI

Pueblo Indian - PIRO

Pueblo Iindian village - ACOMA

Pueblo people - TIWA

Puerto Rican seaport - PONCE

Puff adder - HOGNOSE

Pulitzer novelist - AGEE

Pulpit - AMBO

Pulverize - TRITURATE

Pumpkin or squash - PEPO

Pundit - SWAMI

Punish - AMERCE

Punish by fine - AMERSE

Punishment stick - FERULE

Punjabi beleiver - SIKH

Punkie - GNAT

Pupa graduate - IMAGO

Purple seaweed - NORI

Purpose - NONCE

Purposeful - TELIC

Put forward as fact - POSIT

Put on clothes - DIGHT

Puzzle - REBUS

Pygmy antelope - ORIBE

Pyramus' lover - THISBE

Pyrenees Republic - ANDORRA

Q.E.D word - ERAT

Quadriceps locales - LEGS

Quality of taste - SAPOR

Quarter acre of land - ROOD

Quarter of a denarius - SESTERSE

Quarter-pint - GILL

Queen of Carthage - DIDO

Queen of France - REINE

Queen of Hades - HECATE

Queen of heaven - HERA

Queen of Italy - ELENA

Queen of Jordan - NOOR

Queen of Norway - SONJA

Queen of Persia - ESTHER

Queen of Spain - ENA

Queen of Sparta - LEDA

Queen of Thebes - NIOBE

Queen of the fairies - TITANIA

Queue - BRAID

Quibble - CAVIL

Quickglance or impression - APERCU

Quickly - PRESTO

Quip - EPIGRAM or SALLY

Quisling - TRAITOR

Quivering - ASPEN

Qumram inhabitant - ESSENE

Quorum in a synagog - MINYAN

RNA component - URACIL

Rabbit - CONEY

Rabbit-eared bandicoot - BILBY

Rabbit ears - DIPOLE

Rabbit fur - CONY or LAPIN

Rabbit kin - AGOUTI

Rabbit's tail - SCUT

Raccoon kin - COATI

Raccoon like mammal - PANDA

Rachel's father - LABAN

Radame's beloved - AIDA

Radioactivity unit - CURIE

Radon, originally - NITON

Raga rythem-maker - TABLA

Rainbow goddess - IRIS

Rainbow trout - STEELIE

Rain forest vine - LIANE

Rajah's wife - RANI

Rake - ROUE

Rams-horn horn - SHOFER

Range of Kyrgyzstan - ALAI

Range ridge - ARETE

Rank in taste - RAMMISH

Rapacious seabird - SKUA

Rare-earth element - TERBIUM

Ravine - BARRANCA or NULLAH

Rayed flower - ASTER or OXEYE

Razor-billed auk - MURRE

Razor-billed birds - AUKS

Reach in amount – RUN TO

Readily - LIEF

Reading desk – AMBO

Real - PUKKA

Recess in a church - APSE

Recital halls - ODIA

Recluse - ANCHORET or EREMITE

Recorded proceedings - ACTA

Recoverable cargo cast adrift - LAGAN

Recurring musical phrases - LEITMOTIV

Rectangular paving stone - SETT

Rectangular pier or pilaster - ANTA

Red - CERISE

Red bood cell component - HEME

Red cedar - SAVIN

Red chalcedony - CARNELIAN

Red deer - HART

Red dye - EOSIN

Red dye plant - MADDER

Red giant star - MINA

Red pigment - OCHER

Red quartz - JASPER

Red rockfish - TAMBOR

Red sea port - JIDDA or SUEZ

Red soil - LATERITE

Redactor - EDITOR

Reddish brown - RUSSETY

Reddish-brown gemstone - SARD

Reddish deer - ROES

Reddish hartebeest - TORA

Reddish orange - JACINTH

Reddish rash - ROSEOLA

Redolent compound - ESTER

Reedy pond - SLUE

Refractive unit - DIOPTER

Refuge - EMIGRE

Refuges - ASYLA

Refuse - OFFAL

Regan's dad - LEAR

Regarding - ANENT

Region of Egypt and Sudan - NUBIA

Region of France - ALSACE

Region of old France - DANELAW

Region of South America - PATAGONIA

Region of Spain - CASTILE

Region south of the Sahara - SAHEL

Region that includes Ephesus - IONIA

Regional life - BIOTA

Related maternally - ENATE

Related on the father's side - AGNATE

Relating to grandparents - AVAL

Relating to lungs - LOBAR

Relating to summer - ESTIVAL

Relating to the cheekbone - MALAR

Release a claim to - REMISE

Release Mechanism - DETENT

Relevant - APROPOS

Relict - WIDOW

Religious booklet - ORDO

Religious convert - PROSELYTE

Religious flight - REGIRA

Religious recluse - EREMITE

Religious residence - PRIORY

Religious retreat - ASHRAM

Relinquish - DEMIT

Reliquary - ARCA

Remaining out of sight - PERDU PERDU

Remarkable - UNCO

Remarkable person - PHENOM

Remission - REMITTAL

Remove in printing - DELE

Renaissance instrument - REBEC

Repetition - ROTE

Representative - TYPAL

Reproductive cells - GAMETES

Research baloon - SONDE

Resin - ANIME

Resin used in varnish – SANDARAC

Resonant of voice - OROTUND

Respected one - DOYEN

Restrain - BATE or TRAMMEL

Retardanto - SLOWER

Retinal cells - RODS

Retired - AMERITUS

Retired professors - EMERITI

Reused wool - MUNGO

Rhine feeder - AARE, MOSEL, MOSELLE or RUHR

Rhone feeder - ISERE or SAONE

Rhythmic pattern of a stanza - METER

Rib - COSTA

Ribbed cloth - TRICOT

Ribbed fabric - FAILLE or REP

Rice dish - KEDGEREE or RISOTTO

Rice like pasta - ORZO

Rich fertilizer - GUANO

Rich ice cream - TORTONI

Rich king - CROESUS

Rich: Sp. - RICO

Rich tapestry - ARRAS

Rich-voiced - OROTUND

Rich yeast bread - STOLLEN

Riches - PELF

Riddle - KOAN

Ridge - ARETE

Ridge with a cliff - CUESTA

Ridges - WEALS

Riding crop - QUIRT

Rigel's constellation - ORION

Right hand page - RECTO

Rigid disciplinarian - MARTINET

Ring of color - AREOLA

Ring shape - ANNULAR

Ring stone - SARD

Ring-tailed lemur - MAKI

Ring worm - TINEA

Rio Grande feeder - PECOS

Ripple pattern on a stamp - MOIRE

Risque - SCABROUS

Ritual washbasin - LAVABO

Rival of Sparta and Athens - ARGOS

River at Runnymede - THAMES

River deposit - ALLUVIUM

River in Africa - NIGER or UELE

River in Alaska - YUKON

River in Albania - DRIN

River in Albuqueque - RIO GRANDE

River in Amiens - SOMME

River in Ann Arbor - HURON

River in Arezzo - ARNO

River in Arizona - GILA

River in Arles - RHONE

River in Asia - AMUR, OXUS or YALU

River in Australia - NAMOI

River in Austria - ENNS

River in Avignon - RHONE

River in Baghdad - TIGRIS

River in Bath - AVON

River in Belarus - NEMAN

River in Belgium - LYS, LESSE, OISE or YSER

River in Berlin - HAVEL or SPREE

River in Bolivia - BENI or RIO

River in Bonn - RHINE

River in Boston - CHARLES

River in Botswana - OKAVANGO

River in Brazil - PARA

River in Breslau - ODER

River in British Columbia - FRASER or SKEENA

River in Burma - IRRAWADDY

River in Caen - ORNE

River in Canada - LIARD

River in Cardiff - TAFF

River in Carlsbad - PECOS

River in Carolina - NEUSE

River in Chanilly - OISE

River in Chile - LOA

River in China - AMUR, HAN, HSI, HUANG, ILI or WEI

River in Cologne - RHINE

River in Columbia - CAUCA or META

River in Cornwall - TAMAR

River in Cuxhaven - ELBE

River in Dallas - TRINITY

River in Devon - EXE

River in Dresden - ELBE

River in East Asia - AMUR

River in England - AIRE, AVON, EXE, OUS OUSE, SARRY or SEINE

River in Essen - RHUR

River in Ethiopia - OMO

River in Europe - EGER

River in Flanders - YSER

River in Flores - REO

River in France - LOIRE, LYS, OISE, SAONE, SELLE or YSER

River in Frankfurt - ODER

River in Geneva - RHONE

River in Germany - EDER, ELBE, EMS, ILLE, ISAR, RHONE, RUHR, SAAR or WESER

River in Glasgow - CLYDE

River in Grenoble - ISERE

River in Hades - LETHE

River in Hamburg - ELBE

River in Hartes - EURE

River in Holland - LEK

River in Hungary - EGER

River in Iberia - MINHO

River in Illinois - KASKASKIA

River in Indiana - MAUMEE or WABASH

River in Interlaken - AARE

River in Ireland - ERNE or SHANNON

River in Italy - ARNO, NERA or RUBICON

River in Kansas - OSAGE

River in Karnak - NILE

River in Kashmir - INDUS

River in Kazakhstan - URAL or CHU

River in Kenya - TANA

River in Khabarovsk - AMUR

River in Khartoum - NILE

River in Koln - RHINE

River in Korea - KAN or YALU

River in Krakow - VISTULA

River in Leeds - AIRE

River in Leningrad - SEVA

River in Lisbon - TAGUS

River in Louisville - OHIO

River in Lyon - RHONE or SAONE

River in Maine - SACO

River in Mali - NIGER

River in Manchester - MERSEY

River in Manchuria - AMUR or YALU

River in Memphis - NILE

River in Mongolia - ARIVER

River in Montana - MARIAS or TETON

River in Munich - ISAR

River in Nantes - LOIRE

River in Nebraska - PLATTE

River in New Brunswick - RARITAN

River in Newcastle - TYNE

River in New Jersey - PASSAIC

River in New York - AUSABLE, GENESEE or TIOGA

River in Normandy - ORNE

River in North Carolina - PEEDEE

River in North Dakota - GOOSE or SHEYENNE

River in North Korea - YALU

River in Ohio - SCIOTO

River in Opole - ODER

River in Orel - OKA

River in Orenburg - URAL

River in Orleans - LOIRE

River in Orsk - URAL

River in Pakistan - INDUS

River in Paris - SEINE

River in Pennsylvania - TIOGA

River in Perth - TAY

River in Peru - SANTA

River in Pittsburg - OHIO

River in Poland - NEISSE or ODER

River in Richmond - JAMES

River in Roanne - LOIRE

River in Rochester - GENESEE

River in Romania - OLT or MURES

River in Rome - TIBER

River in Rostov - DON

River in Russia - DON, LENA, NEVA, OKA, SERET or URAL

River in Rutgers - RARITAN

River in Rybinsk - VOLGA

River in Saragossa - EBRO

River in Saxony - WESER

River in Scotland - AFTON, CLYDE or TAY

River in Siberia - LENA or AMUR

River in Silesia - ODER

River in Soissons - AISNE

River in Solothurn - AARE

River in South Africa - LIMPOPO or VAAL

River in South Carolina - SANTEE

River in Spain - EBRO

River in Staffordshire - TRENT

River in Stettin - ODER

River in St. Petersburg - NEVA

River in Stratford - HOUSATONIC

River in Suffern - RAMAPO

River in SW Asia - ARAS

River in Sweden - TORNE

River in Terre Haute - WABASH

River in Texas - SABINE

River in Thailand - NAN

River in Thun - AAR

River in Tibet - INDUS

River in Timbuktu - NIGER

River in the Congo - UELE

River in the Punjab - RAVI

River in Toledo - MAUMEE

River in Tours - LOIRE

River in Turkey - ARAS

River in Tuscany - ARNO

River in Ukraine - DONETS, ONESTR or STYR

River in Venezuela - APURE, ARO or ORINOCO

River in Wroclaw - ODER

River in Verdun - MEUSE

River in Virginia - OTTER

River in Warsaw - VISTULA

River in Washington - SPOKANE

River in West Virginia - OHIO

River in Yakutsk - LENA

River in York - OUSE

River in Yorkshire - AIRE, OUSE or URE

River in Zaire - EULE

River into Issyk-kul - CHOW

River into Lake Utah - PROVO

River into the Severn - AVON

River into the Snake - GROS VENTRE

River into the Oise - AISNE

River into the Wash - OUSE

River islets - AITS or RIAS

River near Lethe - STYX

River near Nottingham - TRENT

River near Rutgers - RARITAN

River near Monterey - SALINAS

River nymph - NAIAD or NAIS

River of Aragon - EBRO

River of Argentina - PARANA

River of Brandenburg - ODER

River of England - OUSE

River of Flanders - YSER

River of Florence - ARNO

River of forgetfulness - LETHE

River of France - AUBE

River of Frankfurt - ODER

River of Grand Forks - RED

River of Hades - LETHE

River of Hesse - EDER

River of Indiana - WABASH

River of Ireland - ERNE

River of Leeds - AIRE

River of Oblivion - LETHE

River of Portugal & Spain - TAGUS

River of Sweden - UME

River through Alaska - YUKON

River through Hesse - FULDA

River through Lower Saxony - EMS

River through Northern Ireland - ERNE

River through Opole - ODER

River through Pakistan - INDUS

River through Perth Amboy - RARITAN

River through Pittsburg - OHIO

River through Rouen - SEINE

River through Switzerland - RHINE

River through the Savoy Alps - ISERE

River through Toledo - MAUMEE

River through Tours - LOIRE

River through Wales - SEVERN

River to Donegal Bay - ERNE

River to Korea Bay - YALU

River to Lake Baikal - SELENGA

River to Lake Ontario - OSWEGO

River to Siegen - EDER

River to the Amazon - JAPURA or NEGRO

River to the Adriatic - ADIGE

River to the Arabian sea - INDUS

River to the Arctic Ocean - LENA

River to the Balltic - ODER

River to the Black sea -
  DANUBE or DNEPR

River to the Caspian Sea -
  KURA, URAL or VOLGA

River to the Chesapeake -
  POTOMAC

River to the Colorado - GILA

River to the Congo - UBANGI

River to the Danube - DRAVE,
  ENNS or ISAR

River to the Dniester - SECRET

River to the Ebro - ARAGON

River to the Elbe - EGER or
  OSTE

River to the English Channel -
  EXE or SOMME

River to the Euphrates - TIGRIS

River to the Fulda - EDER or
  WESER

River to the Gironde -
  GARONNE

River to the Gulf of Finland -
  NEVA

River to the Gulf of Lions -
  RHONE

River to the Hudson -
  MOHAWK

River to the Irish Sea - DEE

River to the Laptev Sea - LENA

River to the Ligurian Sea - ARNO

River to the Mediteranian -
  EBRO

River to the Mississippi - OHIO,

ST.CROIX or YAZOO

River to the Missouri -
  KANSAS or PLATTE

River to the Moselle - SAAR

River to the North Sea - ELBE,
  EMS, GREAT, MEUSE,
  ODER, OUSE, RHINE
  TEES, WESER or YSER

River to the Odor - OPPA or
  WARTA

River to the Ohio - WABASH

River to the Oise - AIRE,
  AISNE or CAM

River to the Orinoco - AARO
  or CARONI

River to the Ouse - AIRE or
  CAM

River to the Rennes - ILLE

River to the Rhine - AARE,
  MOSEL or RUHR

River to the Rhone - ISERE or
  SAONE

River to the Rio Grande - PECOS

River to the St.Lawrence -
  OTTAWA

River to the Sea of Okhotsk -
  AMUR

River to the Seine - AUBE, EURE, MARNE or OISE

River to the Severn - AVON

River to the South China Sea - MEKONG

River to the Ubangi - UELE

River to the Volga - KAMA, OKA or SAMARA

River to the Yangtze - HAN

River to the Yellow Sea - YALU

Riverbank plant - SEDGE

Riverleaf - HEPATICA

RNA component - URACIL

RNA constituent - ADENINE

Robin relative - VEERY

Rock boring tool - TREPAN

Rock braking tool - GAD

Rock garden plant - SEDUM

Rock mineral - FELDSPAR

Rock plant - LICHEN

Rock salt - HALITE

Rock shelter - ABRI

Rocky barren plateau - FJELD

Rocky peak or crag - TOR

Rochy ridge - ARETE

Rodent - AGOUTI

Roll of coins - ROULEAU

Romaine - COS

Roman body armour - LORICA

Roman bronze - AES

Roman Catholic tribunal - ROTA

Roman coin - AES or SESTERCE

Roman commander - AGRIPPA

Roman commoner - PLEB

Roman courtyard - ATRIA

Roman dictator - SULLA

Roman emporer - OTHO, NERVA or TRAJAN

Roman emperor after Galba - OTHO

Roman emperor after Trajan - HADRIAN

Roman festival - FERIA

Roman galley - BIREME or TRIREME

Roman god - AMOR, DIS or LAR

Roman god of festivity & Revelry - COMUS

Roman god of the sea - NEPTUNE

Roman god, to a poet - JOVE

Roman goddess - BONA, DEA or PAX

Roman goddess of horses - EPONA

Roman goddess of war - BELLONA

Roman gods - DEI

Roman guardian spirits - GENII

Roman hades - ORCUS

Roman hero - AENEAS

Roman historian - LIVY

Roman household gods - LARES or PENATES

Roman judge or magistrate - EDILE or PRAETOR

Roman market place - FORA

Roman moon goddess - LUNA

Roman official - AEDILE

Roman philosopher - SENECA

Roman poet - CATO or OVID

Roman politician or censor - CATO

Roman road - ITER

Roman robe - STOLA

Roman ruler - OTHO

Roman sea god - NEPTUNE

Roman senate - CURIA

Roman squares - FORA

Roman statesman - CATO

Roman token - TESSERA

Roman tunic - STOLA

Romanian coin - BANI or LEU

Romanian round dance - HORAH

Romanov emperor - TSAR

Rome's port - OSTIA

Roofing material - TERNE

Rookie - TYRO

Rooms in a harem - ODAS

Rooster - CHANTICLEER

Root - RADIX

Root vegetable - CELERIAC or SALSIFY

Rootrot - EDEMA

Rope fibre - ABACA, BAST, COIR or OAKEM

Rope plant - AGAVE

Rorqual - SEI WHALE

Rose bay - OLEANDER

Rose colored dye - EOSIN

Ross island volcano - EREBUS

Roster - ROTA

Rotary enginer name - WANKEL

Rough earthenware - RAKU

Round mass - BOLUS

Round windows - OCULI

Rounded molding - OVOLO

Royal crown - DIADEM

Royal treasury - FISC

Rubber trees - ULES

Ruby - CARMINE

Rubylike jemstone - SPINEL

Rudimentary seed - OVULE

Ruffles on shirts - JABOTS

Ruined city in Jordan - PETRA

Ruins of Thebes - LUXOR

Ruler of Tunis - DEY

Ruling clique member - OLIGARCH

Rum cake - BABA

Rumanian coin - LEY

Rumba-like dance - BEGUINE

Rumor - ONDIT

Rump - NATES

Run away from debt - LEVANT

Run quickly - HARE

Rural - BUCOLIC

Rural diety - FAUN

Russian alphabet - CYRILLIC

Russian assembly - DUMA

Russian ballet - KIROV

Russian brew - KVASS

Russian city - OREL

Russian commune - MIR

Russian comrade - TOVARISH

Russian convention - RADA

Russian cooperative - ARTEL

Russian crepe - BLINI

Russian dog breed - BORZOI

Russian farm - ARTEL

Russian forest - TAIGA

Russian hemp - RINE

Russian inland sea - ARAL

Russian lake - ONEGA

Russian legislative body - DUMA

Russian measure of distance - VERST

Russian pancake - BLINI

Russian parliament - DUMA

Russian peasant - KULAK or MOUJIK

Russian prison - GULAG

Russian range - ALAI or URAL

Russian retreat - DACHA

Russian river - OKA or URAL

Russian saint - OLGA

Russian sea - AZOV

Russian summer home or villa - DACHA

Russian village - MIR

Russian wolfhound - BORZOI

Rustling sound - SUSURRUS

Rye fungus - ERGOT

Sabbath bread - CHALLAH

Sacrament vessel - PYX

Sacramental oil - CHRISM

Sacred Bookks of Hinduism - VEDA

Sacred Buddhist Mountain - OMEI

Sacred bull of Egypt - APIS

Sacred chest - ARCA

Sacred chorale - MOTET

Sacred Egyptian bird - IBIS

Sacred Egyptian bull - APIS

Sacred Hindu writings - VEDA

Sacred poem - PSALM

Sacred: Pref. - HAGIO

Sacred river of Kubla Khan - ALPH

Sacred song - MOTET

Sacred story set to music - ORATORIO

Sacred text - TORA

Sacred tree of India - BO

Sacrifice - IMMOLATE

Sad song - DIRGE

Saddle part - CANTLE

Safecracker - YEGG

Saga - GEST

Sage - AGNOSTIC, RAMONA, SALVIA or SAVANT

Sagebrush genus - ARTEMISIA

Saharan wind - SIROCCO

Sailing vessel - XEBEC

Sailor's saint - ELMO

Salad cheese - FETA

Salad style - NICOISE

Salad veggie - ESCAROLE

Salamander - EFT or NEWT

Salinger heroine - ESME

Sally - QUIP

Salmon that has spawned - KELT Salt - NACL or OLEATE

Salt containing gold - AURATE or AUREATE

Salt: Fr. - SEL

Salt tree - ATLE

Saltpeter - NITER

Samhita - VEDA

Samoan capital & sea port - APIA

Samoan coin - TALA

Samoan currency - SENE

Samoan island - UPOLU

Samoan port - APIA

Samoan skirt - LAVALAVA

Samuel's teacher - ELI

Samurai code - BUSHIDO

Sand-laden wind - SIMOOM

Sandarac tree - ARAR

Sandpiper - REEVE

Sandpiper's cousin - RHALAROPE

Sandy ridge - ESKER

Sarandac tree - ARAR

Satelite of Jupiter - ELARA, EUROPA or LEDA

Satelite of Mars - DEIMOS

Satalite of Neptune - TRITON or HEREID

Satelite of Saturn - DIONE, HELENE, RHEA or TYR

Satelite of Uranus - ARIEL, OBERON, MIRANDA, TITANIA or UMBRIEL

Satiate - CLOY

Saudi Arabian coin - RIYAL

Savage - LUPINE

Sawbones saw - TREPHINE

Saxony River - WESER

Saxony seaport - EMDEN

Scale on the underside of a snake - SCUTE

Scandinavian coin - ORE

Scandinavian god of strife - TYR

Scandinavian rugs - RYAS

Scan-line pattern - RASTER

Scar - CICATRIX or POCK

Scenic walk - PASEO

Schmaltz - BATHOS

Scholar - PEDANT

Scholarly - ERUDITE

Scholarly book - TOME

Scholarly paper - TREATISE

Schonbrunn palace site - VIENNA

School of Buddhism - MAHAYANA

School of whales - GAM or POD

Schoolmaster's rod - FERULE

Scope - AMBIT

Score after deuce - ADIN

Scorpion, E.G. - ARACHNID

Scottish boat - SKAFFIE

Scottish broadsword - CLAYMORE

Scottish chieftan - THANE

Scottish church - KIRK

Scottish dagger - DIRK, SKEAN or SNEE

Scottish dowry - TOCHER

Scottish hawke - GOS

Scottish highlander - GAEL

Scottish hillside - BRAE

Scottish island - ARRAN, IONA or SKYE

Scottish port - AYR

Scottish resort - OBAN

Scottish spa - TROON

Scottish tenant farm – CROFT

Scottish tree - ARN

Scottiosh uncles - EMES

Scoundrel - LOSEL

Scourge - KNOUT

Scree - TALUS

Scriptual manuscripts - CODICES

Scriptures reader - LECTOR

Scup - PORGIE

Scythe handle - SNATH

Sea bird - PETREL

Sea cow - DUGONG

Sea cucumber - TREPANG

Sea duck - SCOTER

Sea eagle - ERNE

Sea east of the Caspian - ARAL

Sea god - NEPTUNE

Sea goose - GANNET

Sea holly - ERYNGO

Sea in Russia - AZOV

Sea lettuce - ULVA

Sea nymph - NEREIDES or OCEANID

Sea off Corfu - IONIAN

Sea otter - KALAN

Seagulls - MEWS

Seaport in Belgium - GHENT

Sea polyp - ANEMONE

Seaport in Brittany - BREST

Seaport in India - MADRAS

Sea port in Jordan - AQABA

Sea port in West Glamorgan - SWANSEA

Seaport of Ghana - TEMA

Sea port of Italy - GENOA or RIMINI

Sea port on Hokkaido - OTARU

Sea port on the Bay of Biscay - LAROCHELLE or SANTANDER

Seaplane inventor Glenn - CURTISS

Sea urchins - ECHINI

Seal - SIGIL

Sealing substance - LUTE

Seaside shrub - GORSE

Seasonal laborer - BRACERO

Seasoning paste - MISO

Seaweed extract or product - AGAR or POTASH

Second crop of hay - ROWEN

Secret - ARCANUM

Secret stuff - ARCANA

Sect of Islam - SHIA

Secular - LAIC

Secular priest - ORATORIAN

Seed appendage - ARIL

Seed coat or cover - TESTA

Seed plant - SESEME

Seed scars - HILA

Seedlet - OVULE

Seine - NET

Seine feeder - AUBE, EURE, MARNE, OISE or SAONE

Self destructive instinct - THANATOS

Self evident truth - AXION

Self: pref. - AUT

Semi-aquatic rodent - CAPYBARA

Semicircular bench - EXEDRA

Semiconductor additives -
    DOPANTS

Semimetalic element - BORON

Semiprecious gem - BALAS

Senile sort - DOTARD

Senior member - DOYEN

Sense of touch - TACTUAL

Sentimentaal: Fr. - GARDE

Seoul soldier - ROK

Seraglio - HAREM or ZENANA

Seraglio unit - ODA

Serbian folk dance - KOLO

Serf - THRALL

Serf, of old - ESNE

Servant slave - THRALL

Serving tray - SALVER

Sesame plant - BENNE or TIL

Sesame seed paste - TAHINI

Seth's brother - ABEL

Seth's son - ENOS

Setting for Hamlet -
    ELSINMORE

Seven: Sp. - SIETE

Severn tributary - AVON or
    WYE

Seville attraction - ALCAZAR

Sewing machine inventor -
    HOWE

Sexless word - EPICENE

Shad like fish - ALEWIVES

Shaddock fruit - POMELO

Shade of brown - SEPIA

Shaded walk - ALAMEDA

Shaggy rug - RYA

Shakespear's foot - IAMB

Shakespearean king - ALONZO

Shakespearean sprite - ARIEL

Shalom - PEACE

Sham: Pref. - PSEUDO

Shank - CRUS

Shanks - CRURA

Sharp crest - ARETE

Sharp ridge - ARRIS

Shasta - DAISY

Sheath - THECA

Shed, as skin - SLOUGH

Sheepfold - COTE or REE

Sheepish - OVINE

Sheepskin leather - ROAN

Sheer fabric - NINON

Sheet - PONE

Sheik's garmet - ABA

Shell-less marine snail -
    NUDIBRANCH

Shelter for birds - COTE

Sherry of Spain - XERES

Shield bearing or border -
    ORLE

Shield boss - UMBO

Shield of Zeus - AEGIS

Shield with a coat of arms - ESCUTCHEON

Shiite leader - AYATOLLAH

Shinbone - TIBIA

Shinto temple gateway - TORII

Ship-shaped clocks - NEFS

Ship's boat - PINNACE

Ship's deck - ORLOP

Shipworm - BORER or TEREDO

Shivering - AGUEY

Shoe Part or strip - WELT

Shooter marble - RAREE

Shore bird - AVOCET, CURLEW, DOTTREL, ERNE, PLOVER, RAIL, SORA or TERN

Short billed rail - CRAKE

Short billed wading bird - PLOVER

Short cape - MANTELEY

Short, erect tail - SCUT

Short fibre - NOIL

Short legged horse - COB

Short lived things - EPHEMERA

Short operatic solo - ARIETTA

Short prose tale - NOVELLA

Short song - ARIETTA

Short story - CONTE

Short synopsis - APERCU

Shortage - DEARTH

Shorten - TRUNCATE

Short tailed lemur - INDRI

Short tailed rodent - VOLE

Shoshonean - KOSO

Shoulder blades - SCAPULAE

Showy African plant - COLEUS

Showy display - ECLAT

Showy flower - CANNA

Showy trinket or ornament - GAUD

Showy plant - CANNA

Shredded tobacco - SHAG

Shrew - HARRIDAN, TERMAGANT or VIRAGO

Shrew's genus - SOREX

Shrewish woman - HARPY or VIRAGO

Shrill noise - STRIDOR

Shrine at Mecca - KAABA

Shrub - SUMAC

Shrubby thicket - CHAPARRAL

Siamese coin - TICAL

Siamese coins - ATTS

Siamese fighting fish - BETTA

Siamese temple - WAT

Siberiea flower - URAL

Siberian forest - TAIGA

Siberiean River - AMUR

Sicilian fortified wine - MARSALA

Sicilian Mountain - ETNA

Sicilian resort - ENNA

Sicilian sea port - SYRACUSE

Siddhartha author - HESSE

Side pedals - ALAE

Sidereal altar - ARA

Sign of royalty - DIADEM

Sikkim antelope - SEROW

Silent in music - TACET

Silk cotton - CEIBA

Silk dye - EOSIN

Silk fabric - FAILLE, HONAN, SURAH or TULLE

Silk like fabric - RAMIE

Silk scarf - FOULARD

Silk tree - MIMOSA

Silken - SERIC

Silkworm - ERIA

Silkworm moth - CECROPIA

Silky fabric - PONGEE

Silly poetry - DOGGEREL

Silver - ARGENT

Silver in heraldry or silvery white - ARGENT

Silver peso - DURO

Silver refiner - CUPEL

Silvery white - ARGENT

Simple organism - MONAD

Simple planetarium - ORRERY

Simple wind instrument - TONETTE

Sinew -THEW

Single-celled microorganism - MONAD

Single named supermodel - IMAM

Single-seeded fruit - DRUPE

Sinus cavity - ANTRUM

Sioux Indians - OTOS

Sister: Lat. SOROR

Sister of Aaron - MIRIAM

Sister of Apollo - ARTEMIS

Sister of Ares - ERIS

Sister of Antigonnes - ISMEME

Sister of Caliope or Clio - ERATO or THALIA

Sister of Cordelias - REGAN

Sister of Erato - CLIO or URANIA

Sister of Goneril - REGAN

Sister of Helios - EOS or SELENE

Sister of Laetes - OPHELIA

Sister of Margaux - MARIEL

Sister of Melpomene - ERATO

Sister of Mertes - OHPILEA

Sister of Moses - MIRIAM

Sister of Napoleon - SOEUR

Sister of Nephthys - ISIS

Sister of Osiris - ISIS

Sister of Orestes - ELECTRA

Sister of Paris - SOEUR

Sister of Pollus - HELEN

Sister of Polyhymnia - ERATO

Sister of Rachael - LEAH

Sister of Snow White - ROSERED

Sister of Terpsichore - ERATO

Sister of Thalia - ERATO

Sister of Tante - MERE

Sister of Urania - ERATO

Sister of Venus - SERENA

Sitar accompaniment - TABLA

Sitting in art - SEDENT

Situated at the tip - APICAL

Situated below – NETHER

Six: Sp. - SIES

Six-line poem - SESTET

Six penny piece - TANNER

Size of paper - DEMY

Skein of yarn - CLEW

Ski run - PISTE

Skillful - HABILE

Skin defect - WEN

Skin disease - TINEA

Skin: pre. -DERMA

Skin spot - NEVUS

Skin woe - TINEA

Skirt insert - GODET or GORE

Scull bone - INION

Skullcap - COIF

Skull point - INION

Sky: Fr. - CIEL

Sky altar - ARA

Sky whale - CETUS

Slag - DROSS or SCORIA

Slave - MOIL

Slayer of Castor - IDAS

Sleek dog - SALUKA

Sleep: Comb.form - NARCO

Sleepy - TORPID

Sleeveless robe - ABA

Slender and pointed - STYLOID

Slender bristle - ARISTA

Slender cat - REX

Slender dagger - PONIARD

Slender graceful woman - SYLPH

Slender pointed weapon - STYLET

Slender stem - PETIOLE

Slight trace - SOUPCO

Sloe-flavored liqueur - PRUNELLE

Slothful - OTIOSE

Slow dances - HABANERAS

Slow musical movement -
LARGO

Slow passage in music - ADAGIO

Slow primate - LORIS

Slow stroll - PASEO

Slowing, in music -
LENTANDO

Slowish - ANDANTE

Slowly, musically - LENTO

Slowly, to Bach - ADAGIO

Sluggish - TORPID

Slur over a syllable - ELIDE

Small amount - DRIB,
MODICUM or SOUPCON

Small antelope - ORIBI

Small ape - GIBBON

Small barracudas - SPETS

Small bird - PEWEE or
TOMTIT

Small bone - OCCICLE

Small buffalo - ANOA

Small case - ETUI

Small computer program -
APPLET

Small deer - ROES

Small diving bird - DABCHICK
or MURRELET

Small drum - TABLA or TABOR

Small eel - GRIG

Small Eurasian duck - SMEW

Small Eurasian ruminant -
ROEDER

Small evergreen tree - CITRON

Small falcon - KESTREL or
MERLIN

Small finch - LINNET or SERIN

Small fish - SMELT or SPRAT

Small flag - FANION

Small Florida orange - SATSUMA

Small freshwater fish - DACE

Small fruit - ACHENE

Small goose - BRANT

Small green bird - VIREO

Small gull - MEW

Small hand drum - TABLA

Small hawk - KITE

Small heron - BITTERN

Small herring - SPRAT

Small hill - KOPJE

Small insect - MIDGE

Small insect-eating bird - VIREO

Small lake or pond - MERE

Small lamp - ETNA

Small laquer box - INRO

Small liquid measure - MINIM

Small marine animal - SALP

Small merganser - SMEW

Small monkey - TITI

Small napsack - MUSETTE

Small old world lizard - AGAMA

Small open boat - SHALLOP

Small ox - ANOA

Small parrot - LORIKEET

Small perfume bottle - FLACON

Small razor-billed bird -AUKET

Small rodent - LEROT or VOLE

Small Russian turnovers -
  PIROSHKI

Small sailing craft - PINNACE

Small salamander - NEWT

Small salmon - COHO

Small sandpiper - STINT

Small seabird - PETREL

Small shed - COTE

Small slender dagger - PONIARD

Small song bird - PIPIT, VIREO
  or WREN

Small space - AREOLA

Small struffed triangular
  turnover - SAMOSA

Small sturgeon - STERLET

Small stream - RUNNEL

Small table - GUERIDON

Small toucan - ARACARI

Small town - PODUNK

Small whale - SEI

Small wild ox - ANOA

Small woods - COPSE

Smallest bit - JOT

Smelly - OLID

Smog - MIASMA

Smoked salmon - NOVA

Smoking pipe - CALABASH

Smooth transition - SEGUE

Smoothly, in music - LEGATO

Snack - NOSH

Snake - MAMBA

Snake hair women - FURIES

Snake: Pref. - OPHI

Snipe's kin - GODWIT

Snow leopard - OUNCE

Snow field - NEVE

Snow white dog - SAMOYED

So much, musically - TANTO

Soak - IMBRUE

Soaks - RETS

Soap ingredient - OLEATE

Soap plant - AMOLE

Soap stone - TALC

Soap substitute - AMOLE

Soapberry tree - AKEE

Social climber - PARVENU

Social outcast - PARIAH

Sod - SWARD

Sodium carbonate - TRONA

Sodium cloride - NACL

Sodium hydroxide - NAOH

Soft metallic element - CESIUM

Soft palate - VELUM

Soft part of the palate - UVULA

Soft roe - MILT

Soft sheer fabric - BATISTE

Soft velvet - PENNE

Softly in music - PIANO

Solar diety or disc- ATEN

Solar lunar equalizer - EPACT

Solar plexus - RETE

Solar system model - ORRERY

Soldier from down under - ANZAC

Solfeggio - SCALE

Solidified lava - BASALT

Solvent substance - ACETAL

Some collegians - ELIS

Some musical passages - TUTTIS

Some triangles - SCALENE

Something to eat - VIAND

Somewhat, in music - POCO

Sommelier - CUPBEARER

Son of Aaron - ELEAZAR

Son of Abraham - ISAAC or ISHMAEL

Son of Adam - SETH

Son of Agamemnon - ORESTES

Son of Agrippina - NERO

Son of Aphrodite - AENEAS, EROS or PRIAPUS

Son of Apollo - ION

Son of Arba - ANAK

Son of Ares - EROS

Son of Bathsheba - SOLOMON

Son of Bilhah - DAN

Son of Cain - ENOCH

Son of Cronos - PLUTO or ZEUS

Son of Daedalus - ICARUS

Son of David - ABOLOM

Son of EBER - PELEG

Son of Eliphaz - OMAR

Son of Frigg - BALDER

Son of Gad - ERI

Son of Germanicus - CALIGULA

Son of Ham - CANAAN

Son of Hecaba - PARIS

Son of Hera - ARES

Son of Hirohito - AKIHITO

Son of Indira - RAJIV

Son of Isaac - EDOM or ESAU

Son of Jacob - ASHER, BENJAMIN, DAN, LEVI or SIMEON

Son of Japheth - TIBAL

Son of Jehiel - NER

Son of Joktan - OBAL

Son of Joseph - EPHRAM

Son of Judah - ONAN

Son of Kish - SAUL

Son of Lapetus - ATLAS

Son of Leah - LEVI or SIMEON

Son of Loki - NARE

Son of Lot - MOAB

Son of Noah - HAM, JAPHETH or SHEM

Son of Odin - BALDER, BRAGI, THOR or TYR

Son of Osiris - HORUS

Son of Polonius - LAERTES

Son of Poseidon - ORION or TRITON

Son of Priam - PARIS

Son of Prince Valiant - ARN

Son of Rachel - BENJAMIN

Son of Rebekah - ESAU

Son of Rhea - PLUTO

Son of Salah - EBER

Son of Sarah - ISAAC

Son of Seth - ARAM or ENOS

Son of Shem - ELAM

Son of Shiza - ADINA

Son of Telamon - AJAX

Son of Uranus - TITAN

Son of Uther - ARTHUR

Son of Venus - AMOR

Son of Zebulun - SERED

Son of Zeus - APOLLO, ARES or HERCULES

Sonata movement - RONDO

Song of praise - PAEAN

Songbird - OSCINE or VIREO

Songlike - ARIOSE

Songs - LAYS

Song thrush - MAVIS

Sonnet finale or part - SESTET

Sonora native - YAQUI

Soothing tea - CHAMOMILE

Soothsayer - AUGER, SEER or SIBYL

Sorceress in Greek myth - CIRCE

Sorceress of Colchis - MEDEA

Sorrowful poem - ELEGY

Sort of blue - CERULEAN

Soul - ANIMA or PNEUMA

Sound characteristic - TIMBRE

Sound: Prefix - SONO

Sound of rippling water - PURL

Sound quality - TIMBRE

Soup pasta - ORZO

Soup served cold - SCHAV

Sour mash - ALEGAR

Sour tasting - ACERB

Sourness - VERJUICE

Source of agar - REDALGAE

Source of bast fibre - RAMIE

Source of Blue Nile - TANA

Source of caviar - STERLET

Source of hemp - ABACA

Sourse of royal purple - MUREX

Sourse of the Mississippi - ITASCA

South African flower - IXIA

South African fox - ASSE

South African grassland - VELDT

South African iris - IXIA

South African monkey - VERVET

South African stockade - KRAAL

South American bear - OSO

South American dolphin - DORADOR

South American finch - RED SISKIN

South American fish - ACARA

South American Indians - AUCAS or ONAS

South American mammal - VICUNA

South American monkey - SAI or TITI

South American plain - LLANO

South American plateau region - ALTIPLANO

South American raptor - HARPY EAGLE

South American rodent - CAVY, COYPU or PACA

South American sloths - AIS

South American tuber - OCA

South east wind - EURUS

South Indian language - TAMIL

South Korean soldier - ROC or ROK

South of France - MIDI

South Korean port - PUSAN

South Pacific area - OCEANIA

South Pacific boat - PRAU

South sea island - JAVA

South west wind - AFER

Southern constellation - ARA, APUS, ARGO or MENSA

Southwestern beans - FRIJOLES

Southwestern plant - CHIA

Southwestern promenade - PASEO

Southwestern salamander - AXOLOTL

Soverign - SKIV

Soviet cooperative - ARTEL

Soybean-based paste - MISO

Space between leaf veins - AREOLA

Space between two teeth - DIASTEMA

Spadefoot, for one - TOAD

Spanish Almighty - DIOS

Spanish aunt - TIA

Spanish bears - OSO

Spanish conifer - PINO

Spanish dance - JOTA

Spanish dances - SARABANDS

Spanish dish - PAELLA

Spanish eyes - OJOS

Spanish grocery - BODEGA

Spanish gypsy - GITANO

Spanish hall - SALA

Spanish health - SANO

Spanish hors d'oeuvres - TAPAS

Spanish house - CASA

Spanish inn - POSADA

Spanish king - RAY

Spanish kiss - BESO

Spanish lady - DONA

Spanish mackerel - PINTADO

Spanish muralist - SERT

Spanish naval base - VIGO

Spanish nobleman - GRANDEE

Spanish queen - ENA or REINA

Spanish rice - ORROZ

Spanish Road - CAMINO

Spanish sausage - CHORIZO

Spanish scarf - MANTILLA

Spanish seaport - CADIZ

Spanish she-bear- OSA

Spanish sherry - OLOROSO

Spanish silver - PLATA

Spanish silver dollar - DURO

Spanish six - SEIS

Spanish snacks - TAPAS

Spanish stew - PAELLA

Spanish sword - ESPADA

Spanish tar - BREA

Spanish town - AVILA

Spanish town mayor - ALCALDE

Spanish uncle - TIO

Spanish wine - MALAGA or
    RIOJA

Spanish wine bag - BOTA

Sparkly rock - GNEISS

Sparoid fish - SAR

Sparton queen - LEDA

Sparton serf or slave - HELOT

Spauning area - REDD

Speach beginnings - EXODIA

Speaker's platform - BEMA or
    PODIA

Spear - ASSEGAI

Specialized idiom or Vocabulary
    - ARGOT

Specialties - METIERS

Species - GENERA

Speck - MOTE

Specs with a handle - LORGNETTE

Speer with a long blade - ASSAGAI

Spend thrift - WASTREL

Sphere of operation - AMBIT

Spice girl - POSH

Spice girl Halliwell - GERI

Spice used in incense - STACTE

Spiced tea - CHAI

Spicy sausage - KIELBASA

Spicy Stew - OLIO

Spider, to biologist - ARANEID

Spider's nest - NIDUS

Spigot - SPILE

Spinachlike plant - ORACH

Spine - RACHIS

Spinel variety - BALAS

Spiny anteater - ECHIDNA

Spiny lizard - IGUANA

Spiny lobster - LANGOUSTE

Spiny plant - ALOE

Spiny sea creature - URCHIN

Spiny leafed flower - AGAVE

Spiny-shelled gastropod - MUREX

Spiny shrub - FURZE or GORSE

Spiny trees - ACACIAS

Spiral-horned antelope ELAND, KUDU or NYALA

Spiral-horned buck - ADDAX

Spiral-horned sheep - ARGALI

Spiral-shelled mollusk - NAUTILUS, TRITON or WHELK

Spire ornament - EPI

Spirit of the time - ZEITGEIST

Spiritual leader - RABBI or REBBE

Spitchcock - EEL

Split - RIVE

Splitting tool - FROE

Spoil - VITIATE

Sponge - CADGE

Sponsorship - EGIS

Spoor - PISTE

Spore sac - ASCUS

Spotted cat - PARD

Spotted reddish deer - SIKA

Spotted wildcat - MARGAY or SERVAL

Spread hay to dry - TED

Spreads news of - BRUITS

Spring flower - SCILLA

Sprinkles - SPARGES

Sprite - FAY or PERI

Spumous - SUDSY

Spur part - ROWEL

Spurious wing - ALULA

Square - ISOGON

Square column - ANTA

Square stone - ASHLAR

Sri Lanka export -
  TOURMALINE

Sri Lanka native - TAMIL

St. Kitts sister island - VEVIS

St. Petersburg's river - NEVA

St. Theresa's home - AUILA

Stable worker - HOSTLER or
  OSTLER

Staccatos opposite - LEGATO

Staffordshire's river - TRENT

Stage leap - JETE

Staircase post or support -
  NEWEL

Stairway in Italy - SCALA

Stand of trees - COPSE

Stannum - TIN

Stanzas of sonnets - SESSTETS

Star in Aquila - ALTAIR

Star in Argo - CANOPUS

Star in Auriga - CAPELLA

Star in Cannes - ETOILE

Star in Cetus - MIRA

Star in Cygnus - DENEB

Star in Draco - ADIB

Star in Eridanus - ACHERNAR

Star in Gemini - CASTOR

Star in Lyra - VEGA

Star in Orion - RIGEL

Star in Persius - ALGOL

Star in Scorpio - ANTARES

Star in Taurus - ALDEBARAN

Star in Virgo - SPICA

Star of France - ETOILE

Star: Pref. - ASTR

Starch - AMYLOSE

Starch tree - SAGO

Starchy foodstuffs - SAGOS

State: Fr. - ETAT

State in Indian - ASSAM

State of drowsiness - KEF

State of being old - SENESCENT

Stately dance - PAVANE

Statue support - SOCLE

Steel gray element - NIOBIUM

Steel making furnace -
  BESSEMER

Steel mill by-product - DROSS

Steep slope - SCARP

Steller altar - ARA

Stem angle - AXIL

Stench - FETOR or MALODER

Stenuation - SNEEZE

Steppenwolf author - HESSE

Steps for crossing a fence - STILE

Steroids - LIPIDS

Steveadore's group - ILA

Stew - SLUMGULLION

Stew pot – OLLA

Stiff hair - SETA

Stimulating nut - KOLA

Stir up sediment - ROIL

Stirrup bone - STAPES

Stomachs of ruminants - OMASA

Stone Age implement - NEOLITH

Stone coffin - CIST or KIST

Stone fruit - DRUPE

Stone marker - STELA

Stone landmark or mound - CAIRN

Stone splinter - SPALL

Stonecrop plant - SEDUM

Stoppage - STASIS

Stores fodder - ENSILES

Storksbill - GERANIUM

Stout club - CUDGEL

Strait of Messina monster - SCYLLA

Stranger: pref. XENO

Strap on a saddle - LATIGO

Stratagem - RUSE

Stravinski ballet - AGON

Straw for hats - SENNIT

Straw mats - TATANIS

Strawberry geranium - SAXIFRAGE

Stray calf - WAIF

Stray dog - PYE

Stream overflows - FRESHETS

Street kid - GAMIN

Street show - RAREE

Street urchin - WAIF

Stretch material LYCRA

Strict herbivore - VEGAN

String in Bologna - SPAGO

Stringed instruments - VIOLS

Stringed keyboard instrument - CLAVIER

Strip blubber - FLENSE

Strip of gears - UNRIG

Strip tease - ECDYSIAT

Striped antelope - NYALA or KUDU

Strong fiber - BAST or RAMIE

Strong-scented herb or plant - RUE

Strong suit - METIER

Student's cubicle - CARREL

Student's language aid - PONY

Stuffed grape leaves - DOLMA

Stuffs oneself - STODGES

Sturdy chiffon - NINON

Subartic forest - TAIGA

Subatomic particle - BARYON, HADRON, MESON, MUON, PION, or POSITRON

Subordinate diety - DAEMON

Sub-Saharan region - SAHEL

Successor of Moses - JOSHUA

Successor of Ramses - SETI

Sudden flood - SPATE

Sudden uprising - PUTSCH

Suez port - SAID

Sugar in tea: e.g. - SOLUE

Sugarcane byproduct - BAGASSE

Sulawesi - CELEBES

Sultanate on Borneo - BRUNEI

Summary - PRESCIS

Summer capital of India - SIMLA

Summer ermine - STOAT

Summerlike - ESTIVAL

Summet - VERTEX

Summons to prayer - AZAN

Sun dial essential part - GNOMON

Sun flower - HELIANTHUS

Sun god - ATEN

Sun hat - TOPI

Sun helmet - TERAI

Sun: pref. - HELIO

Sunken fence - HAHA

Sunni leader - IMAM

Sunscreenasdditive or Ingredient - PABA

Supernatural power - MANA

Supreme Teutonic god - WOTAN

Surf sound - ROTE

Surgical antiseptic - THIMEROSAL

Surgical insert - STENT

Surgical instrument - PROBANG or TROCAR

Surgical knife - LANCET

Surgical probe - STYLET

Surround - EMBAY

Surveying instument - ALIDADE

Survivor - RELICT

Sushi wrapping - NORI

Suspenders - GALLUSES

Swamp gas or thing - MIASMA

Swan Genus - OLOR

Swan Lake maiden - ODILE

Sward - SOD

Swedish coin - ORE

Swedish seaport - MALMO

Sweet flag - CALAMUS

Sweet bun or roll - BRIOCHE

Sweet Spanish wine - MALAGA

Sweetheart - INSMORATA

Sweetly melodic - ARIOSO

Swift falcon - PEREGRINE

Swift horses - HOUYHNHNMS

Swiftness - CELERITY

Swimming - NATANT

Swindle - MULCT

Swindler - GANEF

Swiss canton - BASEL, LUCERNE or URI

Swiss cheese - GUYERE

Swiss city - BERNE

Swiss dish - RACLETTE

Swiss river - AARE or AAR

Swiss snowfield - FIRN

Sword handle - HAFT

Symbol of life - ANKH

Synagogue - SCHUL or SHUL

Synagogue platform - BEMA or BEMATA

Synecdoche - TROPE

Synthesizer - MOOG

Synthetic alumina-based gem - BOULE

Synthetic fabric - ARNEL

Synthetic garnet - YAG

Synthetic rubber - BUTYL

Synthetic rubber ingredient - STYRENE

Syphonic movement - RONDO or SCHERZO

Table constellation - MENSA

Table linen - NAPERY

Table scrap - ORT

Tahitian seaport - PAPEETE

Tahitian wrapped skirt - PAREU

Tail bone - COCCYX

Tailess cat - MANX

Tailess mammal - LORIS

Taillike - CAUDAL

Tailor: Lat. - SARTOR

Taiwan strait island - AMOY or MATSU

Taj Mahal site - AGRA

Taking effect legally - NISI

Tale - CONTE

Talk raucously - YAWP

Talkative - PRATE

Tall cactus - SAGUARO

Tall coarse herb - COW PARSNIP

Tall seasoning plant - LOVAGE

Tallow acid - OLEIC

Tamarisk - ATLE

Tammany bigwig - SACHEM

Tangy fish sauce - ALEC

Tapestry - ARRAS

Tapestry thread - WEFT

Tapioca sourse - CASSAVA

Taradiddle - FIB or LIE

Taro root - EDDO

Taro's tuber - CORM

Tarsal bones - CUBOIDS

Tastiest turtle part - CALIPASH

Tasty - SAPID

Tasty crust - GRATIN

Tasty dish - VIAND

Ta-ta in Turin - CIAO

Tautog or whitefish -CHUB

Tautomeric compound - ENOL

Tawny - ECRU

Tawny thrush - VEERY

Tea - BOHEA

Tea plant - CAMOMILE

Tear away - AVULSE

Tearful - LACHRYMOSE

Tearful woman - NIOBE

Technology hater - LUDDITE

Tedium - ENNUI

Teeth: pref. - DENTI or DENTO

Temple - FANE or NAOS

Ten Commandments -
DECALOGUE

Ten decibels - BEL

Ten to the 100th power -
GOOGOL

Ten year period - DECENNIUM

Tenant farm in Scotland -
CROFT

Tenant farmer in India - RYOT

Tendon-bone connector - BURSA

Tennessee flower - IRIS

Tennis situation - ADIN

Terminal portion of the small
Intestine - ILEUM

Termagant VERAGO

Testify - DEPONE

Teton Sioux tribe - OGLALA

Tetra variation - NEON

Teutonic god of thunder -
DONAR

Teutonic sky god - TIU

Teutonic war god - WOTAN

Texas armadillo - PEBA

Texas border city - DEL RIO

Texas border river - SABINE

Texctile dyeing substance- EOSIN

Tex-Mex treat - FAJITA

Thailand money - BAHTS

That: Fr. - CETTE

That: Sp. - ESA

That is: Lat. - IDEST

Thatched-roofed hut - JACAL

Thatching palm - NIPA

The act of measuring -
MENSURATION

The forearm - CUBITUS

The Furies - ERINYES or
EUMENIDES

The great unwashed - PLEBS

The gums - ULA

The Museof astonomy - URANIA

The Norse gods - AESIR

The soul - ANIMA

Theatre area - RIALTO

Theatre curtain or drop - SCRIM

Theban god - AMENRA

Then: Fr. - DONC

Thermal energy unit - JOULE

These: Fr. - CES

Theseus's wife - PHAEDRA

Thessaly Mountain -OSSA

Thick piled rug - RYA

Thickening agent - AGAR or SAGO

Thicket - COPPICE or COPSE

Thighbone - FEMUR

Thin fibrous bark - TAPPA

Thin line - STRIA

Thin material - ORGANZA

Thin membrane - PELLICLE

Third canonical hour - TERCE

Third in rank - TERTIARY

This: Sp. - ESTA

Thistlelike plant - TEASEL

Thoroughgoing - ARRANT

Those: Fr. - CES

Thousandth of an inch - MIL

Thrall, of old - ESNE

Thrash - LARRUP

Trattoria dessert - SPUMONI

Thread: pref. - NAMATO

Three masted sailing ship - XEBEC

Threefold - TRINE

Three-headed dog - CERSERUS

Three-legged ornamental table - TEAPO

Thoroughwort - BONESET

Three lines of poetry - TERCET

Three-panel picture - TRIPTYCH

Threesome - TRIAD

Three stringed instruments - REBEC or SAMISET

Three toes bird - RHEA

Three toed sloths - AIS

Three trios - ENNEA

Three wheeled rickshaw - CYCLO

Thrifty - PROVIDENT

Throat dangler - UVULA

Throughout, musically - SEMPRE

Throwback - ATAVISM

Thumb of the nose - SNOOK

Thrushlike warbler - OVENBIRD

Thus - SIC

Tiara - DIADEM

Tiberius' tailor - SARTOR

Tibetan animals - YAKS

Tibetan Buddhism - LAMAISM

Tibetan antelope or gazelle - GOA

Tibetan goat - SEROW

Tick - ACARID

Tidal bore - EAGRE

Tidal wave - TSUNAMI

Tiger genus - FELID

Tight curls - FRIZZ

Tile shaping stand - CRISS

Timbuktu's country - MALI

Time being - NONCE

Time keeper - HOROLOGER

Tinge with gold - AUREATE

Tinny - STANNIC

Tiny blood vessel - VENULA

Tiny dumplings - GNOCCI

Tiny Japanese mushroom - ENOKI

Tiny marine animal - ROTIFER

Tirade - SCREED

Titanium ore - RUTILE

Titled Italian family - ESTE

To be - ESSE

To be: Fr. - ETRA

To endure - ABY

To the end, in music - ALFINE

To the point - ADREM

Toast for the holidays - WASSAIL

Tobacco kiln - OAST

Tocsin - ALARM

Today: Sp. - HOY

Together musicaly - ADUE

Toil - TRAVAIL

Tokyo airport - NARITA

Tokyo, long ago - EDO

Tokyo rice roll - SUSHI

Tolkien beastie - ORC

Tolkien forest creature - ENT

Tolkien ring bearer - FRODO

Tomalley source - LOBSTER

Tomboy - HOYDEN

Tonguelike organ – LINGUA

Too much, musically – TANTO or TROPPO

Tool for bending or shaping metal - SWAGE

Tooth material - APATITE

Tooth shaped - DENTOID

Torch cup - CRESSET

Tortilla cooker - COMAL

Tough, durable wood - LARCH

Tough fiber - BAST

Tough fibrous plant - HEMP

Tough grass - ESPARTO

Touring car - PHAETON

Toward the mouth - ORAD or ORADE

Tower guard - WARDER

Town in Belgium - YPRES

Town in Italy - EBOLI

Town in Montana - MISSOULA

Town in Oklahoma - ADA

Town near Padua - ESTE

Town near Salerno - EBOLI

Town on Lake Maggiore - LOCARNO

Town on Lake Victoria - ENTEBBE

Town on the Penobscot - ORONO

Town on the Uzbeck - OSH

Town on the Vire - St. Lo

Track alternative - OTB

Trail mix - GORP

Trained personnel - CADRE

Trajectory shape - PARABOLA

Tranquil - IRENIC

Transition - SEGUE

Transparent fabric - TOILE

Transparent gemstone - BERYL

Transparent olivine - PERIDOT

Transparent substance - HYALINE

Transplant - ECESIS

Trap SPRINGE

Trattoria dessert - TORTONI

Trash - DRECK

Tree frog - HYLA

Tree: pref. - DENDRO

Tree-like cactus - CHOLLA

Tree protruberamce - KNUR

Tree resembling the elm - ZELKOVA

Tree sap spigot - SPILE

Tree shaded promenade - ALAMEDA

Tree snake - LORA

Tree stump - BOLE

Tree tissue - XYLEM

Tree toad - HYLA

Tree trunk - BOLE

Tree trunk canoe - PIOGUE

Tree with a large trunk - BAOBAB

Tree with nutlike seeds - PINON

Tree with whitish wood - HORNBEAM

Tree worshiper - ANIMIST

Treelike cactus - SAGUARO

Trellis for shrubs - ESPELIER

Trelliswork arbors - PERGOLAS

Tremblor - SEISM

Tremor condition - PALSY

Triangle with 3 unmeven sides - SCALENE

Triangular - DELTAIC

Triangular hat – TRICORN

Triangular kerchief or shawl - FICHU

Triangular sail - LATEEN

Triangular

Tribal chief - SACHEM

Tribal healer - SHAMAN

Tribe of Israel - ASHER, DAN, GAD, JUDAH or LEVI

Tribe unit - SEPT

Tribunal of prelates - ROTA

Trifles - DOITS

Trig. Angle - ARCSINE

Trig. Function - COSEC

Trigon - HARP

Trigonometric function - SINE

Trilled call - CHIRR

Trimming cord - GIMP

Trinity - TRIUNE

Trinket - BIBELOT, GAUD or GEWGAW

Tristan's love - ISEULT or ISOLDE

Troche - PASTILLE

Trojan king - PRIAM

Trojan War hero - AENEAS

Trojan War name - NESTOR

Troop's camp - ETAPE

Tropical Asian tree - TOON

Tropical bird - TOUCAN

Tropical blackbird - ANI

Tropical bloomer - CANNA

Tropical butterfly - ZEBRA

Tropical desert - BIOME

Tropical disease - YAWS

Tropical fibers - ISTLES

Tropical fish - SCAD

Tropical flower - PROTEA

Tropical fruit - ACKEE

Tropical lizard - ANOLE or IGUANA

Tropical palm - ARECA

Tropical parrot - MACAW

Tropical rainforest - BIOME

Tropical resin - ELEMI

Tropical rodent - AGOUTI

Tropical shrub - ACACIA, CASSIA, FICUS,

 LANTANA or SENNA

Tropical tern - NOADY

Tropical tree - AKEE, BALSA, CACAO,

COLA, MANGROVE, PALM or TAMERIND

Tropical tuber - TARO

Tropical wildcat - EYRA

Tropical wood - EBOMY

Troubador love song - ALBA

Troup's rest area - ETAPE

Troy, to the Greeks - ILIUN

True finch - SISKIN

Trump in card games - BASTA

Trumpet pennant - TABARD

Truncated pyramid - FRUSTUM

Truthful - VERIDICAL

Tuba - HELICON

Tubular pasta - PENNE

Tudor queen - MARY

Tuesday's god - TYR

Tumultuous uprising - EMEUTE

Tunes: Sp. - AIRES

Tunic of chain mail - HAUBERK

Tunisean seaport - SFAX

Turbot - BRILL

Turf - GREENSWARD

Turkic people - TATARS

Turkic tongue - ALTAIC

Turkish bigwig - BEY or PASHA

Turkish cap - CALPAC

Turkish cavalryman - SPAHI

Turkish chamber - ODA

Turkish coin - PARA

Turkish decree - IRADE

Turkish garment - CAFTAN

Turkish general or title - AGHA, AMEER or BEY

Turkish hospis or hostel - IMARET

Turkish inn - IMARET or SERAI

Turkish leader - AGA

Turkish liqueur - RAKI

Turkish officer - EMEER

Turkish official or title - AGHA or PASHA

Turkish palace - SERAI

Turkish regiment - ALAI

Turkish saber - YATAGHAN

Turkish title - DEY or EFFENDI

Turkish unit of weight - OKA

Turmoil - WELTER

Turn on a pivot SLUE

Turn outward - SPLAY

Turns inside out - EVERTS

Turtle shell - SCUTE

Tuscan river - ARNO

Twenty third OT book - ISAIAH

Twice baked bread - RUSK

Twice, musically - BIS

Twig broom - BESOM

Twill weaves fabric - TOILE

Twilled fabric - SERGE

Twinned crystal - MACLE

Twisted pasta - ROTINI

Two dimenional - PLANAR

Two faced god - JANUS

Two handed card game - ECARTE

Two handed jar - AMPHOR

Two handed soup bowl - ECUELLE

Two player card game - BEZIQUE

Two: Sp. - DOS

Two toed sloth - UNAU

Two wheel cart - TUMBREL

Two wheeled carriage - CALESA

Two year old sheep - TEG

Twosome - DYAD

Type measure - PICA

Type of algae - DIATON

Type of antelope - SAIGA

Type of apple - WINESAP

Type of bean - HARICOT

Type of beetle - CHAFER or SCARAB

Typre of camera - SLR

Type of daisy - OXEYE or SHASTA

Type of feather - PINNA

Type of flask or vessel - DEWAR

Type of flower cluster - CYME

Type of Larva - REPIA

Type of lily - SEGO

Type of mushroom - CEP or ENOKI

Type of pair - DYAD

Type of shark - TOPE

Type of sugar - HEXOSE

Type of tie - BOLA

Type of triangle - SCALENE

Type of whale - SCRAG

Type of wheat - SPELT

Type stroke or typeface detail - SERIF

Typee sequel - OMOO

Types of deer - ROES

Tyro - NAIF

Tyrolian garb - DIRNDLE

Ukrainian seaport - ODESSA

Ultimate battle - RAGNAROK

Ulysses's home - ITHICA

Umbrella - AEGIS

Unaccented part - ARSIS

Uncle of Levi - ESAU

Uncle of Saul - NER

Unctuous flattery – SMARM

Underground chamber - KIVA

Understanding - KEN

Understood - IMPLICIT

Underworld region - EREBUS

Underworld River - STYX

Undressed hide - KIP

Uneven - EROSE

Unfilled part of a wine cask - ULLAGE

Unflappable - STOLID

Unfledged bird - EYAS

Unglazed chine - BISCUITWARE

Unhealthy atmosphere - MIASMA

Unicorn constellation - MONOCEROS

Uninteresting - VAPID

Uniqque - SUI GENERIS

Unit of compacitance - FARAD

Unit of conductance - MHO

Unit of electric charge - COULOMB

Unit of energy - BEV, BTU, ERG, JOULE,

RAD or WATT

Unit of flux - TESLA

Unit of force - DYNE

Unit of heat - THERM

Unit of illumination - LUX or PHOT

Unit of induction - TESLA

Unit of land measure - MORGEN

Unit of light - LUMEN

Unit of loudness - PHON or SONE

Unit of magnetic flux - TESLA

Unit of potential - VOLT

Unit of pressure - TORR

Unit of radiation - REM

Unit of radiation exposure - ROENTGEN

Unit of radioactivity - CURIE

Unit of refraction - DIOPTER

Unit of volumn - STERE

Unit of wisdom - PEARL

Unit of work - ERG

Units of illumination - LUCES

Units of vers - MORAS

Universal soul - ATMAN

Unless, in law - NISI

Unnatural sleep - SOPOR

Unquestioning follower - MYRMIDON

Unshod - DISCALCED

Unspoken - TACIT

Unstable meson - KAON

Unsubstantial image - EIDOLON

Untamed - FERAL

Untanned hide - KIP

Unwelcomed one - PARIAH

Upas tree poison - ANTIAR

Upholstery fabric - FRISE

Upon: Fr. - SUR

Upper jaw - MAXILLA

Upside down "e" - SCHWA

U.S.A.F. org. - SAC

U.S.N. officers: abbr. - CDRS

U.S. playwright - INGE

U.S.S.R. co-op - ARTEL

Utah lake city - OREM

Utah lily - SEGO

Utah mountain range - UINTA

Vaccines - SERA

Vacuum tube gas - ARGON

Vagabond - PICARD

Vague rumor - ONDIT

Vain - OTIOSE

Valley in Britain - COOMB

Vampire - LAMIA

Vanished - EVANESCED

Variable star - ALGOL

Variety of chalcedony - SARD

Variety of grass - FESCUE

Variety of hornblende - URALITE

Variety of lettuce - COS

Variety of lily - SEGO

Variety of peach - FREESTONE

Variety of sheep - MERINO

Variety of whale - SEI

Various areas - LOCA

Varnish ingredient - ANINE, COPAL, ELEMI,

 LAC, RESIN or TUNG OIL

Varnish material - ELEMI

Vase handle - ANSA

Vase on a pedestal - TAZZA

Vat - TUN

Vatican palace - LATERAN

Vedigris - PATINA

Vegas constellation - LYRA

Veil worn by Muslim women - YASHMAK

Velvet finish - PANNE

Venetian district - RIALTO

Venetian gold coin - DECUT

Venomous snake - FERDELANCE, KRAIT or TAIPAN

Ventilated felt hat - TERAI

Venus as the evening star - HESPERUS

Verbena plant - LANTANA

Verdi opera - ERNANI

Vermin poisin - RATSBANE

Vernacular - ARGOT

Verse with 17 syllables - HAIKU

Very: German - SEHR

Very hairy - PILOSE

Very, in music - ASSAI or MOLTO

Very, in Vichy - TRES

Very loud, musically - FORTISSIMO

Very necessary things - DESITERATA

Very pale dry sherry - FINO

Very pale green - CELADON

Very successful - BUFFO

Vesicle - CYST

Vessel - DEWAR

Vessel or duct - VAS

Vessels - PROA or XEBEC

Vestment - ORALE

Vetch - TARE

Vet's dose - BOLUS

Vicious woman - ARRIDAN

Vienna, to Germans - WIEN

Vietnam city - HANOI or HUE

Vietnamese attire or dress - AODAI

Vigor - BRIO

Vigorously - AMAIN or CON BRIO

Viking poet - SKALD

Vile rumor CANARD

Village - DORP or THORP

Vinegary: pref. - ACETO

Vineyard - CRU

Viol part - CHOLE

Violin bow part - FROG

Violin of the middle ages - REBEC

Virgil creation - IDYLL

Virgil epic - AENEID

Virgil's hero - AENEAS

Virginia rabbit stew - BRUNSWICK

Virginia willow - COSIER or ITEA

Virgo's brightest star - SPICA

Vishnu incarnation - AVATAR or RAMA

Visigoth sacker of Rome - ALARIC

Visored helmet - ARMET

Vitamin A - RETINOL

Vivacity - BRIO

Voiceless - SURD

Volcanic crater - CAULDERA

Volcanic earth - TRASS

Volcanic glass - OBSIDIAN

Volcanic material - MAGMA

Volcanic rock - BASALT or TRASS

Volcanic valley - ATRIO

Volcano goddess - PELE

Volcano in Peru - EL MISTI

Volcano near Manilla - TAAL

Volcano on Antartica - EREBUS

Volga feeder - OKA

Volitile solvent - ACETAL

Voltage: Abbr. - EMF

Volumn - TOME

Voluptuaries - SYBARITES

Voodoo - MOJO

Voodoo amulets or spells - MOJOS

Voodoo fetish - OBEAH

Vouchsafe - DEIGN

Vortex - GYRE

Votive stone - STELE

Vulcan's chimney - AETNA

WWII rifle - GARAND

Wading bird - IBIS, RAIL, SORA or STILT

Wagnarian goddess - ERDA

Wagnerian melod - LEITMOTIF

Wagon shaft - THILL

Wail - ULULATE

Waist coat - GILET

Wales Lake or pool - LLYN

Walk-on-water lizard - BASILISK

Walkway between rows of trees - ALLEE

Wall handing - ARRAS

Wall treatment - WAINSCOT

Walls of ripened fruit - PERICARD

Wampum - PEAG

Wander about - DIVACATE

Wanton - PAPHIAN

Ward off - FORFEND

Warlock - NECROMANCER

Warm brown tone - SEPIA

Warm sweetened wine - NEGUS

Warning, old style - ALARUM

Warning bell - TOCSIN

Washington City or river - YAKIMA

Wasp - VESPID

Waste allowance - TRET

Water: Sp. - AGUA

Water buffalo - ARNA

Water-carved gulch - ARROYO

Water colored with gum - GOUACHE

Water goddess - EGERIA

Water nymph - NAIAD or NEREID

Water pipe - HOOKA

Water wheel - NORIA

Watered silk - MOIRE

Waterfall - LINN or SAULT

Waterloo Marshall - NEY

Waterproof wool cloth - LODEN

Wattle - DEWLAP

Watusi garmet - DASHIKI

Wavy, in heraldry - UNDE

Waxy: pref. - CER

Weak - EFFETE

Wealthy one - NABOB

Weapon handle - HAFT

Weasel cousin - ERMINE or MARTEN

Weasel relative - MINK or TAYRA

Weather baloon - SONDE

Weaver's bobbin - PIRN

Weaver's reed - SLEY

Weblike membrane - TELA

Web-site workers - SYSOPS

Weed of the mint family - HENBIT

Weeper of myth - NIOBE

Weevil - CURCULIO

Weight allowance - TARE or TRET

Weighty volumn - TOME

Welfare - WEAL

Well-groomed - SOIGNE

Well in France - BIEN

Welsh county - GWENT

Welsh wales - OYMRU

West African desert - NAMIB

West African language - HAUSA

West African monkey - MONA

West coast oak - ENCINA

West Indian palm - GRUGRU

West Indian plant - ANIL

West Indian shrub - INGA

West Indies fish - ABOMA

West Indies island - SABA

West Indies magic - OBEAH

Western Pacific republic - PALAU

Western Samoan capital - APIA

Western Samoan currency - TALA

Wet compress - STUPE

Whale constellation - CETUS

Whale herd - GAM or POD

Whalebone - BALEEN

Whales and dolphins - CETACEANS

Whales' blowhole - SPIRACLE

Whatnot - ETAGERE

Wheat used for livestock feed - SPELT

Wheel assembly - BOGIE

Whimper - PULE

Whimpering cry - MEWL

Whimsical humor- DROLLERY

Whine and complain - KVETCH

Whip handle - CROP

Whip used for flogging - KNOUT

White fish - CISCO

White lie - TARADIDDLE

White meat mold - GALANTINE

White metallic element - INDIUM

White oak - ROBLE

White of the eye - SCLERA

White poplar - ABELE or ALDER

White sage - RAMONA

White sauce - BECHAMEL

White Sea arm - ONEGA BAY

White sheep - MERINO

White spotted rodent - PACA

White wine - MACON

Whiten - ETIOLATE

Whole - UNITARY

Wicker basket - SKEP

Wickerwork encased bottle - DEMIJOHN

Wickerwork willow - OSSIER

Wide mouth - MAW

Wife of Abraham - SARAH

Wife of Amphion - NIOBE

Wife of Balder - NANNA

Wife of Brutus - PORTIA

Wife of Cadmus - HARMONIA

Wife of Caesar - UXOR

Wife of Ceausescu - ELENA

Wife of Cronus - RHEA

Wife of David Bowie - IMAM

Wife of Dionysus - ARIADNE

Wife of Dyland Thomas - CAITLIN

Wife of Esau - ADAH

Wife of Ethan - UMA

Wife of Geraint - ENID

Wife of Hephaestus - APHRODITE

Wife of Hercules - HEBE

Wife of Homer - MARGE

Wife of Iago - EMILIA

Wife of Jacob - LEAH or RACHEL

Wife of Jason - MEDEA

Wife of Jupiter - HERA or JUNO

Wife of Julius - CALPURNIA

Wife of Lamech - ADAH

Wife of Lohengrin - ELSA

Wife of Menelaus - HELEN

Wife of Nero - OCTAVIA

Wife of Oberon - TITANIA

Wife of Odysseus - PENELOPE

Wife of Orpheous - EURYDICE

Wife of Osiris - ISIS

Wife of Ovid - UXOR

Wife of Paris - OENONE

Wife of Petruchio - KATE

Wife of Priam - HECUBA

Wife of Prince Valiant - ALETA

Wife of Saturn - OPS

Wife of Sir Geraint - ENID

Wife of Siva - KALI

Wife of Theseus - PHAEDRA

Wife of Thor - SIF

Wife of Tyndareus - LEDA

Wife of Uranus - GAIA

Wife of Vulcan - VENUS

Wife of Wagner - COSIMA

Wife of Woody - SOONYI

Wife to Caesar - UXOR

Wifely - UXORIAL

Wig - PERUKE

Wild - FERAL

Wild ass - KIANG or ONAGER

Wild buffalo - ARNEE

Wild cat with tufted ears - CARACAL

Wild dog of India - DHOLE

Wild edible mushroom - CEP

Wild goat - IBEX or TAHR

Wild goose - BRANT

Wild herb - YARROW

Wild ox - ANOR, ANOA or YAK

Wild sheep - AOUDAD, ARGALI, SHA or URIAL

Wild silkworm - ERIA

Wildebeest - GNU

Willingly - FAIN

Willow - OSIER

Willow genus - ITEA

Wimper - PULE

Wind blown soil - LOESS

Wind instrument - OCARINA

Windflower - ANEMONE

Window divider - MULLION

Wine blender - OENO

Wine bottle or flask - OLPE

Wine cabinet - CELLARET

Wine cask - TUN

Wine from Spain - MALAGA

Wine grape - COLOMBARD or PINOT

Wine pouch - BOTA

Wine: pref. - OEN or OENO

Wine press residue - MARC

Wine sediment - LEES

Wine Stewart - SOMMELIER

Wine vessels - AMAS

Winemaking byproduct - ARGOL

Wing - ALA

Wing part - ALULA

Wing: Fr. - AILE

Winged - ALATE or ALAR

Winged ant - ALATE

Winged elm - WAHOO

Winged god - EROS

Winged goddess - NIKE

Winged horse - ARION or PEGASUS

Winged wader - STILT

Winglike - ALAR, ALATE or OLAR

Winglike structure - ALA

Wings - ALAE

Wink - NICTITATE

Winter apples - RUSSETS or WINESAPS

Winter coat material - LODEN

Winter melon - CASABA

Wipe out - EFFACE

Wire measuure - MIL

Wiry African grasses - ESPARTOS

Wise lawyer - SOLON

Wise Man - MAGUS

Wishbone - FOURCHETTE

Wispy clouds - CIRRI

Witch: Sp. - BRUJA

Witch bird - ANI

Witchcraft - OBEAH

Witchs day - SABBAT

Witch's diety - HECATE

Witchs' home - ENDOR

With: Fr. - AVEC

With: prefix - SYL

With child - GRAVID

With the bow, musically - ARCO

With full force - AMAIN

Within: Pre. - INTRA

With notched edges - EROSE

Withered - SERE

Within: Pre. - INTRA

Witty - JOCOSE

Witty remark - MOT

Wizard - MAGE

Wolfhound - BORZOI

Wolfsbane - ACONITE

Women's fur cape - PELERINE

Women's shoe - CHOPINE

Woman's shoulder scarf - FICHU

Wonder worker - MAGUS or THAMATURGE

Wonk - NERD

Wood knot - KNAR

Wood nymph - DRYAD

Wood sorrel - OCA, OKA or OXALIS

Wooded grove - RABBET

Wooden bench - SETTLE

Wooden goblet - MAZER

Wooden pegina masonary wall - NOG

Woodland diety - FAUN, PAN or SATYR

Woodpile measure - STERE

Woods nyph - DRYAD

Woodwind inventor - SAX

Woody - ALLER

Woody fibre -BAST

Woody plant tissue - XYLEM

Woody's son - ARLO

Woof - WEFT

Wool coat - LODEN

Wool: Lat. or Sp. - LANA

Wooly - HIRSUTE or LANOSE

Word form for "all" - OMNI

Word form for "ancient" - PALEO

Word form for beyond - META

Word form for "billionth" - NANO

Word form for "bird" - AVI or ORNITH

Word form for "blood" - HEMO

Word for for "blossom" - FLOR

Word form for "blue" - CYANO

Word form for "bone" - OSTEO

Word form for "bristle" - SETI

Word form for "bull" - TAURO

Word form for "Chinese" - SINO

Word form for "coil" - SPIRO

Word form for "crop" - AGRO

Word form for "culture" - ETHNO

Word form for "ear" - OTO

Word form for "earth" - GEO

Word form for "egg" - OVI

Word form for "environment" - ECO

Word form for "equal" - PARI

Word form for "false" - PSEUD

Word form for "farming" - AGRI

Word form for "five" - PENTA

Word form for "flight" - AERO

Word for for "foot" - PEDO

Word form for "healing" - IATRO

Word form for "heavens" - URANO

Word form for "high" - ALTI

Word form for "inner" - ENTO

Word form for "image" - ICONO

Word form for "large" - MARCO

Word form for male - ANDO

Word form for "Mars" - AREO

Word form for "milk" - LACT

Word form for "mouth" - ORI

Word form for "nationality" - ETHNO

Word form for "nerve" - NEURO

Word form for "nose" - NASO

Word form for "one billionth" - NANO

Word form for "outer" or "outside" - ECTO

Word form for "peculiar" - IDIO

Word for for "people" - ETHNO

Word form for "personal" - IDIO

Word form for "recent" - NEO

Word form for "right" - ORTH

Word form for "sacred" - HIERO

Word form for "skin" - DERM

Word for for "sleep" - HYPNO

Word form for "small" - MICRO

Word form for "straight" - ORTHO

Word form for "soil" - AGRO

Word form for "sun" - HELIO

Word form for "ten" - DECA

Word form for "thought" IDEO

Word form for "twenty" - ICOSA

Word form for "vinegar" - ACETO

Word form for "wine" - OENO

Word form for "within" - ENTO

Word of mouth - PAROL

Word origin - ETYMON

Word's last syllable - ULTIMA

Work hard - MOIL

Working stiff - POLE

Workshop - ATELIER

World's deepest lake - BAIKAL

World's small nation - NAURU

Worn out - EFFETE

Worshiper of Vishnu - BHAKTA

Worsted fabric - ETAMINE

Woven fabric - WEFT

Wrangle - BRABBLE

Wrapped in waxy cloth - CERED

Wreath for the head - ANADEM

Wrinkled - RUGOSE

Wrinkles - RUCKS

Wrist bone - TRAPEZOID

Wrist bones - CARPI

Writer's works - OEUVE

Writing desk - ESCRITOIRE

Written exposition - TREATISTE

Wrong doer - MISCREANT

Wrong:Pref. - MIS

Xiamen - AMOY

X-ray discoverer - ROENTGEN

X-ray measurements - REMS

Xylophone's relative - CELESTAS

Yacht pole - FID

Yale students - ELIS

Yaren's atoll - NAURU

Yashmak - VEIL

Yearling sheep - TEG

Yeast enzyme - LACTASE

Yeast-raised coffee cake - KUCHEN

Yellow billed rail - SORA

Yellow clay - ADOBE

Yellow fever mosquito - AEDES

Yellow fruit - PAWPA

Yellow plumlike fruit - LOQUAT

Yellow primrose - OXLIP

Yellowish green - BISCAY or RESEDA

Yellowish pigmant - OCHRE

Yellowish pink - RUFOUS

Yellowish red dye - ANATTO

Yemen seaport - ADEN

Yiddish synagogue - SHUL

Yiddish thief - GANEF

Yoga posture - ASANA

Yogert fruit drink - LASSI

Yorkshire River - AIRE or URE

Young actress - ONGENUE

Young barracuda - SPET

Young cod - SCROD

Young eel - ELVER

Young falcon - EYAS

Young female swine - GILT

Young fowl - POULT

Young: Fr. - JEUNE

Young goat - KID

Young Guinea fowl - KEET

Young haddock - SCROD

Young hare - LEVERET

Young hawk - EYAS

Young herring - BRIT

Young hog - SHOAT

Young oyster - SPAT

Young pig - ELT or SHOAT

Young salmon - GRILSE, PARR, SAMLET or SMOLT

Young sheep - TEGS or YEAN

Young sow - GILT

Young swan - CYGNET

Young turkey - POULT

Young wolf - WHELP

Youthful - CALLOW

Yucca cousin - AGAVE

Yucca-like plant - SOTOL

Yugoslavian money -PARA

Yuletime quaff - WASSAIL

Zebu's genus - BOS

Zen enlightenment - SATORI

Zen paradox - KOAN

Zeno's home - ELEA

Zeus' blood - ICHOR

Zeus' mother - RHEA

Zhivago love - LARA

Zinger - REPOSTE

Zoroastrian sacred texts - AVESTA

Zoroastrians - PARSIS

Zulu warriors - IMPI

PEOPLE IN PUZZLES

Abolitionist Harriet - TUBMAN

Accordionist Floren - MYRON

Actor Ackland - KOSS

Actor Acord - ART

Actor Adam - ARKIN

Actor Adams - EVAN

Actor Adrian - ZMED

Actor Afleck - BEN

Actor Alain - DELON

Actor Alastair - SIM

Actor Albright - NEGRON

Actor Alejandro - REY

Actor Ames - LEON

Actor Andrew - SHUE

Actor Andrews - DANA

Actor Antonio - SABATO

Actor Armand - ASSANTE

Actor Arnold - STANG or TOM

Actor Asimov - ISAAC

Actor Asther - NILS

Actor Astin - SEAN

Actor Auberjonois - RENE

Actor Avery - VALActor Ayres - LEW

Actor Axton - Hoyt

Actor Azaria - HANK

Actor Bana - ERIC

Actor Banderas - ANTONIO

Actor Bannen - IAN

Actor Barker - LEX

Actor Barry - Gene

Actor Bates - ALAN

Actor Beery - NOAH or WALLACE

Actor Benedict - DIRK

Actor Bllows - GIL

Actor Benicio Del - TORO

Actor Billy - ZANE

Actor Black - CLINT

Actor Blore - ERIC

Actor Bogosian - ERIC

Actor Booth - EDWIN

Actor Borgnine - ERNEST

Actor Bragher - ANDRE

Actor Branagh - KENNETH

Actor Brasselle - KEEFE

Actor Braugher - ANDRE

Actor Bendon - FRASER

Actor Brazzi - ROSSANO

Actor Brendon - SMALL

Actor Brian - KEITH

Actor Bridges - BEAU, JEFF or LLOYD

Actor Brooks - ALBERT

Actor Bruce - DERN, NIGEL or WILLIS

Actor Buckholz - HORST

Actor Buddy - EBSEN

Actor Burgess - MEREDITH

Actor Burton - LEVAR or RICHARD

Actor C. Thomas - HOWELL

Actor Cain - DEAN

Actor Cameron - KIRK

Actor Cariou - LEN

Actor Carl - WEATHERS

Actor Carridine - DAVID or KEITH

Actor Carroll - LEO G.

Actor Carver - BRENT

Actor Carvey - DANA

Actor Cary - ELWES

Actor Casper Van - DIEN

Actor Chad - EVERETT

Actor Charleson - IAN

Actor Cheech - MARIN

Actor Christian - SLATER

Actor Christopher - REEVE

Actor Clint - WALKER

Actor Cronyn - HUME

Actor Claude - AKINS or RAINS

Actor Clu - GULAGER

Actor Cobb - LEE J

Actor Conrad - Nagel, ROBERT or VEIDT

Actor Conreid - HANS

Actor Coppel - BERNIE

Actor Corin - NEMEC

Actor Cory - HAIM

Actor Cosner - KEVIN

Actor Crane - BOB

Actor Cronyn - HUME

Actor Crothers - SCATMAN

Actor Culken - KIERAN

Actor Cuny - ALAIN

Actor Curry - TIM

Actor Curtis - TONY

Actor D. B. SWEENEY

Actor Daly - TIM

Actor Damon - MATT

Actor Dan - DURYEA

Actor Danson - TED

Actor David Ogden - STIERS

Actor Davis - BRAD or OSSIE

Actor Davenport - NIGEL

Actor Day - Lewis - DANIEL

Actor Dean - CAIN

Actor Del Tor - BENICIO

Actor Delois - DOM

Actor Delon - ALAIN

Actor Denis - OHARE

Actor Denver - PYLE

Actor Depardieu - GERARD

Actor Derek - JACOBI

Actor Diamond - DUSTIN

Actor Dillon - MATT or MELINDA

Actor Donahue - TROY

Actor Donald - CRISP

Actor Douglas - KIRK

Actor Dourif - BRAD

Actor Dow - TONY

Actor Dullea - KEIR

Actor Duryea - DAN

Actor Ed - CROSS

Actor Edmund - KEAN

Actor Eldred - GREGORY PECK

Actor Elizondo - HECTOR

Actor Edwards - VINCE

Actor Elwes - CARY

Actor Ely - RON

Actor Epps - OMAR

Actor Eric - BLORE

Actor Erik - ESTRADA

Actor Erwin - STU

Actor Esai - MORALES

Actor Estevez - EMELIO

Actor Ethan - HAWKE

Actor Everett - SLOANE

Actor Farrell - COLIN

Actor Fernando - REY

Actor Fiennes - RALPH

Actor Firth - COLIN

Actor Fishburn - LAWRENCE

Actor Franco - NERO

Actor Frederic - MARCH

Actor Frobe - GERT

Actor Gabby - HAYES

Actor Garcia - ANDY

Actor Gary - COLE or OLDMAN

Actor George - ARLISS, HEARN,

SANDERS or TAKEI

Actor Gerard - GIL

Actor Gibson - MEL

Actor Gilliam - STU

Actor Glenn - SCOTT or STRANGE

Actor Goldblum - JEFF

Actor Gossett - LOU

Actor Green - LORNE or SETH

Actor Gregory - PECK

Actor Gross - ARYE

Actor Guinness - ALEC

Actor Gulager - CLU

Actor Guttenberg - STEVE

Actor Gyllenhaal - JAKE

Actor Haas - LUKAS

Actor Hadley - REED

Actor Haim - COREY

Actor Handler - EVAN

Actor Hanff - HELENE

Actor Hardison - KADEEM

Actor Harmon - MARK

Actor Harris - MEL

Actor Harrison - REX

Actor Hartnett - JOSH

Actor Hauer - RUTGER

Actor Hawk - ETHAN or NATHAN

Actor Hawthorn - NIGEL

Actor Heflin - VAN

Actor Henreid - PAUL

Actor Herbert - LOM

Actor Herschel - BERNARDI

Actor Heydaya - PAN

Actor Hoffman - DUSTIN

Actor Holm - IAN

Actor Homolka - OSCAR

Actor Horsley - LEE

Actor Howard - DUFF, KEN or TREVOR

Actor Hunter - IAN

Actor Irwin - STU

Actor Ivor - NOVELLO

Actor Jack or Tim - HOLT

Actor Jacobi - DEREK or LOU

Actor Jacques - TATI

Actor Jaffe - SAM

Actor Jake - WEBBER

Actor James - CAAN, SPADER or WOODS

Actor Jannings - EMIL

Actor Jarod - LETO

Actor Jeremy - IRONS

Actory Jerome - COWAN

Actor Jerry - ORBACH

Actor Jimmy - SMITS

Actor Joe - PESCI

Actor Joel - GREY

Actor John_____Davies - RHYS

Actor Johnny - DEPP

Actor Johnson - DON

Actor Jonathan - PRYCE

Actor Jones - DEAN

Actor Jose - FERRER

Actor Jude - LAW

Actor Julia - RAUL

Actor Karas - ALEX

Actor Katz - OMRI

Actor Kaufman - ANDY

Actor Keach - STACY

Actor Keaton - BUSTER

Actor Keir - DULLEA

Actor Kelly - GENE

Actor Kilmer - VAL

Actor Kingsley - BEN

Actor Kinnear - GREG

Actor Kinski - KLAUS

Actor Kirby - BRUNO

Actor Klemperer - WERNER

Actor Kline - KEVIN

Actor Kopell - BERNIE

Actor Koteas - ELIAS

Actor Kotto - YAPHET

Actor Kristofferson - KRIS

Actor Kruger - OTTO

Actor Law - JUDE

Actor Ladd - ALAN

Actor Lasalle - ERIQ

Actor Leary - DENIS

Actor LeBlanc - MATT

Actor Lee Browne - ROSCOE

Actor Liam - NEESON

Actor Linden - HAL

Actor Liota - RAY

Actor Lloyd - NOLAN

Actor Lowe - CHAD or ROBERT

Actor Lucas - HAAS

Actor Lyon - Ben

Actor M_____Walsh - EMMET

Actor MacDonald - CAREY

Actor MacLachlan - KYLE

Actor MacMurray - FRED

Actor Mantegna - JOE

Actor March - HAL

Actor Mark - ADDY

Actor Mark_____Baker - LINN

Actor Markham - MONTE

Actor Martin - LANDAU, RITTor ROSS

Actor Marvin - LEE

Actor Matt - DILLON

Actor Matthau - WALTER

Actor Max Von - SYDOW

Actor Maxwell - GAIL

Actor Maynard - KEN

Actor McGowen - ALEC

Actor McGregor - EWAN

Actor McKellen - IAN

Actor McKern - LEO

Actor McRaney - GERALD

Actor McShane - IAN

Actor Mel - FERRER

Actor Merlin - OLSEN

Actor Michael - ANSARA, CAINE, PARE or RENNIE

Actor Milo - O'SHEA

Actor Minaco - AINO

Actor Mineo - SAL

Actor Mintz - ELI

Actor Misha - AUER

Actor Mitchell - SASHA

Actor Mix - TOM

Actor Montalban - RICARDO

Actor Montand - YVES

Actor Moore - DUDLEY

Actor Morales - ESAI

Actor Moranis - RICK

Actor Morgan - HARRY or
FREEMAN

Actor Morita - PAT

Actor Mr. T. - TERO

Actor Mullavey - GREG

Actor Muni - PAUL

Actor Murphy - AUDIE or
EDDIE

Actor Murray - DON

Actor Navarro of old - RAMON

Actor Nazimova - ALLA

Actor Neeson - LIAM

Actor Neville - BRAND

Actor Nicky - KAT

Actor Nolan - LLYOD

Actor Nolte - NICK

Actor Norton - Edward

Actor Novarro - RAMON

Actor Novello - IVOR

Actor O'Brien - EDMOND or
HUGH

Actor O'Donnell - CHRIS

Actor Omar - EPPS

Actor O'Shea - MILO

Actor Pacino - AL

Actor Palminteri - CHAZZ

Actor Parker - FESS

Actor Patrick - BERGIN

Actor Paul - MUNI

Actor Pendleton - NAT

Actor Perlman - RON

Actor Perry - LUKE

Actor Peter - BOYLE, GRAVES
or O'TOOLE

Actor Philip - AHN

Actor Phillippe - RYAN

Actor Pop - IGGY

Actor Portier - SIDNEY

Actor Power - TYRONE

Actor Price - LONNY or
VINCENT

Actor/Producer Peter -
USTINOV

Actor Quinn - AIDAN or
ANTHON

Actor Rachins - ALAN

Actor Rainer - LUISE

Actor Raines - CLAUDE

Actor Ramis - HAROLD

Actor Ramon - BIERI

Actor Ray - ALDO or LIOTTA

Actor Reeves - KEANU

Actor Reginald - OWEN

Actor Regis - PHILBIN or TOOMEY

Actor Reynolds - BERT

Actor Rhames - VING

Actor Rhodes - HARI or HARRY

Actor Richard - BELZER, EGAN, GERE or KIEL

Actor Richmond - DEON

Actor Rickman - ALAN

Actor Rip - TORN

Actor Ritchard - CYRIL

Actor Ritter - JOHN or TEX

Actor Robbe-Grillet - ALAIN

Actor Robert - ERIC, DONAT or RYAN

Actor Roberts - ERIC

Actor Roger - REES

Actor Romero - CESAR

Actor Roscoe - ATES

Actor Rupert - EVERETT

Actor Russell - KURT

Actor Ryan - ONEAL

Actor Santori - LENI

Actor Scheider - ROY

Actor Schreiber - LIEV

Actor Scott - BAIO or BAKULA

Actor Sewell - RUFUS

Actor Sharif - OMAR

Actor Shepard - SAM

Actor Shimerman - ARMIN

Actor Silver - RON

Actor Silvers - PHIL

Actor Singer - LORI or MARC

Actor Sizemore - TOM

Actor Skinner - OTIS

Actor Slaughter - TOD

Actor Sloane - EVERETT

Actor Smith - WIL

Actor Spiner - BRENT

Actor Stamp - TERENCE

Actor Stephen - BOYD or REA

Actor Steve - MCQUEEN

Actor Steven - SEAGAL or WEBBER

Actor Stevenson - MCLEAN

Actor Stoltz - ERIC

Actor Stu - IRWIN

Actor Summerville - SLIM

Actor Sutherland - DONALD or KEIFFER

Actor Tamblyn - RUSS

Actor Tamiroff - AKIM

Actor Tayback - VIC

Actor Terry - KISER

Actor Thicke - ALAN

Actor Thinnes - ROY

Actor Tognazzi - UGO

Actor Tom - ARNOLD, EWELL, HULCE or WOPAT

Actor Turhan - BEY

Actor Ustinov - PETER

Actor Vallone - RAF

Actor Van Peebles - MARIO

Actor Verne - TROYER

Actor Victor - BUONO or MATURE

Actor Vigoda - ABE

Actor Villechaise - HERVE

Actor Ving - RHAMES

Actor Visnjic - GORAN

Actor Vito - SCOTTI

Actor Voight - JON

Actor Waggoner - LYLE

Actor Wahl - KEN

Actor Walker - CLINT

Actor Wallace - BEERY or REID

Actor Wallach - ELI

Actor Walsh - M. EMMET

Actor Walston - RAY

Actor Warner - OLAND

Actor Warren - OATES

Actor Washington - DENZEL

Actor Weaving - HUGO

Actor Welles - ORSON

Actor Wendell - COREY

Actor Werner - OSKAR

Actor Wesley - ADDY

Actor Wheaton - WIL

Actor Willem - DAFOE

Actor William - CLARK GABLE

Actor William - HAINES, INGE or KATT

Actor Williams - TREAT

Actor Williamson - NICOL

Actor Wilson - OWEN

Actor Woods - JAMES

Actor Wyle - NOAH

Actor Yaphet - KOTTO

Actor Young - GIG

Actor Ziering - IAN

Actress Ada - REHAN

Actress Adams - AMY or EDIE

Actress Adoree - RENEE

Actress Aimee - ANOUK

Actress Adrienne - BARBEAU or CORRI

Actress Albright - LOLA

Actress Alexander - ERIKA

Actress Alicia - ANA

Actress Allen - KAREN

Actress Alley - KIRSTIE

Actress Allgood - SARA

Actress Alonzo - CONCHITA

Actress Altieri - ELENA

Actress Alvarado - TRINI

Actress Alyssa - MILANO or PEET

Actress Amanda - BEARSE, PEET or PLUMMER

Actress Amis - BOZ

Actress Amy - MADIGAN

Actress Anderson - LONI or PAMELA

Actress Andesson - BIBI

Actress Andress - URSELA

Actress Angela - BASSETT or LANSBURY

Actress Angelina - JOLIE

Actress Anjelica - HUSTON

Actress Ann - ARCHER or DOREN

Actress Anna - STEN

Actress Anna May - WONG

Actress Anne - HECHE

Actress Annette - O'TOOLE

Actress Annie - POTTS

Actress Anouk - AIMEE

Actress Archer - ANNE

Actress Argento - ASIA

Actress Ari - MEYERS

Actress Arlene - DAHL

Actress Armstrong - BESS

Actress Arquette - ROSANNA

Actress Arthur - BEA

Actress Ashley - OLSEN

Actress Astor - MARY

Actress Audra - LINDLEY

Actress Aulin - EWA

Actress Bainter - FAY

Actress Baird - CORA

Actress Balin - INA

Actress Bancroft - ANNE

Actress Bara - THEDA

Actress Barbara - BARRY or BOSSAN

Actress Barkin - ELLEN

Actress Barrie - MONA

Actress Barrymore - ETHEL

Actress Bartok - EVA

Actress Basinger - KIM

Actress Benning - ANNETTE

Actress Berle - REID

Actress Bergen - CANDICE

Actress Berger - SENTA

Actress Bernadette - PETERS

Actress Berry - HALLE

Actress Beryl - REID

Actress Best - EDNA

Actress Beulah - BONDI

Actress Black - KAREN

Actress Blair - LINDA

Actress Blakley - RONEE

Actress Blanchett - CATE

Actress Bloom - CLAIRE

Actress Blythe - ANN or DANNER

Actress Bondi - Beulah

Actress Bonet - LISA

Actress Bow - CLARA

Actress Brega - SONIA

Actress Brennan - EILEEN

Actress Brewster - PAGET

Actress Brianne - LEARY

Actress Burke - BILLIE or DELTA

Actress Burstyn - ELLEN

Actress Burton - KATE

Actress Busch - MAE

Actress Caldwell - ZOE

Actress Cameron - DIAZ

Actress Campbell - NEVE or TISHA

Actress Candy - AZZARA

Actress Cannon - DYAN

Actress Capshaw - KATE

Actress Cardinale - CLAUDIA

Actress Carey - AMIE

Actress Carman - ELECTRA

Actress Carol - KANE

Actress Carrie - NYE

Actress Carrere - TIA

Actress Carter - LINDA or NELL

Actress Cate - BLANCHETT

Actress Cates - PHOEBE

Actress Catherine_____- Jones - ZETA

Actress Chalke - SARAH

Actress Charlotte - RAE

Actress Chase - ILKA

Actress China - CHOW

Actress Christina - RICCI

Actress Christine - ELISE or LAHTI

Actress Clair - DANES

Actress Claire - INA

Actress Clarke - MAE

Actress Close - GLENN

Actress Collette - TONI

Actress Conn - DIDI

Actress Copley - TERI

Actress Croft - LARA

Actress Crouse - LINDSAY

Actress Curtain - JANE

Actress Daly - TYNE

Actress Dame Edith - EVANS

Actress Damita - LILI

Actress Danes - CLAIRE

Actress Daniels - BEBE

Actress Danner - BLYTHE

Actress Danning - SYBIL

Actress Darby - KIM

Actress Dash - STACY

Actress Davis - GEENA or ESSIE

Actress Dawber - PAM

Actress_____Dawn Chong - RAE

Actress Debra - PAGET

Actress Delaney - KIM

Actress Delaria - LEA

Actress Delta - BURKE

Actress Demornay - REBECCA

Actress Dench - JUDI

Actress Diamond - SELMA

Actress Diane - LADD or LANE

Actress Dianne - WIEST

Actress Dickenson - ANGIE

Actress Dillon - MELINDA

Actress Divorak - ANN

Actress Dolenz - AMI

Actress Dolorea - DEL RIO

Actress Donahoe - AMANDA

Actress Donahue - ELINOR

Actress Doris - DAY

Actress Dorothy - MALONE or PROVINE

Actress D'Orsay - FIFI

Actress Downey - ROMA

Actress Dressler - MARIE

Actress Duce - ELEONORA

Actress Dunaway - FAYE

Actress Duncan - SANDY

Actress Dunne - IRENE

Actress Durbin - DEANNA

Actress Eartha - KITT

Actress Edna - BEST

Actress Eggar - SAMANTHA

Actresss Ekberg - ANITA

Actress Ekland - BRITT

Actress Elaine - STRITCH

Actress Eleniak - ERIKA

Actress Eleonora - DUSE

Actress Elg - TAINA

Actresss Elizabeth - ASHLEY, PENA or SHUE

Actress Ella - RAINES

Actress Ellen - DEGENERES

Actress Emma - SAMMS

Actress Erin - MORAN

Actress Esther - MOIRE or ROLLE

Actress Evans - LINDA

Actresss Eve - ARDEN

Actress Faris - ANNA

Actess Faye - ALICE

Actress Feldshuh - TOVAH

Actress Felicia - FARR

Actress Ferrel - TYRA

Actress Fionnula - FLANAGAN

Actress Fiore - ELENA

Actress Fiorentino - LINDA

Actress Fleming - RHONDA

Actresss Flynn Boyle - LARA

Actress Foch - NINA

Actress Fontanne - LYNNE

Actress Fonteyn of old - MARGOT

Actress Foster - JODIE

Actress Freeman - MONA

Actress Fricker - BRENDA

Actress Garbo - GRET

Actress Gay Harden - MARCIA

Actress Genevieve - BUJOLD

Actress Georgia - ENGEL

Actresss Geraldine - PAGE

Actress Gershon - GINA

Actress Gertrude - BERG

Actress Getty - ESTELLE

Actress Gia - SCALA

Actress Gibbs - MARLA

Actress Gilbert - MELISSA or SARA

Actress Gill - THEA

Actress Gilpin - PERI

Actress Gimpel - ERICA

Actress Glen - CLOSE

Acress Goddard - PAULETTE

Actress Gold - MISSY

Actress Goldberg - WHOOPI

Actress Goodman - DODY

Actresss Graff - ILENE

Actress Grant - LEE

Actress Gray - ERIN or NAN

Actress Gretta - GARBO

Actress Grier - PAM

Actress Grimes -TAMMY

Actress Gwyn - NELL

Actress Gyllenhaal - MAGGIE

Actress Hagan - UTA

Actress Hall - DEIDRE

Actress Harmon - ANGIE

Actress Harper - TESS

Actress Harris - ZELDA

Actress Hartley - MARIETTE

Actress Hartman - LISA

Actress Hasso - SIGNE

Actress Hatcher - TERI

Actress Hawn - GOLDIE

Actress Hayek - SALMA

Actress Hayworth - RITA

Actress Headly - GLENNE

Actress Heche - ANNE

Actress Heckart - EILEEN

Actress Helen _____Carter - BONHAM

Actress Helen - HAYES, MIRREN, SLATERS or TWELVETREES

Actress Helgenberger - MARG

Actress Hendren - TIPPI

Actress Henner - MARILU

Actress Hildegarde - NEFF

Actress Holden - AMANDA

Actress Holm - CELESTE

Actress Holmes - KATIE

Actress Hooks - JAN

Actress Hunt - HELEN or LINDA

Actress Hunter - HOLLY, KIM or TYLO

Actress Hussey - OLIVIA

Actress Huxtable - ADA

Actress Hymes - LEILA

Actress Ina - BALIN

Actress Iona - SKYE

Actress Irene - PAPAS

Actress Jackson - GLENDA or KATE

Actress Jane - CARR

Actress Janet - MCTEER

Actress Janis - ELSIE or PAIGE

Actress Jeanne - EAGLES

Actress Jeffreys - ANNE

Actress Jennifer - ALBA, BEALS, LOPEZ or SALT

Actress Jessica - ALBA, LANGE or TANDY

Actresss_____Jessica Parker - SARAH

Actress Jill - WHELAN

Actress Jillian – ANN

Actress Joan - CHEN

Actress Jo Ann - PFLUG

Actress Joanne - DRU or KERNS

Actress Jodie - FOSTER

Actress Johnson - CELIA

Actress Jolie - ANGELINA

Actress Jovovich - MILLA

Actress Joyce - DEWITT

Actress Judd - ASHLEY

Actress Judi - DENCH

Actress Judith - IVEY

Actress Julia - ORMOND

Actress Jurado - KATY

Actress Kaminska - IDA

Actress Kate - REDDING

Actress Kathy - BATES

Actress Katie - SAGAL

Actress Kazan - LAINIE

Actress Kedrova - LILA

Actress Keanon - STACI

Actress Keeton - DIAME

Actress Kelly - MOIRA

Actress Kennedy - MIMI

Actress Kidman - NICOLE

Actress King - MABEL

Actress Knightly - KEIRA

Actress Kristen - ILENE

Actress Kruger - ALMA

Actress Kurtz - SWOOZIE

Actress Ladd - DIANE or CHERYL

Actress Lake - VERONICA

Actress LaMarr - HEDY

Actress Lancaster - ELSA

Actress Landi - ELISSA

Actress Lansbury - ANGELA

Actress Lasser - LOUISE

Actress Laughlin - LORI

Actress Laura - DERN

Actress Laurie - PIPER

Actress Lawless - LUCY

Actress Lawrence - CAROL

Actress Lea - DELARIA

Actress Leachman - CLORIS

Actress Lee - LILA or RUTA

Actress_____Lee Nolin - GENA

Actress Legienne - EVA

Actress Leigh - JANET or VIVIEN

Actress Lena - OLIN

Actress Lenore - ULRIC

Actress Lenska - RULA

Actress Leoni - TEA

Actress Leslie - CARON

Actress Lillie - BEA

Actress Linda - DANO, EDER, LAVIN or PURL

Actress Lindley - AUDRA or CAROL

Actress Lindsay - CROUSE, LOHAN or WAGNER

Actress Linney - LAURA

Actress Lisi - VIRNA

Actress Locke - SONDRA

Actress Lockhart - JUNE

Actress Locklear - HEATHER

Actress Logan - ELLA

Actress Lollobrigida - GINA

Actress Long - NIA or Shelley

Actress Lotte - LENYA

Actress Loughlin - LORI

Actress Louise - FLETCHER, LASSER or STUBBS

Actress Luana - ANDERS

Actress Lucy - ARNEZ or LIU

Actress Luise - RAINER

Actress Lupino - IDA

Actress Lupone - PATTI

Actress Lyon - SUE

Actress MacDowel - ANDIE

Actress Madeleine - STOWE

Actress Madigen - AMY

Actress Madlyn - RHUE

Actress Magnani - ANNA

Actress Maples - MARLA

Actress Marceau - SOPHIE

Actress Marisa - TOMEI

Actress Markey - ENID

Actress Marlee - MATLIN

Actress Marsh - JEAN

Actress Marsha - HUNT

Actress Martha - HYER

Actress Martin - ANDREA, NAN or PAMELA SUE

Actress Martinelli - ELSA

Actress Mary - ASTOR or URE

Actress Mary Kay - PLACE

Actress Mason - MARSHA

Actress Massey - ILONA

Actress Matlin - MARLEE

Actress Maude - ADAMS

Actress May - ELAINE

Actress Mazar - DEBI

Actress McCambridge - MERCEDES

Actress McClanahan - RUE

Actress McClurg - EDIE

Actress McKenna - SIOBHAN

Actress Meg - RYAN or TILLY

Actress Mendez - EVA

Actress Menken - ADAH

Actress Mercedes - RUEHL

Actress Merkel - UNA

Actress Merrill - DINA

Actress Messing - DEBRA

Actress Metcalf - LAURIE

Actress Meyer - Dina

Actress Meyers - ARI

Actress Mia - SARA

Actress Michael - LEARNED

Actress Milano - ALYSSA

Actress Miles - SARAH or VERA

Actress Mimi - ROGERS

Actress Mimieu - YVETTE

Actress Minnelli - LIZA

Actress Mitzi - GAYNOR or MCCALL

Actress Molly - PICON

Actress Monk - DEBRA

Actress Montez - LOLA

Actresss Moore - TERRY

Actress Moran - ERIN

Actress Moreau - JEANNE

Actress Moreno - RITA

Actress Morris - ANITA

Actress Munson - ONA

Actress Myer - DINA

Actress Myers - ARI

Actress Naldi - NITA

Actress Nancy - KWAN or OLSON

Actress Nazimova - ALLA

Actress Neagle - ANNA

Actress Negri - POLA

Actress Nell - GWYN

Actress Nelligan - KATE

Actress Nettleton - LOIS

Actress Neuwirth - BEBE

Actress NG - IRENE

Actress Nia - PEEBLES

Actress Nicollette - SHERIDAN

Actress Nielsen - ASTA or BRIGITTE

Actress Normand - MABEL

Actress North - SHEREE

Actress Olin - LENA

Actress Oliver - EDNA MAY

Actress Olivia d'_____ - ABO

Actress Olivia - HUSSEY

Actress O'Neal - TATUM

Actress O'Shea - TESSIE

Actress Ostereald - BIBI

Actress Owen - RENA

Actress Pacula - JOANNA

Actress Page - ERICKA or GERALDINE

Actress Pamela - ANDERSON, DES BARRES or REED

Actress Papas - IRENE

Actress Paquin - ANNA

Actress Park-Lincoln - LAR

Actress Parker - SUSY

Actress Parsons - ESTELLE

Actress Patsy - KENSIT

Actress Paula - PRENTISS

Actress Pedrova - OLGA

Actress Peeples - NIA

Actress Peggy - CASS

Actress Penelope - CRUZ

Actress Perez - ROSIE

Actress Petty - LORI

Actress Pfeiffer- DEDEE

Actress Phoebe - CATES

Actress Pier - ANGELI

Actress_____ Pinket Smith - JADA

Actress Piper - LAURIE

Actress Pitts - ZASU

Actress Plato - DANA

Actress Plumb - EVE

Actress Plummer - AMANDA

Actress Polo - TERI

Actress Portia de - ROSSI

Actress Portman - NATALIE

Actress Potts - ANNIE

Actress Powers - MALA

Actress Prentiss - PAULA

Actress Purviance - EDNA

Actress Rainer - LUISE

Actress Raines - ELLA

Actress Ramirez - MARISA

Actress Redgrave - LYNN or VANESSA

Actress Reed Hall - ALAINA

Actress Rehan - ADA

Actress Reid - TARA

Actress Reinking - ANN

Actress Reischl - GERI

Actress Remini - LEAH

Actress Renee - ADOREE

Actress Reva - ROSE

Actress Richards - DENISE

Actress Richardson - MIRANDA or NATASHA

Actress Rinna - LISA

Actress Rita - GAM or MORENO

Actress Ritter - THELMA

Actress Roberts - TANYA

Actress Rogers - MIMI

Actress Roker - ROXIE

Actress Rosie - O'DONNELL or PEREZ

Actress Rowlands - GENA

Actress Rossellini - ISABELLA

Actress Ruby - KEELER

Actress Rule - JANICE

Actress Russel - KERI

Actress Russo - RENE

Actress Ruth - ROMAN

Actress Ryan - JERI or MEG

Actress Ryder - WINONA

Actress Sagal - KATIE

Actress Sally Ann - HOWES

Actress Salma - HAYEK

Actress Salome - JENS

Actress Salonga - LEA

Actress Sammantha - EGGAR

Actress Samms - EMMA

Actress Sara - MIA

Actress Sara Jessica - PARKER

Actress Sarandan - SUSAN

Actress Scacchi - GRETA

Actress Scala - GIA

Actress Schell - MARIA

Actress Schneider - ROMY

Actress Sedgwick - EDIE or KYRA

Actress Sevigne - CHLOE

Actress Shane - LIN

Actress Sharon - GANS, STONE or TATE

Actress Shearer - MOIRA

Actress Sheedy - ALLY

Actress Sheppard - DELIA

Actress Shields - BROOKE

Actress Shire - TALIA

Actress Shirley - AURORA

Actress Shue - ELISABETH

Actress Siddons - SARAH

Actress Signe - HASSO

Actress Signoret - SIMONE

Actress Silverstone - ALICIA

Actress Silvia - SIDNEY or SYMS

Actress Singer - LORI

Actress Skye - IONE

Actress Slezak - ERIKA

Actress Smart - JEAN

Actress Smith - JACLYN or MAGGIE

Actress Sobieski - LEELEE

Actress Sofer - RENA

Actress Sommer - ELKE

Actress Sondra - LOCKE

Actress Sonya - BRAGA

Actress Sorvino - MIRA

Actress Spacek - SISSY

Actress Spelling - TORI

Actress Stanley - KIM

Actresss Stapleton - JEAN

Actress Stella - ADLER

Actress Stephanie - BEECHAM

Actress Stevens - INGER or STELLA

Actress Stewart - ALANA

Actress Stimson - SARA

Actress Stone - SHARON

Actress Strassman - MARCIA

Actress Streep - MERYL

Actress Stritch - ELAINE

Actress Struthers - SALLY

Actress Sue_____Langdon - AN

Actress _____Sue Martin - PAMELA

Actress Susan - ANTON, DEY or LUCCI

Actress Suvari - MENA

Actress Suzanne - SOMERS

Actress Swenson - INGA

Actress Sykes - WANDA

Actress Ta - LEONI

Actress Taina - ELG

Actress Talbot - NITA

Actress Talia - SHIRE

Actress Talmadge – NORMA

Actress Tatania - ALI

Actress Taylor - ELIZABETH, LILI, RENEE

or REGINA

Actress Tea - LEONI

Actress Tessie - O'SHEA

Actress Texada - TIA

Actress Thomas - MARLO

Actress Thompson - EMMA, LEA or SADA

Actress Thorndyke - SYBIL

Actress Thurman - UMA

Actress Tierney - Gene or MAURA

Actress Tilly - MEG

Actress Tippi - HEDREN

Actress Tracy - ULLMAN

Actress Trevor - CLAIRE

Actress Tuesday - WELD

Actress Turner - LANA

Actress Turturro - AIDA

Actress Tyler - LIV

Actress Tyson - CICELY

Actress Ullman - LIV

Actresss Una - MERKEL

Actress Uta - HAGAN

Actress Valli - ALIDA

Actress Van Devere - TRISH

Actress Van Doren - MAMIE

Actress Vardalus - NIA

Actresss Velez - LUPE

Actress Verdon - GWEN

Actress Verdugo - ELENA

Actress Veronica - HAMIL or LAKE

Actress Vidal - THEA

Actress Virginia - MAYO

Actress Virna - LISI

Actress Vivian - LEIGH or VANCE

Actress Volz - NEDRA

Actress Wallace - DEE

Actress Wannamaker - ZOE

Actress Ward - SELA

Actress Watson - EMILY or EMMA

Actress Watts - NAOMI

Actress Weist - DIANNE

Actress Wendy - BARRIE

Actress Wettig - PATRICIA

Actress Whitman - MAE

Actress Williams - CARA, EDY, ESTHER, JOBETH or KELLY

Actress Winger - DEBRA

Actress Winningham - MARE

Actress Winona - RYDER

Actress Winslet - KATE

Actress Winwood - ESTELLE

Actress Witherspoon - CORA or REESE

Actress Witt - ALICIA

Actress Wood - LANA

Actress Woodard - ALFRE

Actress Woods - NAN or REN

Actress Worth - IRENE

Actress Wray - FAY

Actress Wright - TERESA

Actress York - SUSANNAH

Actress Yothers - TINA

Actress Zellweger - RENEE

Actress Zeta-Jones - CATHARINE

Actress Zetterling - MAI

Actress Ziemba - KAREN

Admiral Zumait - ELMO

Albert & Tipper - GORE

Alda - ROBERT or ALAN

Alex & Felix - ADLER

Ali - BABA

Allen - TIM

Allen or Tim - CONWAY

Aluminum discoverer - OERSTED

American naturalist - MUIR

Amin - IDI

Amy or James - LOWELL

Anarchist Goldman - EMMA

Andrea_____Sarto - DEL

Andretti - MARIO

Angus - DEI

Animator Avery - TEX

Animator Bluth - DON

Animator Groening - MATT

Announcer Costas - BOB

Annoucer Dawson - LEN

Announcer Don - PARDO

Anthologist Alberto - MANGUEL

Anthropologist Fossey - DIAN

Anthropologist Margaret - MEAD

Anthropologist Montagu - ASHLEY

Anthropologist Morris - DESMOND

Anthropologist Strauss - LEVI

Aoki of Golf - ISAO

Archibald of basketball - NATE

Architect Alva - AALTO

Architect Benjamin - LAROBE

Architect Brammante - DONATO

Architect Buckminster - FULLER

Architect Christopher - WREN

Architect I. M. _____ - PEI

Architect Jacobsen - ARNE

Architect James - HOBAN

Architect Jones - INIGO

Architech Leoh_____Pei - MING

Architect Maya - LIN

Architect Mies van de - ROHE

Architect Oscar - NIEMEYER

Architect Pei - IEOH

Architect Pelli - CESAR

Architect Richard - MEIER

Architect Saarinen - EERO or ELIEL

Architect Samuel - SLOAN

Architect Soleri - PAOLO

Architect Van der Rohe - MIES

Architect Wagner - OTTO

Architect William Van - ALEN

Arlene or Roald - DAHL

Art collector Broad - ELI

Art deco designer - ERTE

Artist Adams - OLETA

Artist Alex - KATZ

Artist Andrew - WYETH

Artist Annigoni - PIETRO

Artist Arp - HANS

Artist Ben - SHAHN

Artist Bonheur - ROSA

Artist Cezanne - PAUL

Artist Chagal - MARC

Artist Del Sarto - ANDREA

Artist Duffy - RAOUL

Artist Edgar - DEGAS

Artist Edouard - MANET

Artist Edvard - MUNCH

Artist Elbers - JOSEF

Artist Emily - CARR

Artist Eric - SLOANE

Artist Franz - MARC

Artist Gaugan - PAUL

Artist Grant - WOOD

Artist Guido - RENI

Artist Gustave - DORE

Artist Harring - KEITH

Artist Homer - WINSLOW

Artist Hopper - EDWARD

Artist Jan - STEEN or
VERMEER

Artist Jasper - JOHNS

Artist Joan - MIRO

Artist John - SARGENT

Artist Kahlo - FRIDA

Artist LaLique - RENE

Artist Lewitt - SOL

Artist Lichtenstein - ROY

Artist Magritte - RENE

Artist Mark - ROTHKO

Artist Matisse - HENRI

Artist Max - ERNST

Artist Modigliani - AMEDEO

Artist Mondrian - PIET

Artist Monet - CLAUDE

Artist Nadelman - ELIE

Artist Neiman - LEROY

Artist Nolde - EMIL

Artist Paul - KLEE

Artist Picasso - PABLO

Artist Poussin - NICOLAS

Artist Rivera - DIEGO

Artist Rockwell - KENT or
NORMAN

Artist Rouseau - HENRI

Artist Sedgewick - EDIE

Artist Smit - ARIE

Artist Vermeer - JAN

Artist Verones - PAOLO

Artist Warhol - ANDY

Artist Watteau - ANTOINE

Artist Wyeth - JAMIE

Asner or Wynn - ED

Astrologer Dixon - JEAN

Astrologer Goodman - LINDA

Astrologer John - DEE

Astrologer Sidney - OMARR

Astronaut Armstrong - NEAL

Astronaut Buzz - ALDRIN

Astronaut Carpenter - SCOTT

Astronaut Collins - EILEEN

Astronaut Dr. Mae - JEMISON

Astronaut Gagarin - YURI

Astronaut Garriott - OWEN

Astronaut Jamison - MAE

Astronaut Jernigan - TAMARA

Astronaut Roosa - STU

Astronaut Sally - RIDE

Astronaut Shannon - LUCID

Astonaut Slaton - DEKE

Astronaut Sullivan - KATHRYN

Astronaut Walter - SCHIRRA

Astronomer Hubble - EDWIN

Astronomer Johannes - KEPLER

Astronomer Lowell - PERCIVAL

Astronomer Martin - REES

Astronomer Penzias - ARNO

Astronomer Sir Martin - RYLE

Astronomer Tycho - BRAHE

Atheist Madalyn Murray - OHAIR

Attorney Dershowitz - ALAN

Attorney Melvin - BELLI

Attorney Roy - COHN

Auberjonois - RENE

Author Abba - EBAN

Author Achebe - CHINUA

Author Adler - FREDA or RENATA

Author Alan - PATON

Author Alcott - LOUISA

Author Alexandra - SHANA

Author Algren - NELSON

Author Alice - ADAMS

Author Alighieri - DANTE

Author Alison LURIE

Author Allende - ISABEL

Author Alther - LISA

Author Alvin - TOFFLER

Author Ambler - ERIC

Author Amis - MARTIN

Author Amy - TAN

Author Anais - NIN

Author Anchee - MIN

Author Andersen - HANS

Author Andre - MAUROIS

Author Andric - IVO

Author Angelou - MAYA

Author Anita - LOOS

Author Anna - SEWELL

Author Anya - SETON

Author Arendt - HANNAH

Author Arthur - CLARKE

Author Asch - SHOLEM

Author Asimov - ISAAC

Author Asquith - ROS

Author Auel - JEAN

Author Austen - JANE

Author Ayn - RAND

Author Babel - ISAAC

Author Bacon - DELIA

Author Bagnold - ENID

Author Balzac - HONORE

Author Barker - CLIVE

Author Bates - ARLO

Author Beattie - ANN

Author Beckett - SAMUEL

Author Belloc - HILAIRE

Author Bellows - SAUL

Author Belva - PLAIN

Author Berenstain - STAN

Author Bernard - MALAMUD

Author Betti - UGO

Author Bierce - AMBROSE

Author Binchly - MAEVE

Author Blixen - KAREN

Author Bloom - ALLAN

Author Blyton - ENID

Author Booth - TARKINGTON

Author Boyle - KAY or TISH

Author Bracken - PEG

Author Braveman - KATE

Author Bret - ELLIS or HARTE

Author Brookner - ANITA

Author Brown - DEE

Author Buchanan - EDNA

Author Buck - PEARL

Author Buscaglia - LEO

Author Butler - ROBERT- OLEN

Author Cainan - ETHAN

Author Caldwell - ERSKINE

Author Caleb - CARR

Author Calvino - ITALO

Author Canette - ELIAS

Author Capek - KAREL

Author Capet - KARE

Author Capote - TRUMAN

Author Carl - SAGAN

Author Carnegie - DALE

Author Carolyn - KEENE

Author Carr - CALEB

Author Carson - RACHEL

Author Castaneda - CARLOS

Author Castillo - ANA

Author Cather - WILLAS

Author Chalmers - IRENA

Author _____Chandler Harris - JOEL

Author Charles - READE or OLSON

Author Chomsky - NOAM

Author Chopin - KATE

Author Clark - BLAISE

Author Clancy - TOM

Author Cleveland - AMORY

Author Clifford - ODETS

Author Collins - WILKIE

Author Comfort - ALEX

Author Connell - EVAN

Author Conrad - JOSEPH

Author Cornelius - RYAN

Author Coulter - ANN

Author Cross - AMANDA

Author Currie - EDWINA

Author Cussler - CLIVE

Author Dahl - ROALD

Author Daniel - KEYES

Author Davis - ADELLE

Author De Beauvoir - SIMONE

Author De Foe - DANIEL

Author De Hartog - JAN

Author De La Roche - MAZO

Author Deighton - LEN

Author Devereau - JUDE

Author Dexter - PETE

Author Dian - FOSSEY

Author Dideon - JOAN

Author Dillard - ANNIE

Author Dinesen - ISAK

Author Don - DeLILLO

Author _____Donald Walsch- NEALE

Author Du Maurier - DAPHNE

Author Earl _____Biggers - DERR

Author Eberhart - MIGNON

Author Eda - LESHAN

Author Edward D. - HOCH

Author Edwin - OCONNOR

Author Eleanor - ESTES

Author Eliau - ARIE

Author Elinor - WYLIE

Author Ellen - RASKIN

Author Ellison - HARLAN or RALPH

Author Ellsberg - DANIEL

Author Emily - CARR

Author Ephron - DELIA or NORA

Author Erica - JONG

Author Erich - SEGAL

Author Ernest - POOLE

Author Ernie - PYLE

Author Eudora - WELTY

Author Fannie - FLAGG

Author Fallaci - ORIANA

Author Farley - MOWAT

Author Fleming - IAN

Author Follett - KEN

Author Fosse - DIAN

Author France - ANATOLE

Author Francoise - SAGAN

Author Frank - NORRIS

Author Franz - KAFKA

Author Frederik - POHL

Author Fromm - ERIC

Author Fugard - ATHOL

Author Gardner - EARL

Author Garson - KANIN

Author Gay - TALESE

Author George - ELIOT, ORWELL or SAND

Author Germaine - GREER

Author Germaine de - STAEL

Author Gertrude - STEIN

Author Gibbons - KAYE

Author Gilchrist - ELLEN

Author Gish - JEN

Author Glasgow - ELLEN

Author Glyn - ELINOR

Author Godden - RUMER

Aauthor Godwin - GAIL

Author Goncharov - IVAN

Author Gore - VIDAL

Author Grafton - SUE

Author Graham - GREENE

Author Grass - GUNTER

Author Gray - ZANE

Author Greene - GAEL

Author Greg - EGAN

Author H. H. Munroe - SAKI

Author Hagan - UTA

Author Haley - ALEX

Author Hammond - INNES

Author Hamsun - KNUT

Author Hanff - HELENE

Author Harland - ELLISON

Author Harper - LEE

Author Havelock - ELLIS

Author Hawthorn - NATHANIEL

Author Henrik - IBSEN

Author Henry - ROTH

Author Herman - HESSE

Author Heyerdahl - THOR

Author Hillerman - TONY

Author Hite - SHERE

Author Hoag - TAMI

Author Hoff - BENJAMIN

Author Hoffer - ERIC

Author Hoffman - ABBIE

Author Hood - ANN

Author Horatio - ALGER

Author Hubbard - LRON

Author Hulme - KERI

Author Hunter - EVAN

Author Hurston _____ NEALE - ZORA

Author Huxley - ALDOUS

Author Ian - FLEMING or MCEWAN

Author Ingall Wilder - LAURA

Author Ira - LEVIN

Author Isaac - ASIMOV

Author Jack - LONDON

Author _____Jackson Braun - LILIAN

Author Jacob - RIIS

Author Jaffe - RONA

Author James - AGEE, ATLAS, MANN or PATTERSON

Author Janowitz - TAMA

Author Jane - SMILEY

Author Jaquelin - SUSANN

Author Jay - ANSON

Author Jean - AUEL or RHYS

Author Jessamyn - WEST

Author Johann - WYSS

Author Johanna - SPYRI

Author John Dickson - CARR

Author John Dos - PASSOS

Author John - LECARRE, LYLY or UPDIKE

Author John Kennedy - TOOLE

Author Jones - LEROI

Author Jong - ERICA

Author Jorge - AMANDO

Author Jorge_____Borges - LUIS

Author Josephine - TEY

Author Joyce - JAMES

Author Joyce Carol - OATES

Author Kafka - FRANZ

Author Kanter - SETH

Author Kauffman - BEL

Author Ken - KESEY

Author Kesey - KEN

Author Khoury - ELIAS

Author Kingsley - AMIS

Author Knight - ERIC

Author Kogawa - JOY

Author Koontz - DEAN

Author Kundera - MILAN

Author Lamott - JUNE

Author Langdon - JANE

Author Lathen - EMMA

Author _____ Lee Hope - LAURA

Author Leguin - URSALA

Author Lesage - ALAIN

Author Leon - ROOKE or URIS

Author Leonard - ELMIR or ELMORE

Author Leshan - EDA

Author Lesssing - DORIS MAY

Author Levin - IRA

Author Lin - YUTANG

Author Lindbergh - ANNE

Author Lofting - HUGH

Author Lofts - NORAH

Author Loos - ANITA

Author Louisa May - ALCOTT

Author Ludlum - ROBERT

Author Ludwig - EMIL

Author Lurie - ALISON

Author Lustbader - ERIC

Author MacDonald - ROSS

Author Malraux - ANDRE

Author Margaret - ATWOOD

Author Marian- ENGEL

Author Marsh - NGAIO

Author Martin - AMIS

Author Mary Lee - SETTLE

Author Maurice - EVANS

Author May - ROLLO

Author McBain - ED

Author McCaffrey - ANNE

Author McCann - COOLUM

Author McCourtney - LORENA

Author McCullers - CARSON

Author McCullough - COLLEEN

Author McDermott - ALICE

Author Melville - HERMAN

Author Melvin - BELLI

Author Michael - ENDE or INNES

Author Mihel - KORDA

Author Miller - SUE or HENRY

Author Mills - ENOS

Author Milne - ALAN

Author Milosz - CZESLAW

Author Montez - LOLA

Author Morrison - TONI

Author Munro - ALICE

Author Murdoch - IRIS

Author Nathaniel - WEST

Author Nelson - ALGREN

Author Neville - SHUTE

Author Ngaio - MARSH

Author Nicolas - GAGE

Author Nin - ANAIS

Author Nino - RICCI

Author Noel - BEHN or COWARD

Author Norman - MAILER

Author Norman Vincent - PEALE

Author O'Brien - EDNA

Author Octavio - PAZ

Author Odets - CLIFFORD

Author O'Faolain - SEAN

Author O'Flaherty - LIAM

Author Olesha - YURY

Author Oz - AMOS

Author Packard - VANCE

Author Pamela_____Barres - DES

Author Parent - GAIL

Author Paretsky - SARA

Author Pasternak - BORIS

Author Paton - ALAN

Author Peter - MAAS

Author Peters - ELLIS

Author Philip - ROTH

Author Piandello - LUIGI

Author Plain - BELVA

Author Prosper - MERIMEE

Author Proust - MARCEL

Author Prudhomme - ENOLA

Author Puzo - MARIO

Author Pyle - ERNIE

Author Quick - AMANDA

Author Radcliffe - ANN

Author Randy - SHILTS

Author Rawlings - MARJORIE

Author Rebecca - WEST

Author Rice - ANNE or ELMER

Author Richard - ADAMS or SCARRY

Author Richard Henry - DANA

Author Roald - DAHL

Author Robbe-Grillet - ALAIN

Author Robert - RUARK or STONE

Author Robert_____Butler - OLEN

Author Roberts - NORA

Author Robertson - DAVIES

Author Robinson - EDEN

Author Roger St. Johns - ADELA

Author Rombauer - IRMA

Author Rosten - LEO

Author Roth - PHILIP

Author Rule - ANN

Author S. S. Van - DINE

Author Sanchez - SONIA

Author Sandel - CORA

Author Sarah_____Jewett - ORNE

Author Schreiner - OLIVE

Author Scott - O'DELL or TUROW

Author Sebold - ALICE

Author Segal - ERICH

Author Sendak - MAURICE

Author Seton - ANYA

Author Sewell - ANNA

Author Shaw - IRWIN

Author Sheehy - GAIL

Author Sheldon - SIDNEY

Author Shelley - MARY

Author Shere - HITE

Author Shilts - RANDY

Author Sholem - ASCH

Author Shreve - ANITA

Author Siddhartha - HESSE

Author Sidney - SHELDON

Author Siegel - BERNIE

Author Sillitoe - ALAN

Author Silvia - PLATH

Author Simenon - Georges

Author Simpson - MONA

Author Sinclair - ROSS or UPTON

Author Sir Thomas - ELYOT

Author Skvorecky - JOSEF

Author Sophie - KERR

Author Spryri - JOHANNA

Author Stanislaw - LEM

Author Stein - GERTRUDE

Author Stephen - CRANE

Author Stewart - ALSOP

Author Stoker - BRAM

Author Stout - REX

Author Susan - SONTAG

Author Suzanne - SOMERS

Author Talese - GAY

Author Tamblyn - RUSS

Author Tan - AMY

Author Tarbell - IDA

Author Tasha - TUDOR

Author Tertz - ABRAM

Author Thomas - MARLO

Author Tolstoy - LEO

Author Toni - MORRISON

Author Trilling - LIONEL

Author Truman - CAPOTE

Author Turgenov - IVAN

Author Turkel - STUDS

Author Tyler - ANNE

Author Umberto - ECO

Author Updike - JOHN

Author Uris - LEON

Author Urquhart - THOMAS

Author Vonnegut - KURT

Author Walker - ALICE or PERCY

Author Wallace - LEW

Author Walter - FARLEY or PATER

Author Walton - IZAAK

Author Waugh - ALEC or EVELYN

Author Weldon - FEY

Author Welty - EUDORA

Author West - NATHANAEL

Author Wharton - EDITH

Author Wilde - OSCAR

Author Wilder - THORNTON

Author Wiesel - ELIE

Author William - GIBSON

Author William H. - WHYTE

Author Winegarten - RENEE

Author Wister - OWEN

Author Wolf - NAOMI

Author Wolfert - IRA

Author Wolff - TOBIAS

Author Yurik - SOL

Author Yutang - LIN

Author Zola - EMILE

Author Zona - GALE

Author Zora _____ Hurton - NEALE

Auto pioneer Ransom - OLDS

Auto racer Gordon - JEFF

Auto racer Petty - KYLE or RICHARD

Auto racer Prost - ALAIN

Automaker Ferrari - ENZO

Automaker Maserati - ERNESTO

Aviator Balbo - ITALO

Aviator Chennault - CLAIRE

Aviator Earhart - AMELIA

Aviator Post - WILEY

B. C. Cartoonist - HAUNT

Baba - ALI

Bacteriologist Dubos - RENE

Bacteriologist Jonas - SALK

Bakkaruba Alicia - ALONZO

Ballpoint pen inventor Lazlo - BIRO

Ballarina Alonzo - ALICIA

Ballarina Fonteyn - MARGOT

Ballarina Galina - ULANOVA

Ballarina Karsavina - TAMARA

Ballarina Markova - ALICIA

Ballarina Markarova - NATALIA

Ballarina Melissa - HAYDEN

Ballarina painter - DEGAS

Ballarina Pavlova - ANNA

Ballarina Plisetskaya - MAYA

Ballarina Rambeat - MARIE

Ballarina Shearer - MOIRA

Ballarina Spessivtzeve - OLGA

Ballet dancer Youskevitch - IGOR

Ballet dancer Bruhn - ERIC

Ball player Dykstra - LEN

Bandleader Baxter - LES

Bandleader Cugot - Xavier

Bandleader Edmundo - ROS

Bandleader Fields - SHEP

Bandleader Kay - KYSER

Bandleader King - PEEWEE

Bandleader Lawrence - WELK

Bandleader Les - ELGART

Bandleader Lester - LANIN

Bandleader Lewis - TED

Bandleader Miller - GLENN

Bandleader Puente - TITO

Bandleader Ray - EBERLE

Bandleader Waring - FRED

Bandleader Winding - KAI

Banjoist Fleck - BELA

Bannister or Moore - Roger

Barak of Israel - EHUD

Barbera's partner - HANNA

Baritone Paquale - AMATO

Baritone Robert - MERRILL

Baseball great Buck - O'NEIL

Baseball great Combs -EARLE

Baseball great Irvin - MONTE

Baseball great Moore - EARL

Baseball great Ralph - KINER

Baseball great Rod - CAREW

Baseball great Tony - GWYNN or OLIVA

Baseball great Honus - WAGNER

Baseball great Vaughan - ARKY

Baseball manager Piniella - LOU

Baseball pitcher Tiant - LUIS

Baseball player Clemente - ROBERTO

Baseball shortstop Vizquel - OMAR

Baseball star Garciaparra - NOMAR

Baseball star Suzuki - ICHIRO

Baseballer Frankie - FRISCH

Basebeller Fred - LYNN

Baseballer Hodges - GIL

Baseballer Johnny - SAIN

Baseballer Magglio or Rey - ORDONEZ

Baseball's Alcindor - LEW

Baseball's Alejandro - PENA

Baseball's Amos - OTIS

Baseball's Bando or Maglie - SAL

Baseball's Banks - ERNIE

Baseball's Bauer - HANK

Baseball's Boggs - WADE

Baseball's Boone - BRET

Baseball's Boyer - CLETE or KEN

Baseball's Bud - SELIG

Baseball's Buddy - ROSAR

Baseball's Carew - ROD

Baseball's Carlton - FISK

Baseball's Cey - RON

Baseball's Combs - EARLE

Baseball's Darling - RON

Baseball's Del - ENNIS

Baseball's Doubleday - ABNER

Baseball's Durocher - LEO

Baseball's Dykstra - LEN

Baseball's Felipe - ALOU

Baseball's Gibson - BOB

Baseball's Grove - LEFTY

Baseball's Guerrero - PEDRO

Baseball's Hank - BAUER

Baseball's Hershiser - OREL

Baseball's Hideo - NOMO

Baseball's Howard - ELSTON

Baseball's Jeter - DEREK

Baseball's Jones - CLEON

Baseball's Jorge - POSADA

Baseball's Jose - CANSECO

Baseball's Lopes - DAVEY

Baseball's Maglie - SAL

Baseball's Martinez - PEDRO or TINO

Baseball's Matsui - KAZ

Baseball's Musial - STAN

Baseball's Olivares - OMAR

Baseball's Ordonez - REY

Baseball's Ott - MEL

Baseball's Palmiero - RAFAEL

Baseball's Petrocelli - RICO

Baseball's Piniella - LOU

Baseball's Preacher - ROE

Baseball's Rafael - PALMIERO

Baseball's Ricky - LEDEE

Baseball's Ripken - CAL

Baseball's Rizzuto - PHIL

Baseball's Roberto - CLEMENTE

Baseball's Robin - YOUNT

Baseball's Rodriguez - ALEX AROD or IVAN

Baseball's Roush - EDD

Baseball's Rusty - STAUB

Baseball's Sal - BANDO

Baseball's Sandberg - RYNE

Baseball's Sandy - ALOMAR

Baseball's Slaughter - ENOS

Baseball's Speaker - TRIS

Baseball's Tommie - AGEE

Baseball's Tony - PENA

Baseball's Travis - LEE

Baseball's Vizquel - OMAR

Baseball's Wilhelm - HOYTE

Baseball star Galarraga - ANDRES

Baseball star Rebecca - LOBO

Basketball coach Pat - RILEY

Basketball great Thomas - ISIAH

Basketball star Baylor - ELGIN

Basketball star Larry - BIRD

Basketball star Ming - YAO

Basketball star Malone - KARL

Basketball's Birdsong - OTIS

Basketball's Gilmore - ARTIS

Basketball's Jason - KIDD

Basketbell's Kemp - SHAWN

Basketball's Olajuwan - AKEEM

Basketball's Patrick - EWING

Basketball's Robertson - OSCAR

Basketball's Thurmond - NATE

Basketball's Unseld - WES

Basketball's Walter - KARA

Bass player Chandler - CHAS

Basso Cesare - SIEPI

Basso Pinza - EZIO

Bathyspherist William - BEEBE

Beattie or Blyth - ANN

Beatty of films - NED

Best or Ferber - EDNA

Betsy or Arnold - PALMER

Betsy or Diana - ROSS

Beverly or George - SANDERS

Bhutto of Pakastan - BENAZAR

Bike racer Lemond - GREG

Biochemist Tiselius - ARNE

Biographer Hawes - ESME

Biographer Leon - EDEL

Biographer Ludwig - EMIL

Biographer Strachey - LYTTON

Biographer Walton - IZAAK

Biologist Metchnikoff - ELIE

Biologist Rachel - CARSON

Blake of TV - AMANDA

Body builder Ferrigno - LOU

Bohr - AAGE NIELS

Bonheur or Ponselle - ROSA

Botinist Gray - ASA

Botinist Mendal - GREGOR

Boulanger of music - NADIA

Bowler Dick - WEBER

Boxer Ali - LAILA

Boxer Archie MOORE

Boxer Barkley - IRAN

Boxer Benvenuti - NINO

Boxer Firpo - LUIS

Boxer Griffith - EMILE

Boxer Holyfield - EVANDER

Boxer Johansson - ENGEMAR

Boxer Laila - ALI

Boxer Marvin - HAGLER

Boxer Max - BAER

Boxer Primo - CARNERA

Boxer Riddick - BOWE

Boxer Roberto - DURAN

Boxer Rodriguez - IVAN

Boxer Schmelling - MAX

Boxer Spinks - LEON

Boxer Stevenson - TEO

Boxer Tyson - MIKE

Boxer Willard - JESS

Boxing champ Billy - CONN

Boxinng champ Hawes - ESME

Boxing champ Riddick - BOWE

Boxing great Carlos - PALOMINO

_____Breckonridge - MYRA

Bridge expert Charles - GOREN

Bridge expert Oswald - JACOBY

Bridge Guru Culbertson - ELY

British actor Peter - CUSHING

British composer - ELGAR or ARNE

British playwrite Barstow - STAN

British PM Tony - BLAIR

Broadcaster Linda - ELLERBEE

Bronte's governess - EYRE

Brooks or Brundage - AVERY

Bruce & Laura - DERN

Bryant or Baker - ANITA

Bulba - TARAS

Buster or Diane - KEATON

Cabinet maker Phyfe - DUNCAN

Cager Frazier - WALT

Cager Gilmore - ARTIS

Cager Montore - EARL

Cager Thomas - ISIAH

Caldwell of Broadway - ZOE

Cambodia's Lon - NOL

Camera maven Land - EDWIN

Camus - ALBERT

Canadian actor Cariou -LEN

Canadian songstress - K.D. LANG

Cantor or Murphy - EDDIE

Car maker Maserati - ERNESTO

Cartoonist Addams - CHAS

Cartoonist Berke - BREATHED

Cartoonist Browne - DIK

Cartoonist Bushmiller - ERNIE

Cartoonist Caniff - MILT

Cartoonist Chast - ROZ

Cartoonist Drake - STAN

Cartoonist Drucker - MORT

Cartoonist Ed - DODD

Cartoonist Feifer - JULES

Cartoonist Foster - HAL

Cartoonist Gardner - REA

Cartoonist Gary - LARSON

Cartoonist Goldberg - RUBE

Cartoonist Gould - CHESTER

Cartoonist Groening - MATT

Cartoonist Guisewite - CATHY

Cartoonist Hoff - SYD

Cartoonist Hollander - NICOLE

Cartoonist Johnny - HART

Cartoonist Keane - BIL

Cartoonist Kelly - WALT

Cartoonist Key - TED

Cartoonist Lazarus - MELL

Cartoonist Malden - BILL

Cartoonist Peter - ARNO

Cartoonist R. - CRUMB

Cartoonist Russell - MYERS

Cartoonist Silverstein - SHEL

Cartoonist Soglow - OTTO

Cartoonist Tex - AVERY

Cartoonist Thomas - NAST

Cartoonist Trudeau - GARRY

Cartoonist Walker - MORT

Cartoonist Will - EISNER

Cartoonist Wilson - GAHAN

Cartoonist Winsor - MCCAY

Carvey or Delaney - DANA

Cecil B. or Agnes De - MILLE

Cellist Casals - PABLO

Cellist Ma - YOYO

Cellist Nathanial - ROSEN

Cellist Rostropovich - SLAVA

Cellist Starker - JANOS

Central idea, in music - TEMA

Chairperson Greenspan - ALAN

Chan portrayer Sidney -TOLER

Chan portrayer Warren - OLAND

Chang's twin - ENG

Channel swimmer Gertrude - EDERLE

Channing - CAROL

Chanteuse Edith - PIAF

Chaplin - Charles or OONA

Chef Deen - PAULA

Chef Ducasse - ALAIN

Chef Emeril - LAGASSE

Chef Jacques - PEPIN

Chemist Mendeleev - DMITRI

Chemist Otto - HAHN

Chemist Remsen - IRA

Chess Champ Capablanca - JOSE

Chess champ Mikhail - TAL

Chess champion Nimzowitsch - ARON

Chess great Spassky - BORIS

Chessmaster Anatoly - KARPOV

Chessmaster Kasparov - GARY or TAL

Chess player Lasker - EMANUEL

Choreographer Ailey - ALVIN

Choreographer Alvin - AILEY

Choreographer Antonio - GEDES

Choreographer Bausch - PINA

Choreographer Bob - FOSSE

Choreographer Champion - GOWER

Choreographer Cunningham - MERCE

Choreographer de Mille - AGNES

Choreographer Fosse - BOB

Choreographer Frederick - ASHTON

Choreographer Graham - MARTHA

Choreographer Jose - LIMON

Choreographer Lubovitch - LAR

Choreographer Michael - KIDD

Choreographer Pan - HERMES

Choreographer Paula - ABDUL

Choreographer Ruth - ST. DENIS

Choreographer Shawn - TED

Choreographer Sir Frederick - ASHTON

Choreographer Ted - SHAWN

Choreographer Tetley - GLEN

Choreographer Tharp - TWYLA

Choreographer White - ONNA

Chou En - LAI

Chris of tennis - EVERT

Cinematographer Charles - LANG

Cinematographer Nykvist - SVEN

Cinematographer Tony - IMI

Clapton of song - ERIC

Clare Boothe - LUCE

Clarinetist Artie - SHAW

Clark of country - ROY

Clockmaaker Terry - ELI

Clockmaker Thomas - SETH

Clothier Straus - LEVI

Coach Amos Alonzo - STAGG

Coach Chuck - NOLL

Coach Ditka - MIKE

Coach Ebank - WEEB

Coach Jackson - PHIL

Coach Karolyi - BELA

Coach Parseghian - ARA

Coach Pat - RILEY

Coach Paterno - LOE

Coach Rockner - KNUTE

Coburg - SAXE

Colonial patriot Silas - DEANE

Colomnist Bobeck - ERMA

Columnist Buckwald - ART

Columnist Charen - MONA

Columnist Frank Pierce - ADAMS

Columnist George - WILL

Columnist Goodman - ELLEN

Columnist Greenfield - MEG

Columnist Herb - CAEN

Columnist Huffington - ARIANNA

Columnist Joseph - ALSOP

Columnist Leshan - EDA

Columnist Maxwell - ELSA

Colomnist Mike - ROYKO

Colomnist Miller - JUDITH

Columnist Molly - IVINS

Columnist Pyle - ERNIE

Colomnist Reese - HELOISE

Columnist Wilson - EARL

Comedian Amsterdam - MOREY

Comedian Bernie - MAC

Comedian Bill - DANA

Comedian Bishop - JOEY

Comedian Bob - HOPE

Comedian Carrey - JIM

Comedian Cohen - MYRON

Comedian David - BRENNER

Comedian Denis - LEARY

Comedian George - CARLIN or GOBEL

Comedian Green - TOM

Comedian Izzard - EDDIE

Comedian MacDonald - NORM

Comedian Margaret - CHO

Comedian Myron - COHEN

Comedian Philips - EMO

Comedian Richard - BELZER

Comedian Rock - CHRIS

Comedian Shandling - GARY

Comedian Shore - PAULY

Comedic actor James - COCO

Comedienne Butler - BRETT

Comedienne Charlotte - RAE

Comedienne Degeneres - ELLEN

Comedienne Dunn - NORA

Comedienne Fields - TOTIE

Comediene Gasteyer - ANA

Comediene Georgia - ENGEL

Comedienne Judy - CANOVA

Comediene Margaret - CHO

Comedienne Martha - RAYE

Comedienne May - ELAINE

Comedienne McClurg - EDIE

Comedienne O'Donnell - ROSIE

Comedienne O'Shea - TESSIE

Comedienne Peggie - CASS

Comedienne Radner - GILDA

Comedienne Rosie - ODONNEL

Comedienne Taylor - RENEE

Comedienne Witherspoon -
  CORA

Commentator Rowland - EVANS

Comic actor Oakie - JACK

Comis actor John - CLEESE

Comic actor Sandler - ADAM

Comic Allen - STEVE

Comic Amsterdam - MOREY

Comic Anderson - LOUIS

Comic Ann - MEARA

Comic Auerbach - ARTIE

Comic Bill - DANA

Comic Boosler - ELAINE

Comic Brad - HALL

Comic Bruce - LENNY

Comic Buddy - HACKETT

Comic Butler - BRETT

Comic Caplan - GABE

Comic Carey - DREW

Comic Carolla - ADAM

Comic Carvey - DANA

Comic Chris - ROCK

Comic Crosby - NORM

Comic Dangerfield - RODNEY

Comic David - SPADE

Comic Fannie - FLAGG

Comic Foxsworthy - JEFF

Comic Freberg - STAN

Comic Gobel - GEORGE

Comic Hartmen - PHIL

Comic Hill - BENNY

Comic Idle - ERIC

Comic Janeane - GAROFALO

Comic Jaques - TATI

Comic Johnson - ARTE

Comic Johny - YUNE

Comic Joslyn - ALLYN

Comic Judy - TUNUDA

Comic Kamen - MILT

Comic Kaplan - GABE

Comic Kibibble - ISH

Comic Kilborn - CRAIG

Comic Kineson - SAM

Comic Kovacs - ERNIE

Comic Lily - TOMLIN

Comic Lovitz - JON

Comic Mandel - HOWIE

Comic Margaret - CHO

Comis Meara - ANNE

Comic Miller - DENNIS

Comic Nora - DUNN

Comic O'Donnell - ROSIE

Comic Perlman - RHEA

Comic Philips - EMO

Comic Radner - GILDA

Comic Rich - HAL

Comic Richard - JENI

Comic Rickles - DON

Comic Rudner - RITA

Comic Russell - NIPSEY

Comic Sandler - ADAM

Comic Sherman - ALLAN

Comic Stewart - JON

Comic Wilson - FLIP

Comic Youngman - HENNY

Comical Schreiber - AVERY

Commentator Limbaugh - RUSH

Commentator Rooney - ANDY

Composer Ahbez - EDEN

Composer Alban - BERG

Composer Albeniz - ISAAC

Composer Alessandro - SCARLATTI

Composer Anderson - LEROY

Composer Arensky - ANTON

Composer Arlen - HAROLD

Composer Bacharach - BURT

Composer Bartok - BELA

Composer Bedrich - SMETANA

Composer Benjamin - BRITTEN

Composer Berg - ALBAN

Composer Berlioz - HECTOR

Composer Bernstein - ELMER

Composer Blake - EUBIE

Composer Boulez - PIERRE

Composer Brian - ENO

Composer Bruch - MAX

Composer Bruckner - ANTON

Composer Cage - JOHN

Composer Camille Saint - SAENS

Composer Carl - NIELSEN or ORFF

Composer _____ Carlo Menotti - GIAN

Composer Cesar - CUI

Composer Charles - IVES

Composer Copland - AARON

Composer Corelli - ARCANGELO

Composer Corngold - ERICH

Composer Coward - NOEL

Composer DeBussy - CLAUDE

Composer Delibes - LEO

Composer Di Capua - EDUARDO

Composer Timitri - TIOMKIN

Composer Dohnanyi - ERNO

Composer Domenico - SCARLATTI

Composer Dvorak - ANTON

Composer Edouardo - LALO

Composer Edvard - GRIEG

Composer Elfman - DANNY

Composer Elton - JOHN

Composer Eric - COATES

Composer Erik - SATIE

Composer Ethelbert - NEVIN

Composer Eugene - YSAYE

Composer Faith - PERCY

Composer Fauer - GABRIEL

Composer Ferde - GROFE

Composer Francis - LAI

Composer Franck - CESAR

Composer Franz - LEHAR

Composer Frederick - LOWE

Composer Friml - RUDOLF

Composer Garner - ERROLL

Composer Georges - ENESCO

Composer Giacomo - PUCCINI

Composer Giancarlo - MENOTTI

Composer Giuscppi - VERDI

Composer Glass - PHILIP

Composer Grieg - EDVARD

Composer Grofe - FERDA

Composer Gustav - HOLST or MAHLER

Composer Haba - ALOIS

Composer Harold - ARLEN

Composer Hayes - ISAAC

Composer Heft - NEAL

Composer Heitor - VILLALOBOS

Composer Hovhaness - ALAN

Composer Howard - HANSON

Composer Jacques - BREL or IBERT

Composer Janacek - LEOS

Composer Jean-Marie - LECLAIR

Composer Jeff - NEVIN

Composer Jones - ISHAM

Composer Joseph - HAYDN or MEYER

Composer Josquin_____ Pres - DES

Composer Jule - STEIN or STYNE

Composer Jules - MASSENET

Composer Karl - ORFF

Composer Kern - JEROME

Composer Khachaturian - ARAM

Composer Kit - ORY

Composer Kodaly - ZOLTAN

Composer Korngold - ERICH

Composer Kurt - WEILL

Composer Lalo - EDOUARD

Composer Legrand - MICHEL

Composer Lehman - ENGEL

Composer Leonard - COHEN

Composer Leos - JANACEK

Composer Lieberman - ROLF

Composer Lucas - FOSS

Composer Luigi - NONO

Composer Mahler - GUSTAV

Composer Markovitch - IHOR

Composer Mascagni - PIETRO

Composer Maurice - JARRE or RAVEL

Composer Max - REGER or STEINER

Composer Mendelssohn - FELIX

Composer Menken - ALAN

Composer Milhaud - DARIUS

Composer Milton - AGER

Composser Morricone - ENNIO

Composer Mussorgsky - MODESTE

Composer Mustgrave - THEA

Composer Muzio - CLEMENTI

Composer Ned - ROREM

Composer Newborn - IRA

Composer Nino - ROTA

Composer Novello - IVOR

Composer Nuno - JAIME

Composer Peter - NERO

Composer Philip - GLASS

Composer Ponchielli - AMILCARE

Composer Porter - COLE

Composer Prokofiev - SERGIE

Composer Puccini - GIACOMO

Composer Puente - TITO

Composer Quincy - JONES

Composer Rachmanninoff - SERGEY

Composer Randy - NEWMAN

Composer Ravel - MAURICE

Composer Respighi - OTTORINO

Composer Richard - DRIGO or WAGNER

Composer Rimsky - Korsakov - NIKOLAI

Composer Rorem - NED

Composer Rota - NINO

Composer Rubenstein - ANTON

Composer Rudolph - FRIML

Composer Saint-Saens - CAMILLE

Composer Sammy - FAIN

Composer Satie - ERIK

Composer Scarlatti - ALESSANDRO

Composer Schifrin - LALO

Composer Schumann - ROBERT

Composer Shostakovich - DMITRI

Composer Siegmeister - ELIE

Composer Sir Edward - ELGAR

Composer Speaks - OLEY

Composer Strauss - JOHANN or OSKAR

Composer Stravinski - IGOR

Composer Styne - JULE

Composer Taylor - DEEMS

Composer Thomas - ARNE

Composer Thomson - VIRGIL

Composer Tiompkin - DMITRI

Composer Tchaikovsky - PETER ILICH

Composer Ulysses - KAY

Composer Victor - HERBERT

Composer Villa-Lobos - HEITER

Composer Von Dohnanyi - ERNST

Clomposer Weben - ATON

Composer Weill - KURT

Composer William - BOYCE

Composer Zimbalist - EFREM

Computer pioneer Lovelace - ADA

Concertist Campbell - TEVIN

Conductor Alberto - EREDE

Conductor Anderson - LEROY

Conductor Andre - PREVIN

Conductor Ansermet - ERNEST

Conductor Antal - DORATI

Conductor Barenboim - DANIEL

Conductor Boulanger - NADIA

Conductor Boult - ADRIAN

Conductor Caldwell - SARAH

Conductor Claudio - ABBADO

Conductor Davis - COLIN

Conductor de Waart - EDO

Conductor Dorati - ANTAL

Conductor Erno - PAPEE

Conductor Fritz - REINER

Conductor Georg - SOLTI

Conductor Hefti - NEAL

Conductor James - LEVINE

Conductor Jarvi - NEEME

Conductor Klemperer - OTTO

Conductor Kostelanetz - ANDRE

Conductor Koussevetzky - SERGE

Conductor Kubelik - RAFAEL

Conductor Kurt - ADLER, MASUR or WIELL

Conductor Lehman - ENGEL

Conductor Leibowitz - RENE

Conductor Leinsdorf - ERICH

Conductor Lukas - FOSS

Conductor Markovitch - IGOR

Conductor Marriner - NEVILLE

Conductor Mehta - ZUBIN

Conductor Mitropoulos - DIMITRI

Conductor Ormandy - EUGENE

Conductor _____ Pekka Salonen - ESA

Conductor Pierre - Boulez

Conductor Previn - ANDRE

Conductor Riccardo - MUTI

Conductor Seiji - OZAWA

Conductor Sir Thomas - BEECHAM

Conductor Toscanini - ARTURO

Conductor Walter - BRUNO

Conductor Zubin - MEHTA

Congressman Gingrich - NEWT

Contralto Marian - ANDERSON

Convey - BERT

Cook Rombauer - IRMA

Coolidge of song - RITA

Cornelia_____Skinner - OTIS

Cornetist Beiderbecke - BIX

Corporal O'Reilly - RADAR

Cosmetician Curtis - HELENE

Cosmonaut Gagarin - YURI

Cosmonaut Leonov - ALEXI

Cosmonaut Markarov - OLEG

Coty M. - RENE

Count in music - BASIE

Country's Brooks - GARTH

Country's Jennings - WAYLON

Country star McCann - LILA

Country star West - DOTTIE

Couric of NBC - KATIE

Cousteau's middle name - YVES

Couturiere Schiaparelli - ELSA

Cover girl Carol - ALT

Coward or Harrison - NOEL

Cowboy Rogers - ROY

_____"Crazy Legs" Hirsch - ELROY

Critic Barnes - CLIVE

Critic Ebert - ROGER

Critic Greene - GAEL

Critic Harold - ROSENBERG

Critic Hentoff - NAT

Critic John - SIMON

Critic Kael - PAULINE

Critic Kenneth - TYNAN

Critic Pauline - KAEL

Critic Reed - REX

Critic Sheraton - MIMI

Critic Susan - SONTAG

Critic Taylor - DEEMS

Critic Trilling - LIONEL

Critic Walter - KERR

Crooner King Cole - NAT

Crooner Michael - BOLTON

Crooner Perry - COMO

Cruise - TOM

Cuban patriot Jose - MARTI

Cubist Fernand - LEGER

Cubist Rubic - ERNO

Cuthbertson of bridge - ELY

Cyclist Armstrong - LANCE

Cyclist Ballanger - FELICIA

Cyclist Floyd - LANDIS

Cyclist Lemond - GREG

DDE's arena - ETO

Da Gama - VASCO

Dadaist Hans - ARP

Dadaist Jean - ARP

Dadaist Max - ERNST

Dallas - STELLA

Daly of TV - TYNE

Dame Everage - EDNA

Dame Myra - HESS

Dame Sitwell - EDITH

Dancer Abdul - PAULA

Dancer Alvin - AILEY

Dancer Bausch - PINA

Dancer Ben - VEREEN

Dancer Castle - IRENE

Dancer Coles - HONI

Dancer Cunningham - MERCE

Dancer DeMille - AGNES

Dancer Duncan - ISADORA

Dancer Gilda - GRAY

Dancer Honi - COLES

Dancer Jean Marie - RENEE

Dancer Jose - LIMON

Dancer Kaye - NORA

Dancer Leanide - MASSINE

Dancer Lola - MONTEZ

Dancer McKechne - DONNA

Dancer Miller - ANN

Dancer Montez - LOLA

Dancer Ninjinski - VASLAV

Dancer Pavlova - ANNA

Dancer Petit - ROLAND

Dancer Prowse - JULIET

Dancer Reinking - ANN

Dancer Rita - MORENO

Dancer Robbins - JEROME

Dancer Shawn - TED

Dancer Sheara - MOIRA

Dancer Taina - ELG

Dancer Tamblyn - RUSS

Dancer Ted - SHAWN

Dancer Vaslav - NIJINSKY

Dancer Vereen - BEN

Dancer Verdon - GWEN

Daniel of the LPGA - BETH

Danson or Koppel - TED

David Bowie's wife - IMAM

Dawson or Deighton - LEN

De Balzac - HONORE

Decathlete Johnson - RAFER

Decorator De Wolf - ELSIE

Degeneres - ELLEN

De Leon - PONCE

De Valera - EAMON

Dennis - DAY

Dentist Dr. Ida - GRAY

Derek or Diddley - BO

Descartes - RENE

Designer Alvar - AALTO

Designer Antonio - CASTILLO

Designer Arpel - ADRIEN

Designer Ashley - LAURA

Designer Barley - LUELLA

Designer Beaton - CECIL

Designer Bill - BLASS

Designer Calvin - KLEIN

Designer Cassini - OLEG

Designer Cerutti - NINO

Designer Charles - EAMES

Designer Clairborne - LIZ

Designer Clark - OSSIE

Designer Danillo - Donati

Designer de Wolfe - ELSIE

Designer Donna - KARAN

Designer Emilio - PUCCI

Designer Geoffrey - BEENE

Designer Gernreich - RUDI

Designer Giorgio - ARMANI

Designer Gucci - ALDO

Designer Hardy - AIMIES

Designer Head - EDITH

Designer Herman - STAN

Designer Herv - LEGER

Designer Hilfiger - TOMMY

Designer Horn - CAROL

Designer Hugo - BOSS

Designer Johnson - BETSEY

Designer Karan - DONNA

Designer Kawakudo - REI

Designer Kenneth - COLE

Designer Klein - ANNE

Desgner Lagerfield - KARL

Designer Lapidus - TED

Designer Laura - ASHLEY

Designer Magli - BRUNO

Designer Mary - QUANT

Designer Melinda - ENG

Designer Miller - NICOLE

Designer Miuccia - PRADA

Designer Mizrahi - ISAAC

Designer Nina - RICCI

Designer Peretti - ELSA

Designer Perry - ELLIS

Designer Picasso - PALOMA

Designer Picone - EVAN

Designer Pierre - CARDIN

Designer Pucci - EMILIO

Designer Rabanne - PACO

Designer Ricci - NINA

Designer Rowan - RENA

Designer Saab - ELIE

Designer Saint Laurent - YVE

Designer Schiaparelli - ELSA

Designer Sharaff - IRENE

Designer Simpson - ADELE

Designer Sui - ANNA

Designer Tahari - ELIE

Designer Vera - WANG

Designer Versace - DONATELLA

Designer Von Furstenberg - EGON

Designer Wang - VERA

Detective Lupin (fiction) - ARSENE

Detective Pinkerton - ALLAN

DeValera - EAMON

Diarist Anais - NIN

Diarist Frank - ANNE

Diarist Samuel - PEPYS

Dicken's pen name - BOZ

Diplomat Hammarskjold - DAG

Diplomat Harriman - PAMELA

Diplomat Mesta - PERLE

Diplomat Silas - DEANE

Deplomat Wallenberg - RAOUL

Diplomat Whitelaw - REID

Director Adrian - LYNE

Director Allegret - MARC

Director Alan - PAKULA

Director Almodovar - PEDRO

Director Amiel - JON

Director Anatole - LITVAK

Director Anderson - WES

Director Andre - MALLE

Director Arthur - PENN

Director Avakian - ARAM

Director Barker - CLIVE

Director Bergman - INGMAR

Director Besson - LUC

Director Blake - EDWARDS

Director Brian de - PALMA

Director Brooks - MEL

Director Browning - TOD

Director Bunuel - LUIS

Director Burrows - ABE

Director Burton - TIM

Director Cameron - CROWE

Director Campion - JANE

Director Chabrol - CLAUDE

Director Clair - RENE

Director Columbus - CHRIS

Director Coppola - SOPHIA

Director Craven - WES

Director Daniel - MANN

Director David - LEANN or LYNCH

Director Davis - OSSIE

Director Demme - TED

Director DePalma - BRIAN

Director DeSica - VICTORIO

Director Donen - STANLEY

Director Doug - LIMAN

Director Edwards - BLAKE

Director - ELI - ROTH

Director Eng - LEE

Director Ephrom - NORA

Director Ferrara - ABEL

Director Forman - MILOS

Director Francesco - ROSI

Director Frank - CAPRA, LLOYD or TASHLIN

Director Fritz - LANG

Director Gance - ABEL

Director Garson - KANIN

Director Gibbons - CEDRIC

Director Grosbard - ULU

Director Gus van - SANT

Director Guthrie - TYRONE

Director Guy - RITCHIE

Director Haines - RANDA

Director Hal - ASHBY

Director Hallstrom - LASSE

Director Harold - RAMIS

Director Heckerling - AMY

Director Herzog - WERNER

Director Hitchcock - ALFRED

Director Hooper - TOBE

Director Howard - HAWKS or RON

Director Jaques - TATI

Director Jean_____Godard - LUC

Director Joel - COEN

Director Joffe - ROLAND

Director John - CARPENTER or SAYLES

Director Jon - AMIEL

Director Jonathan - DEMME

Director Jordan - NEIL

Director Josh - LOGAN

Director Kazan - ELIA

Director Kenton - ERLE

Director King - VIDOR

Director Kubrick - STANLEY

Director Kurosawa - AKIRA

Director Lee - ANG or SPIKE

Director Leone - SERGIO

Director Litvak - ANATOL

Director Louis - MALLE

Director Lubitsch - ERNST

Director Lucas - GEORGE

Director Lumet - SIDNEY

Director Lyne - ADRIAN

Director Malle - LOUIS

Director Mann - DELBERT

Director Marshall - PENNY

Director Martin - RITT

Director May - ELAINE

Director Mazursky - PAUL

Director McAnuff - DES

Director McCarey - LEO

Director Mervyn - LEROY

Director Meyer - RUSS

Director Michael - APTED or MANN

Director Mike - NICHOLS

Director Mimi - LEDER

Director Minnelli - VINCENTE

Director Mira - NAIR

Director Nicholas - MEYER or ROEG

Director Norah - EPHROM

Director Noyce - PHILLIP

Director Pakula - ALAN

Director Parker - ALAN

Director Pasolini - PAOLO

Director Peckinpah - SAM

Director Peter - WEIR or YATES

Director Petri - ELIO

Director Pitlik - NOAM

Director Polanski - ROMAN

Director Pollock - SYD

Director Ponti - CARLO

Director Preston - STURGES

Director Raoul - WALSH

Director Reitman - IVAN

Director Renoir - JEAN

Director Resnais - ALAIN

Director Richard - DONNER, LESTER or TODD

Director Riefenstahl - LENI

Director Rietman - IVAN

Director Robert - ALTMAN

Director Robins - JEROME

Director Rohmer - ERIC

Director Roth - ELI

Director Russ - MEYER

Director Russell - KEN

Director Sam - RAIMI

Director Schary - DORE

Director Scott - RIDLEY

Director Sergio - LEONE

Director Shepard - SAM

Director Sidney - LUMET

Director Spielberg - STEVEN

Director Spike - LEE

Director Stanley - DONEN

Director Stone - OLIVER

Director Sturges - PRESTON

Director Tarantino - QUENTON

Director Trevor - NUNN

Director Vadim - ROGER

Director Van Sant - GUS

Director Vittorio - DESICA

Director Von Sternburg - JOSEF

Director Vontrier - LARS

Director Walsh - RAOUL

Director Wenders - WIM

Director Werner - HERZOG

Director Wertmuller - LINA

Director Whitaker - FOREST

Director Woody - ALLEN

Director Zeffirelli - FRANCO

Director Zoltan - KORDA

Discus champion Al - OERTER

Diva Albanes - LICIA

Diva Baker - ANITA

Diva Borodina - OLGA

Diva Callas - MARIA

Diva Gluck - ALMA

Diva Linda - EDER

Diva Maria - CALLAS

Diva Marton - EVA

Diva Merriman - NAN

Diva Mitchell - LEONA

Diva Moffo - ANNA

Diva Ponselle - ROSA

Diva Ranata - SCOTTO

Diva Roberta - PETERS

Diva Sutherland - JOAN

Diva Te Kanawa - KIRI

Diver Louganis - GREG

Divine - ANDY

Doctor Alzheimer - ALOIS

Doctor Westheimer - RUTH

Dolphin Marino - DAN

Don of football - SHULA

Doris - DAY

Doubleday - ABNER

Douglas of film - KIRK

Drama critic Walter - KERR

Dramatist Arthur Wing - PINERO

Dramatist Ben - JONSON

Dramatist Blitzstein - MARC

Dramatist Cherkhov - ANTON

Dramatist Clifford - ODETS

Dramatist David - HARE or RABE

Dramatist De Vega - LOPE

Dramatist Edward - ALBEE

Dramatist Fugard - ATHOL

Dramatist George - PEELE

Dramatist Guitry - SACHA

Dramatist Henly - BETH

Dramatist Henrik - IBSEN

Dramatist Jonson - BEN

Dramitist Luigi - PIRANDELLO

Dramatist Moss - HART

Dramatist O'Casey - SEAN

Dramatist Thomas - KYD

Drummer Blakey - ART

Drummer Cosy - COLE

Drummer Gene - KRUPA

Drummer Keith - MOON

Drummer Ringo - STARR

Drummer Ulrich - LARS

Drummer Warren - DODDS

Duncan - ISADORE

Durocher - LEO

Dutch painter Karel - APPEL

Earl_____Biggers - DERR

Eban of Israel - ABBA

Economist Eliot - JANEWAY

Economist John_____Mill - STUART

Economist John Maynard - KEYNES

Economist Marx - KARL

Economist Short - ADAM

Economist Smith - ADAM

Editor Brown - TINA

Editor Paley - BABE

Editor Whitelaw - REID

Editor Wintour - ANNA

Editor/Writer Peter - DEVRIES

Educator Collins - MARVA

Educator Horace - MANN

Educator Mary McLeod - BETHUNE

Educator Montessori - MARIE

Educator Willard - EMMA

Egypt's Mubarak - HOSNI

Elevator man Otis - ELISHA

Emcee Garroway - DAVE

Emmy winner Falco - EDIE

English composer - ARNE

English philosopher - LOCKE

English poet Matthew - PRIOR

Engraver Albrecht - DURER

En-Lai - CHOU

Entertainer Allen - STEVE

Entertainer Amos - TORI

Entertainer Blossom - DEARIE

Entertainer Brickell - EDIE

Entertainer Brooks - GARTH

Entertainer Eartha - KITT

Entertainer Falana - LOLA

Entertainer Ivor - NOVELLO

Entertainer Josephine - BAKER

Entertainer Kazan - LAINIE

Entertainer Kotto - YAPHET

Entertainer Massey - ILONA

Entertainer Miles - VERA

Entertainer Moffo - ANNA

Entertainer Myra - HESSE

Entertainer O'Shea - TESSIE

Entertainer Rita - MORENO

Environmentalist Dubos - RENE

Ernie of golf - ELS

Essayist Bacon - FRANCIS

Essayist Repplier - AGNES

Essayist Susan - SONTAG

Estaire - FRED and ESTELE

Ethologist Konrad - LORENZ

Evangelist McPherson - AIMEE

Explorer Amundsen - ROALD

Explorer Balboa - VASCO

Explorer De Gama - VASCO

Explorer Eriksson - LEIF

Explorer Hedin - SVEN

Explorer Hernando - DE SOTO

Explorer Heyerdahl - THOR

Explorer James - COOK

Explorer John - RAE

Explorer Johnson - OSA

Explorer Marquette - PROPERS

Explorer Robert - PEARY

Explorer Sabastian - CABOT

Explorer Shackleton - ERNEST

Explorer Sverdrup - OTTO

Explorer Tasman - ABEL

Explorer William - BEEBE

Explorer Zebulon - PIKE

Expressionist Emil - NOLDE

Feminist Carrie - CATT

Feminist Germaine - GREER

Feminist Lucretia - MOTT

Fernando or Lorenzo - LAMAS

Fields - W.C. or GRACIE

Figure-skater Kulik - ILIA

Figure-skater Midori - ITO

Figure-skater Trenary - JILL

Film critic James - AGEE

Film critic Pauline - KAEL

Filmmaker De Laurentis - DINO

Filmmaker Joel or Ethan - COEN

Filmmaker Van Sant - GUS

Financier Carl - ICAHN

Fire fighter Red - ADAIR

Fitzgerald - ELLA

Fleming or Hunter - IAN

Flemish painter - BOSCH

Flugalhorn player Check -
MABGIONE

Flutist Herbie - MANN

Flutist Jean Pierre - RAMPAL

Flutist Luening - OTTO

Flynn of films - ERROL

Foch or Simone - NINA

Folk singer Burl - IVES

Folk singer Guthrie - ARLO

Folk singer Joan - BAEZ

Folk singer Mitchell - JONI

Folk singer Pete - SEEGER

Folk singer Phil - OCHS or SIMMS

Football analyst Hank - STRAM

Football great Bart - STARR

Football great Graham - OTTO

Football great Len - DAWSON

Football kicker Jason - ELAM

Footballer Aikman - TROY

Footbeller Brian - SIPE

Footballer Ewbanks - WEEB

Footballer Grier - ROSIE

Footballer Hersh - ELROY

Footballer Jones - BERT

Footballer Manchetti - GINO

Footballer Ronnie - LOTT

Footballer Sayers - GALE

Footballer Staubach - ROGER

Footballer Swann - LYNN

Footballer Terrell - OWENS

Footballer Van Brocklin - NORM

Footballer Yepremian - GARO

Football great - Ronnie - LOTT

Ford of fashion - EILEEN

Fountain - PETE

Foxx - REDD

Francis or Dahl - ARLENE

Frankie of music - CARLE or LAINE

Franklin or Hogen - BEN

Fraser of tennis - NEALE

French astronomer - PICARD

French composer Daniel - AUBER

French composer - LALO

French landscapist - COROT

French novelist, Pierre - LOTI

French novelist Zola - EMILE

French painter - INGRES

French philosopher - SOREL

French revelutionist John Paul - MARAT

French sociologist - TARDE

Funnyman Jay - MOHR

Funnyman Martin - SHORT

Gabriel of music - PETER

Gadgeteer Popiel - RON

Game show Monte - HALL

Game show White - VANNA

Gandi - RAJIV

Garfunkel - ART

Garr of filmdom - TERI

General Aarnold - HAP

General Bradley - OMAR

General Clark - WESLEY

General Doubleday - ABNER

General Powell - COLIN

General Rommel - ERWIN

German astronomer - KEPLER

German author - SACHS

German chemist - EIGEN

German composer - WEBER

Gerulaitis, of tennis - VITAS

Gillette - ANITA

Glass maker Antonio - NERI

Gold medalist Lipinski - TARA

Gold Medalist Latrina - WITT

Gold medalist Yagudin - ALEXEI

Gluck of opera - ALMA

Gold medalist Mary Lou - RETON

Gold medalist Miller - SHANNON

Gold medalist Rantanen - HELI

Gold medalist Rudolph - WILMA

Golden Glover Rodriguez - IVAN

Golf pro Hale - IRWIN

Golfer Alcott - AMY

Golfer Aoki - ISAO

Golfer Ballesteros - SEVE or SEVERIANO

Golfer Bernhard - LANGER

Golfer Bob - ESTES or TWAY

Golfer Bobbie - JONES

Golfer Bret - OGLE

Golfer Browne - OLIN

Golfer Bruce - CRAMPTON

Golfer Calvin - PEETE

Golfer Christina - KIM

Golfer Crenshaw - BEN

Golfer Curtis - STRANGE

Golfer Dave - MARR

Golfer Davies - LAURA

Golfer Davis - LOVE III

Golfer Didrikson - BABE

Golfer Dutra - OLIN

Golfer Ed - SNEAD

Golfer Ernie - ELS

Golfer Faldo - NICK

Golfer Garcia - SERGIO

Golfer Harrington - PADRAIG

Golfer Henke - NOLAN

Golfer Hinckle - LON

Golfer Hogan - BEN

Golfer Irwin - HALE

Golfer Isao - AOKI

Golfer Jay - HAAS

Golfer Jerry - PATE

Golfer John - DALY

Golfer Julius - BOROS

Golfer Laura - DAVIES

Golfer Lindley - LETA

Golfer Lopez - NANCY

Golfer Lorena - OCHOA

Golfer Mark – OMEARA

Golfer Mediate - ROCCO

Golfer Michelle – WIE

Golfer Middlecoff - GARY

Golfer Montgomerie - COLIN

Golfer Morgan - GIL

Golfer Nick - FALDO

Golfer Nicklaus - JACK

Golfer Norman - GREG

Golfer North - ANDY

Golfer Palmer - ARNIE

Golfer Patty - BERG

Golfer Pavin - COREY

Golfer Payne - STEWART

Golfer Peter - THOMSON

Golfer Price - NICK

Golfer Rodriquez - CHICHI

Golfer Sam - SNEAD

Golfer Sandy - LYLE

Golfer Sarazen - GENE

Golfer Sorenstam - ANNIKA

Golfer Stadler - CRAIG

Golfer Stewart - PAYNE

Golfer Steve - PATE

Golfer Strange - CURTIS

Golfer Sutton - HAL

Golfer Thomas - BJORN

Golfer Tom - KITE

Golfer Turner - SHERRI

Golfer Uresti - OMAR

Golfer Vijay - SINGH

Golfer Wadkins - LANNY

Golfer Watson - BUBBA

Golfer Walter - HAGEN

Golfer Weir - MIKE

Golfer Woosnan - IAN

Golf's Baker-Finch - IAN

Gorby's Mrs. - RAISA

Governor Ventura - JESSE

Grammy winner Puente - TITO

Gridiron great Greasy - NEALE

Griffith - ANDY

Guevara - CHE

Guitar master Van Halen -
    EDDIE

Guitarist Allman - DUANE

Guitarist Andre - SEGOVIA

Guitarist Atkins - CHET

Guitarist Barrett - SYD

Guitarist Bob - EGAN

Guitarist Campbell - GLEN

Guitarist Carlo - SANTANA

Guitarist Chet - ATKINS

Guitarist Clapton - ERIC

Guitarist Delucia - PACO

Guitarist Duane - EDDY

Guitarist Farlow - TAL

Guitarist Fender - LEO

Guitarist Flatt - LESTER

Guitarist George - BENSON

Guitarist Harvey - MANDEL

Guitarist Hendrix - JIMI

Guitarist Jeff - BECK

Guitarist Jimmy - PAGE

Guitarist Kottke - LEO

Guitarist Lofgren - NILS

Guitarist Mann - AIMEE

Guitarist Montgomery - WES

Guitarist Montoya - CARLOS

Guitarist Nugent - TED

Guitarist Paul - LES

Guitarist Romero - PEPE

Guitarist Santana - CARLOS

Guitarist Segovia - ANDRES

Gutarist Steve - EARLE or VAI

Guitarist Walsh - JOE

Guitarist Watson - DOC

Guthrie - ARLO

Gymnast Comaneci - NADIA

Gymnast Dominique - DAWES

Gymnast Kerri - STRUG

Gymnast Korbut - OLGA

Gymnast Miller - SHANNON

Gymnast Rigby - CATHY

Gynt - PEER

Hall-of-Fame pitcher Early - WYNN

Hall-of-Famer Al - KALINE

Hall-of-Famer Aparicio - LUIS

Hall-of-Famer Averill - EARL

Hall-of-Famer Banks - ERNIE

Hall-of-Famer Bart - STARR

Hall-of-Famer Baylor - ELGIN

Hall-of-Famer Cap - ANSON

Hall-of-Famer Carey - MAX

Hall-of-Famer Clemente - ROBERTO

Hall-of-Famer Combs - EARLE

Hall-of-Famer Dan - ISSEL

Hall-of-Famer Dawson - LEN

Hall-of-Famer Early - WYNN

Hall-of-Famer Earnie - NEVERS

Hall-of-Famer Edd - ROUSH

Hall-of-Famer Ewbank - WEEB

Hall-of-Famer Fingers - ROLLIE

Hall-of-Famer Ford - LEN

Hall-of-famer Fox - BRETT or NELLIE

Hall-of-Famer George - HALAS

Hall-of-Famer Gibson - JOSH

Hall-of-Famer Graham - OTTO

Hall-of-Famer Greasy - NEALE

Hall-of-Famer Groza - LOU

Hall-of-Famer Herber - ARNIE

Hall-of-Famer Hirsch - ELROY

Hall-of-Famer Hoyt - WAITE

Hall-of-Famer Jim - THORPE

Hall-of-Famer Johnny - MIZE

Hall-of-Famer Koufax - SANDY

Hall-of-Famer Lefty - GROVE

Hall-of-Famer Long - HOWIE

Hall-of-Famer Lott - RONNIE

Hall-of-Famer Luckman - SID

Hall-of-Famer Marchetti - GINO

Hall-of-Famer Mel - OTT

Hall-of-Famer Mike - SCHMIDT

Hall-of-Famer Monte - IRVIN

Hall-of-famer Pennock - HERB

Hall-of-Famer Ralph - KINER

Hall-of-Famer Rixey - EPPA

Hall-of-Famer Rod - CAREW

Hall-of-Famer Roush - EDD

Hall-of-Famer Sandberg - RYNE

Hall-of-Famer Thomas - ISIAH

Hall-of-famer Tom - LANDRY

Hall-of-Famer Tony - PEREZ

Hall-of-Famer Traynor - PIE

Hall-of-Famer Unseld - WES

Hall-of-Famer Wagner - HONUS

Hall-of-Famer Waite - HOYT

Hall-of-Famer Walker - DOAK

Hall-of-Famer Warren - SPAHN

Hall-of-Famer Wilhelm - HOYT

Hall-of-Famer Wilson - PHAT

Hall-of-Famer Yogi - BERRA

Hammett to friends - DASH

Hank of baseball - AARON

Harmonica virtuoso Larry - ADLER

Harpsichordist Landowska - WANDA

Hart or Cooper - GARY

Hartman - LISA

Heraldic cross - SALTIRE

Herbie or Horace - MANN

Hershiser of baseball - OREL

Hipnotist Franz - MESMER

Historian Durant - ARIEL

Historian Hannah - ARENDT

Historian Macaulay - CATHARINE

Historian Max - WEBER

Historian Nevins - ALLAN

Historian Toynbee - ARNOLD

Hockey great Potvin - DENIS

Hockey's Bobby - ORR

Hockey's Broten - NEAL

Hockey's Lindros - ERIC

Hockey's Stojanov - ALEK

Hockey star Tikkanen - ESA

Hollywood gossip Barrett - RONA

Hollywood Moore - DEMI or DUDLEY

Hoopster Baylor - ELGIN

Hoopster Gilmore - ARTIS

Hoopster Unseld - WES

Hope of Hollywood - BOB or LANGE

Horatio - ALGER

Horologist Terry - ELLI

Horologist Thomas - SETH

Horoscope columnist Sydney - OMARR

Horse-drawn coach - FIACRE

Hostess Perle - MESTA

Hotelier Helmesley - LEONA

Humorist Ade - GEORGE

Humorist Barry - DAVE

Humorist Bill - ARPS

Humorist Buckwald - ART

Humorist Cleveland - AMORY

Humorist Dorothy - PARKER

Humorist Geroge - ADE

Humorist Hubbard - KIM

Humorist Joe - HAN

Humorist Keillor - GARRISON

Humorist Lardner - RING

Humorist Lebowitz - FRAN

Humorist Rogers - WILL

Humorist Rosten - LEO

Humorist Sahl - MORT

Humorist Sedaris - AMY

Humorist Sherman - ALLEN

Humorist Sherrin - NED

Humorist Ward - ARTEMUS

Hungarian composer - LEHAR

Hungarian leader - Kadar - JANOS

Hurler Hideo - NOMO

Hurler Johnson - RANDY

Hurler Moses - EDWIN

Hurler Nehemiah - RENALDO

Hurler Tiant - LUIS

Hurler Warren - SPAHN

Illusionist Burton - LANCE

Illustrator Beardsly - AUBREY

Illustrator Edward - GOREY

Illustrator Maxfield - PARRISH

Illustrator Ronald - SEARLE

Impresario Sol - HUROK

Impressionist David - FRYE

Impressionist Mary - CASSATT

Impressionist Pierre - RENOIR

Industrialist Cyrus - EATON

Industrialist Harvey - FIRESTONE

Infamous Amin - IDI

Infamous Helmsley - LEONA

Interviewer Couric - KATIE

Inventor Berliner - EMILE

Inventor Borden - GAIL

Inventor Deforst - LEE

Inventor Elisha - OTIS

Inventor Gray - ELISHA

Inventor Howe - ELIAS

Inventor James - EDES

Inventor Land - EDWIN

Inventor McCormack - CYRUS

Inventor Nikola - TESLA

Inventor Otis - ELISHA

Inventor Popeil - RON

Inventor Tesla - NIKOLA

Inventor Tull - JETHRO

Inventor Samuel - MORSE

Inventor Sikorsky - IGOR

Inventor Whitney - ELI

Ireland's De Valera - EAMON

Irene - RYAN

Irish author O'Brien - EDNA

Irwin of the PGA - HALE

Israili Barak - EHUD

Israeli hero Moshe - DAYAN

Italian actress, of old - DUSE

Italian General, Balbo - ITALO

Jackson or Nelligan - KATE

Jacques of song - BREL

James of song - ETTA

Jamie of TV - FARR

Jannings of early films - EMIL

Japanese Nobelist - SATO

Jazz artist Crothers - SCATMAN

Jazz fusion guitarist Klugh - EARL

Jazz great Davis - MILES

Jazz great Sandoyal - ARTURO

Jazz great Thelonious - MONK

Jazz guitarist Montgomery - WES

Jazz legend Chick - COREA

Jazz musician Adderley - NAT

Jazz musician Austen - LOVIE

Jazz pianist Allison - MOSE

Jazz pianist Jankowski - HORST

Jazz pianist Oscar - PETERSON

Jazz singer Anita - O'DAY

Jazz trombonist Jack - TEAGARDEN

Jazz trumpeter Baker - CHET

Jazz trumpeter Jones -THAD

Jazzman Aderley - NAT

Jazzman Allison - MOSE

Jassman Baker - CHET

Jassman Beiderbecke - BIX

Jazzman Blake - EUBIE

Jazzman Blakey - ART

Jazzman Chick - COREA

Jazzman Dave - BRUBECK

Jazzman Garner - ERROLL

Jazzman Hentoff - NAT

Jazzman Hines - EARL

Jazzman _____ Hot Lips Page - ORAN

Jazzman Hubert - LAWS

Jazzman Jackson - MILT

Jazzman Kid - ORY

Jazzman Malone - KARL

Jazzman Montgomery - WES

Jazzman Mose - ALLISON

Jazzman Niehaus - LENNIE

Jazzman Rollins - SONNY

Jazzman Russell - PEE WEE

Jazzman Saunders - MERL

Jazzman Shapiro - ARTIE

Jazzman Tatum - ART

Jazzman Thelonious - MONK

Jazzman Tristano - LENNIE

JazzmanWaller - FATS

Jassman Zoot - SIMS

Jeweler LaLique - RENE

Jockey Arcaro - EDDIE

Jockey Cordero - ANGEL

Jockey Day - PAT

Jockey Julia - KRONE

Jockey Laffit - PINCAY

Jockey Pat - DAY

Jockey Sellers - SHANE

Jockey Smith - ROBYN

Jockey Turcotte - RON

Jockey Valasquez - JORGE

John_____Passos - DOS

John the writer - O'Hara

Johnson - Magic

Josip Broz - TITO

Journalist Abel - ELIE

Journalist Alexander - SHANA

Journalist Alisair - COOKE

Journalist Bierce - AMBROSE

Journalist Blitzer - WOLF

Journalist Bly - NELLY

Journalist Bombeck - ERMA

Journalist Bernstein - CARL

Journalist Brendon - GILL

Journalist Cupcinet - IRV

Journalist Dominick - DUNNE

Journalist Ernie - PYLE

Journalist Fallaci - ORIANA

Journalist Gellhorn - MARTHA

Journalist Glenny - MISHO

Journalist Hamill - PETE

Journalist Herb - CAEN

Journalist Hentoff - NAT

Journalist Horace - GREELEY

Journalist Hume - BRIT

Journalist Jacob August - RIIS

Journalist Joseph & Stuart - ALSOPS

Journalist Kupcinet - IRV

Journalist Lebowitz - FRAN

Jounalist Marvin - KALB

Journalist Pyle - ERNIE

Journalist Riis - JACOB

Journalist Roberts - COKIE

Journalist Roger St. Johns - ADEL A

Journalist Seymor - NERSH

Journalist Sheehy - GAIL

Journalist Shriver - MARIA

Journalist Stewart - ALSOP

Journalist Tarbell - IDA

Journalist Walters - BARBARA

Journalist Whitelaw - REID

Judge Lance - ITO

Julius of golf - BOROS

Jurist Fortas - ABE

Jurist Kenneth - STARR

Justice Bader Ginsberg - RUTH

Justice Scalia - ANTONIN

Justice Thomas - CLARENCE

Karenina - ANNA

Keaton - BUSTER

Kennedy or Waters - ETHEL

Kerr - ANITA

King of Hollywood - VIDOR

King of the Faeries - OBERON

Kruger or Preminger - OTTO

LPGA Carner - JOANNE

LPGA Daniel - BETH

LPGA Hall-of-Famer Patty - BERG

LPGA Juli - INKSTER

LPGA Karrie - WEBB

LPGA star Pak - SERI

Lacosta of tennis - RENE

Lady Hamilton - EMMA

Lahr - BERT

Lagosi or Bartok - BELA

Lamarr of old films - HEDY

Lamb - ELIA

Lambchops Lewis - SHARI

Lance of the court - ITO

Lawman Earp - WYATT

Lawyer Dershowitz - ALAN

Legal Lance - ITO

Lendl of tennis - IVAN

Levin or Gershwin - IRA

Lexicographer Partridge - ERIC

Linguist Chomsky - NOAM

Linguist Mario - PEI

Lithographer Currie - NATHANIEL

Lithographer James - IVES

Lizzy Borden's sister - EMMA

Lollobrigida - GINA

Lon - NOL

Long - HUEY PIERCE

Lorna - DOONE

Lott of politics - TRENT

Luft of song - LORNA

Lyrisist Carole Bayer - SAGER

Lyrisist David - HAL

Lyisist Gershwin - IRA

Lyrisist Green - ADOLPH

Lyrisist Gus - KAHN

Lyrisist Harbach - OTTO

Lyrisist Harburg - YIP

Lyrisist Hart - Lorenz

Lyrisist Kahn - GUS

Lyrisist Lorenz - HART

Lyrisist Rice - TIM

Lyrisist Taupin - BERNIE

Lyrisist Washington - NED

Madam Bovary - EMMA

Madame de _____ - STAEL

Maestro DeWaart - EDO

Maestro Koussevitzky - SERGE

Maestro Leinsdorf - ERICH

Maestro Lorin - MAAZEL

Maestro Mehta - ZUBIN

Maestro Ricardo - MUTI

Maestro Jeiji - OSWA

Maestro Toscanini - ARTURO

Magician Henning - DOUG

Magician Jillette - PENN

Magnani or Moffo - ANNA

Malcolm_____Warner - JAMAL

Malone of baseball - MOSES

Mao_____Tung - TSE

Marathoner Pippig - UTA

Marathoner Rosie - RUIZ

Marathoner Waitz - GRETA

Marathoner, Zatioej - EMIL

Mariah of music - CAREY

Mar_____- Baker - LINN

Markswoman Annie - OAKLEY

Marlon of film - BRANDO

Marquis de - SADE

Marvin - LEE

Masters champion Mark - OMEARA

Mathematician Babbage - CHARLES

Mathematician Blaise - PASCAL

Mathematician Byron - ADA

Mathematician Descartes - RENE

Mathematician George - BOOLE

Mathematician Godel - KURT

Mathematician Gottfried - LIEBNIZ

Mathematician Jon Von - NEUMANN

Mathematician Kummer - ERNST

Mathematician Kurt - GODEL

Mathematician Leonhard - EULER

Mathematician Lovelace - ADA

Mathematician Marin - MERSENNE

Mathematician Newton - ISAAC

Mathematician Robert - HOOKE

Mathematician Stewart - IAN

Mathematician Turing - ALAN

Matty or Felix - ALOU

Maxwell - ELSA

_____ May Alcott - LOUISA

Meg - RYAN

Mentalist Geller - URI

Metcalf of Football - ERIC

Mezzo Frederica von - STADE

Mezzo Obraztsova - ELENA

Mezzo-soprano Marilyn - HORNE

Mezzo-soprano Merriman - NAN

Mezzo-soprano Stevens - RISE

McClurg - EDIE

Mies Vander - ROHE

Millay or Ferber - EDNA

Mime Marcel - MARCEAU

Missionary Junipero - SERRA

Missionary Schweitzer - ALBERT

Mme. Bovary - EMMA

Model Alexis - KIM

Model Banks TYRA

Model Campbell - NAOMI

Model Carangi - GIA

Model Carol - ALT

Model Carre - OTIS

Model Chow - TINA

Model Crawford - CINDY

Model Everhart - ANGIE

Model from Samolea - IMAN

Model Garielle - REECE

Model Herzigova - EVA

Model Kate - MOSS

Model Kim - ELEXIS

Model Lanzoni - FABIO

Model McPherson - ELLE

Model Moss - KATE

Model Parker - SUSY

Model Tyler - LIV

Monica of tennis - SELES

Moody in Allen's alley - TITUS

Moore - DEMI, DUDLEY, MARY TYLER or ROGER

Moran or Gray - ERIN

Moshe of Israel - ARENS

Movie Mogul Adolph - ZUKOR

Movie mogul Laemmle - CARL

Moviie mogul Marcus - LOEW

Movie's Bruce - WILLIS

Mr. Arafat - YASIR

Mr. Sagan - CARL

Mrs. Artie Shaw - LANA

Mrs. Charlie Chaplin - OONA

Mrs. David Bowie - IMAN

Mrs. David Copperfield - DORA

Mrs Gorbachev - RAYSA

Mrs. Marcos - IMELDA

Mrs. Parker-Bowles - CAMILLA

Mrs. Rabin - LEAH

Mrs. Tony Martin - SYD

Ms. LeGallienne - EVA

Ms. Massey - ILONA

Ms. Miles - VERA

Ms. Roger St. Johns - ADELA

Ms. Thorndike - SYBIL

Mubarak of Egypt - HOSNI

Muckraker Tarbell - IDA

Mulrooney of Canada - BRIAN

Munro's pen name - SAKI

Muralist Jose - SERT

Muralist Melchers - GARI

Muralist Rivera - DIEGO

Muscleman Steve - REEVES

Musial - STAN

Music critic Ned - ROREM

Musical Franklin - ARETHA

Musical John - DENVER

Musician Blake - EUBIA

Musician Brian - ENO

Musician Brubeck - DAVE

Musician Chick - COREA

Musician Doherty - PAPAS

Musician Dury - IAN

Musician Lofgren - NILS

Musician Lou - REED

Musician Morissette - ALANIS

Musician Phillips - PAPAS

Musician Redbone - LEON

Musician Schifrin - LALO

Musician Shankar - RAVI

Musician Santamaria - MONGO

Musician Willie - COLON

Musico Guisar - TITO

Naldi of silents - NITA

Nat King - COLE

Naturalist Adamson - JOY

Natualist John - MUIR

Navarro of the silents - RAMON

Navigator Vitus - BERING

NBA great Hayes - ELVIN

NBA's Gilmore - ARTIS
NBA's Miller - REGGIE
NBA's Mourning - ALONZO
NBA's Shaquille - ONEAL
Negri of old films - POLA
New age Irish singer - ANYA
News anchor Connie - CHUNG
Newscaster Ellerbee - LINDA
Newsman Bernard - SHAW
Newsman Blitzer - WOLF
Newsman Brit - HUME
Newsman Charles - OSGOODE
Newsman Donaldson - SAM
Newsman Garrick - UTLEY
Newsman Hughes - RUDD
Newsman Huntley - CHET
Newsman Lehrer - JIM
Newsman Marvin - Kalb
Newsman Sevareid - ERIC
Newsman Ted - KOPPEL
Newsman Vanocur - SANDER
Newsperson Alexandria - SHANA
Newswoman Braver - RITA
Newswoman Lindstrom - PIA
Newswoman Shriver - MARIA
NFL great Kyle - ROTE
NFL kicker Jason - ELAM
Ngo Dinh - DIEM

Nobel bacteriologist - ENDERS
Nobel biochemist Servo - OACHOA
Nobel chemist Harold - UREY
Nobel chemist Von Baeyer - ADOLF
Nobel physicist Isidor - RABI
Nobel winner Bellow - SAUL
Nobel winner Pavlov - IVAN
Nobelist Alverez - LUIS
Nobelist Andre - GIDE
Nobelist Andric - IVO
Nobelist Bellow - SOL
Nobelist Camilo - CELA
Nobelist Canetti - ELIAS
Nobelist Cassin - RENE
Nobelist Clancy - TOM
Nobelist Cordel - HULL
Nobelist Currie MARIE
Nobelist Dulbecco - RENATO
Nobelist Eisaku - SATO
Nobelist Fermi - ENRICO
Nobelist Finsen - NIELS
Nobelist Fo - DARIO
Nobelist Fredrik - BAJER
Nobelist Glashow - SHELDON
Nobelist Gordimer - NADINE
Nobelist Hahn - OTTO
Nobelist Harold - UREY

Nobelist Henri - BERGSON

Nobelist Isador - RABI

Nobelist Jacobus Van't - HOFF

Nobelist John_____Orr - BOYD

Nobelist Joliet-Curie - IRENE

Nobelist Kofi - ANNAN

Nobelist Kurt - ALDER

Nobelist Metchnikoff - ELIE

Nobelist Neruda - PABLO

Nobelist Nevil - SHUTE

Nobelist Octavio - PAZ

Nobelist Onsager - LARS

Nobelist Oscar_____Sanchez - ARIAS

Nobelist Paul - DIRAC

Nobelist Pavlov - IVAN

Nobelist Penzias - ARNO

Nobelist _____Perez Esquivel - ADOLFO

Nobelist Planck - MAX

Nobelist Root - ELIHU

Nobelist Sachs - NELLY

Nobelist Sakharov - ANDREI

Nobelist Sanchez - OSCAR ARIAS

Nobelist Servo - OCHOA

Nobelist Shimon - PEREZ

Nobelist Soyinka - WOLE

Nobelist Wiesel - ELIE

Nobelist Wolfgan - PAULI

Nobelist Yalow - ROSALYN

Nobelist Yasir - ARAFAT

Nolan, of baseball - RYAN

Norwegian Nobelist - LANGE

Novelist Alcott - LOUISA

Novelist Alexandre - DUMAS

Novelist Amado - JORGE

Novelist Amelia - BARR

Novelist Andre - GIDE

Novelist Andric - IVO

Novelist Anita - BROOKNER

Novelist Anne - TYLER

Novelist Anya - SETON

Novelist Austen - JANE

Novelist Ayn - RAND

Novelist Bainbridge - BERYL

Novelist Barker - CLIVE

Novelist Barstow - STAN

Novelist Baum - VICKI

Novelist Beattie - ANN

Novelist Binchy - MAEVE

Novelist Blasco - IBANEZ

Novelist Brand - MAX

Novelist Bret Easton - ELLIS

Novelist Bronte - EMILY

Novelist Brookner - ANITA

Novelist Buck - PEARL

Novelist Buntline - NED

Novelist Caldwell - ERSKINE

Novelist Caleb - CARR

Novelist Camus - ALBERT

Novelist Canin - NATHAN

Novelist Capec - KAREL

Novelist Carr - CALEB

Novelist Castedo - ELENA

Novelist Cather - WILLA

Novelist Calvino - ITALO

Novelist Charles - READE

Novelist Connell - EVAN

Novelist Conroy - PAT

Novelist Cornelius - RYAN

Novelist Cusler - CLIVE

Novelist Dahl - ROALD

Novelist Danielle - STEE

Novelist DeBalzac - HONORE

Novelist De La Roche - MAZO

Novelist Dorothy - EDEN

Novelist Drury - ALLEN

Novelist Dulbecco - RENATO

Novelist du Maurier - DAPHNE

Novelist Elinor - GLYN or WYLIE

Novelist Elizabeth - BOWEN

Novelist Emile - ZOLA

Novelist Ephron - DELIA or NORA

Novelist Eric - AMBLER

Novelist Ernest K. – GANN

Novelist Eugene - SUE

Novelist Fannie - HURST

Novelist Ferber - EDNA

Novelist Flannery - OCONNOR

Novelist France - ANATOLE

Novelist Frances Parkinson - KEYES

Novelist Frankie - FRISCH

Novelist George - ELIOT or SAND

Novelist Georgette - HEYER

Novelist Glasgow - ELLEN

Novelist Glyn - ELINOR

Novelist Gordimer - NADINE

Novelist Gore - VIDAL

Novelist Gould - LOIS

Novelist Grafton - SUE

Novelist Green - GRAHAM

Novelist Gray - ZANE

Novelist Harper - LEE

Novelist Hay - IAN

Novelist Herman - HESSE

Novelist Hoag - TAMI

Novelist Honore - de BALZAC

Novelist Hunter - EVAN

Novelist Hurston - ZORA

Novelist Ishmael - REED

Novelist Jaffe - RONA

Novelist Jamaica - KINCAID

Novelist James - AGEE or JONES

Novelist Janowitz - TAMA

Novelist Jean - AUEL

Novelist Jean-Paul - SARTRE

Novelist John - JAKES

Novelist John - Le CARRE or O'HARA

Novelist John Dickson - CARR

Novelist John_____Passos - DOS

Novelist Jong - ERICA

Novelist Jorge - AMADO

Novelist Josephine - TEY

Novelist Joyce Carol - OATES

Novelist Kathleen - NORRIS

Novelist Kesey - KEN

Novelist Kiklai - GOGOL

Novelist Kingsley - AMIS

Novelist Kobo - ABE

Novelist Koontz - DEAN

Novelist Laurence - STERNE

Novelist Lee - HARPER

Novelist Legerlof - SELMA

Novelist Lequin - URSULA

Novelist Leon - URIS

Novelist Leonard - ELMORE

Novelist Leshan - EDA

Novelist Lessing - DORIS

Novelist Leverson - ADA

Novelist Levin - IRA

Novelist Lindgren - ASTRID

Novelist Lofts - NORAH

Novelist Lurie - ALISON

Novelist Malamud - BERNARD

Novelist Malrau - ANDRE

Novelist Marcel - PROUST

Novelist Margaret - DRABBLE

Novelist McCullough - COLLEEN

Novelist McMillan - TERRY

Novelist Mishima - YUKIO

Novelist Morant - ELSA

Novelist Moravia - ALBERTO

Novelist Murdock - IRIS

Novelist Nevada - BARR

Novelist Nevil - SHUTE

Novelist Ngaio - MARSH

Novelist O'Brien - EDNA

Novelist O'Flaherty - LIAM

Novelist Olsen - TILLIE

Novelist Oz - AMOS

Novelist Paretsky - SARA

Novelist Paton - ALAN

Novelist Peter - BENCHLE, MAAS or STRAUB

Novelist Philip - ROTH or WYLIE

Novelist Phillpotts - EDEN

Novelist Pierre - LOTI

Novelist Quindlen - ANNA

Novelist Radcliffe - ANN

Novelist Raja - RAO

Novelist Ralph - ELLISON

Novelist Rand - AYN

Novelist Reidbanks - LYNNE

Novelist Remarque - ERICH

Novelist Roberts - NORA

Novelist Roche - MAZO

Novelist Rohmer - SAX

Novelist Roxana - DEFOE

Novelist Sandel - CORA

Novelist Santha_____Rau - RAMA

Novelist Sarah _____ Jewett - ORNE

Novelist Segal - ERICH or LORE

Novelist Servero - OCHOA

Novelist Seton - ANYA

Novelist Sewell - ANNA

Novelist Shaw - IRWIN

Novelist Sheldon -SIDNEY

Novelist Shirley Ann - GRAU

Novelist Sholem - ASCH

Novelist Shreve - ANITA

Novelist Shusaku - ENDO

Novelist Sillitoe - ALAN

Novelist Sinclair - UPTON

Novelist Sontag - SUSAN

Novelist Stanley - ELKIN

Novelist Stapleton - OLAF

Novelist Susan - ISAACS

Novelist Svevo - ITALO

Novelist Tan - AMY

Novelist Tennant - KYLIE

Novelist Tilley - OLSEN

Novelist Turgenev - IVAN

Novelist Turow - SCOTT

Novelist Tyler - ANNE

Novelist Umberto - ECO

Novelist Uris - LEON

Novelist Vicki - BAUM

Novelist Victoria - HOLT

Novelist Vidal - GORE

Novelist Virginia - WOOLF

Novelist Vittorini - ELIO

Novelist Wagner - ELIN

Novelist Walker - ALICE

Novelist Waugh - ALEC

Novelist Welty - EUDORA

Novelist Wharton - EDITH

Novelist Willa - CATHER

Novelist Wilson ANGUS

Novelist Wister - OWEN

Novelist Wolfert - IRA

Novelist Zola - EMILE

Novelist Zora_____Hurston - NEALE

Novello of old films - IVOR

Olympian Al - OERTER

Olympian Biondi - MATT

Olympian Blair - BONNIE

Olympain Devers - GAIL

Olympian Jesse - OWENS

Olympian Jim - THORPE

Olympian Johnson - RAFER

Olympian Lewis - CARL

Olympian Lipinski - TARA

Olympian Nurmi - PAAVO

Olympian Street - PICABO

Olympian Zatopek - EMIL

Olympic discus champ Al - OERTER

Olympic great Comaneci - NADIA

Olympic great Janet - EVANS

Olympic runner Johnson - RAFER

Olympic skier Alberto - TOMBA

Olympic skier Maentyranta - EERO

Olympic skier Phil - MAHRE

Olympic skier Sailer - TONI

Olympic swimmer Bionde - MATT

Onassis, briefly - ARI

Ono - YOKO

Opera bass Tajo - ITALO

Opera singer Bostridge - IAN

Opera singer Gedda - NICOLAI

Opera singer Gluck - ALMA

Opera singer Marilyn - HORNE

Opera singer Quilico - LOUIS

Opera singer Te Kenawa - KIRA

Opera star Tebaldi - RENATA

Operetic Eleanor - STEBER

Orator Chauncey - DEPEW

Orchestrator Jule - STYNE

Organist Braga - ENA

Oscar nominee Edward James - OLMOS

Oscar winner Dench - JUDY

Oscar winner Gooding - CUBA

Oscar winner Rainer - LUISE

Otis - AMOS or ELISHA

Outfielder Slaughter - ENOS

Page of music - PATTI

Painter Albert Pinkham - RYDER

Painter Alphonse - MUCHA

Painter Andrea del - SARTO

Painter Anthony Van - DYCK

Painter Appel - KAREL

Painter Berthe - MORISOT

Painter Bonheur - ROSA

Painter Braque - GEORGES

Painter Brueghel - PIETER

Painter Camille - PISARRO

Painter Carot - JEAN BAPTISTE

Painter Chagall - MARC

Painter Claude - MONET

Painter Cornelius de - VOS

Painter Daumier - HONORE

Painter Degas - EDGAR

Painter Dufy - RAOUL

Painter Emile - NOLDE

Painter Fernand - LEGER

Painter Fiorentino - ROSSO

Painter Francis - BACON

Painter Frank - STELLA

Painter Frans - HALS

Painter Franz - MARC

Painter George - INNESS

Painter Georges - SEURAT

Painter Gerard_____Borch -TER

Painter Gino - SEVERINI

Painter Guido - RENI

Painter Guy_____Dubois - PENE

Painter Hals - FRANS

Painter Hans - ARPS

Painter Hieronymus - BOSCH

Painter Hofmann - HANS

Painter Holbein - HANS

Painter Hopper- Edward

Painter Jackson - POLLOCK

Painter James - ENSOR

Painter Jan - STEEN

Painter Jan van der - MEER

Painter Jan Van - GOYEN

Painter Jean - ARP

Painter Jim - DINE

Painter Joan - MIRO

Painter John - SLOAN

Painter John Baptiste - COROT

Painter John La_____ - FARGE

Painter John Singer - SARGENT

Painter Jose Maria - SERT

Painter Joseph - STELLA

Painter Katz - ALEX

Painter Klee - PAUL

Painter Krasner - LEE

Painter Larry - RIVERS

Painter Leroy - NEIMAN

Painter Lichtenstein - ROY

Painter Magritte - RENE

Painter Manet - EDOUARD

Painter Mantegna - ANDREA

Painter Mary - CASSATT

Painter Matisse - HENRI

Painter Maurice - UTRILLO

Painter Max - ERNST

Painter Modigliani - AMEDEO

Painter Mondrian - PIET

Painter Munch - EDVARD

Painter N. C. - WYETH

Painter Neiman - LEROY

Painter Nolde - EMIL

Painter of ballarinas - DEGAS

Painter Paul - KLEE

Painter Picasso - PABLO

Painter Pierre Auguste - RENOIR

Painter Rembrandt - PEALE

Painter Remington - FREDERIC

Painter Richard - ESTES

Painter Rivera - DIEGO

Painter Rober - HENRI

Painter Rockwell - NORMAN

Painter Rossetti - DANTE

Painter Rousseau - HENRI

Painter Rossetti - DANTE

Painter Schiele - EGON

Painter Signorelli - LUCA

Painter Sir Joshua - Reynolds

Painter Sir Peter - LELY

Painter Sir William - ORPEN

Painter Soutine - CHAIM

Painter Steen - JAN

Painter Taddeo - GADDI

Painter Tanguy - YVES

Painter Uccello - PAOLO

Painter Van Doesburg - THEO

Painter Van Eyck - JAN

Painter Vereshchagin - VASILI

Painter Vermeer - JAN

Painter Veronese - PAOLO

Painter Wifredo - LAM

Painter Wyeth - ANDREW

_____Panza - SANCHO

Papas and Ryan - IRENE

Parks or Bonheur - ROSA

Parquet circle - PARTERRE

Pat or Richard - BOONE

Pathologist Sir James - PAGET

Paul of song - ANKA

Peggy of TV - REA

Penn or Connery - SEAN

Percussionist Puente - TITO

Perot - ROSS

Perry of TV - LUKE or COMO

Peter of films - LORRE

Philanthropist Andrew - CARNEGIE

Philanthropist Barton - CLARA

Philanthropist Brady - DIAMONDJIM

Philanthropist Brooke - ASTOR

Philanthropist Cornell - EZRA

Philanthropist Fisher - AVERY

Philanthropist George - SOROS

Philanthropist Hopkins - JOHNS

Philanthropist Rhodes - CECIL

Philanthropist Yale - ELIHU

Philbin - REGIS

Philosopher Auguste - COMTE

Philosopher Bergson - HENRI

Philosopher Blaise - PASCAL

Philosopher David - HUME

Philosopher De Beauvoir - SIMONE

Philosopher Denis - DIDEROT

Philosopher Descartes - RENE

Philosopher Emmanuel - KANT

Philosopher Francis - BACON

Philosopher Georg - HEGEL

Philosopher Georges - SOREL

Philosopher Gottfried - LEIBNIZ

Philosopher Hume - DAVID

Philosopher Immanuel - KANT

Philosopher Jean Paul - SARTRE

Philosopher John Stuart - LOCKE or MILL

Philosopher Josiah - ROYCE

Philosopher Kierkegaard - SOREN

Philosopher Langer - SUSANNE

Philosopher Lao - TSE

Philosopher Mach - ERNST

Philosopher Pascal - BLAISE

Philosopher Smith - ADAM

Philosopher Watts - ALAN

Philosopher Wittgenstein - LUDWIG

Philosopher/writer Hoffer - ERIC

Photographer Adams - ANSEL

Photographer Arbus - DIANE

Photographer Beaton - CECIL

Photographer Cornell - CAPA

Photographer Cunningham - IMOGEN

Photographer Diane - ARBUS

Photographer Dorothea - LANGE

Photographer Gilpin - LAURA

Photographer Goldin - NAN

Photographer Irving - PENN

Photographer Leibovitz - ANNIE

Photographer Paul - STRAND

Photographer Richard - AVEDON

Photographer Walker - EVANS

Physicist Ampere - ANDRE

Physicist Bohr - NIELS

Physicist Edward - TELLER

Physicist Enrico - FERMI

Physicist Ernst - MACH

Physicist Esaki - LEO

Physicist Fermi - ENRICO

Physicist Geiger - HANS

Physicist George - OHM

Physicist Hawking - STEPHEN

Physicist Helsenberg - WERNER

Physicist Isador - RABI

Physicist John - KERR or LOCKE

Physicist Joliot-Curie - IRENE

Physicist Mach - ERNST

Physicist Meitner - LISE

Physicist Nicola - TESLA

Physicist Niels - BOHR

Physicist Niels - BOHR

Physicist Otto - HAHN

Physicist Rutherford - ERNEST

Physicist Sakharov - ANDRE

Physicist Szilard - LEO

Physicist Wolfgang - PAULI

Pianist Alicia - KEYS

Pianist Allison - MOSE

Pianist Andre - WATTS

Pianist Art - TATUM

Pianist Arthur - SCHNABEL

Pianist Barenboim - DANIEL

Pianist Bill - EVANS

Pianist Billy - JOEL

Pianist Bronstein - EVA

Pianist Brubeck - DAVE

Pianist Bruno - ROSSI

Pianist Eubie - BLAKE

Pianist Chasins - ABRAM

Pianist Chick - COREA

Pianist Claudio - ARRAU

Pianist Cliburn - VAN

Pianist Czerny - KARL

Pianist Diane - KRALL

Pianist Emile - GILELS

Pianist Evans - GIL

Pianist Fats - DOMINO

Pianist Fleisher - LEON

Pianist George - SHEARING

Pianist Gilels - EMIL

Pianist Glenn - GOULD

Pianist Handcock - HERBIE

Pianist Hess - MYRA

Pianist Hines - EARL

Pianist Janis - BYRON

Pianist Jankowski - HORST

Pianist Jorge - BOLET

Pianist Jose - ITURBI

Pianist Katie - WEBSTER

Pianist Lupu - RADU

Pianist Marsalis - ELLIS

Pianist Marx - CHICO

Pianist McCann - LES

Pianist Myra - HESS

Pianist Oscar - LEVANT or PETERSON

Pianist Paderewski - IGNACE

Pianist Peter - NERO

Pianist Previn - ANDRE

Pianist Radu - LUPU

Pianist Rosalyn - TURECK

Pianist Rubinstein - ANTON or ARTUR

Pianist Rudolph - SERKIN

Pianist Schnabel - ARTUR

Pianist Serkin - PETER or RUDOLF

Pianist Tatum - ART

Pianist Templeton - ALEC

Pianist Tesh - JOHN

Pianist Thelonious - MONK

Pianist Von Alpenheim - ILSE

Pianist Von Dohnanyi - ERNO

Pianist Watts - ANDRE

Pianist Wilson - TEDDY

Pierre or J. D. - SALINGER

Pike - NEBULON

Pilgrim John - ALDEN

Pinky and Peggy - LEE

Pirate William - KIDD

Pitcher of old Wilhelm - HOYT

Pitcher Al - LEITER

Pitcher Astacio - PEDRO

Pitcher Billy - O'DELL

Pitcher Blackwell - EWELL

Pitcher Blue - VIDA

Pitcher Blyleven - ERT

Pitcher Dave - STIEB

Pitcher David - CONE

Pitcher Fingers - ROLLIE

Pitcher Gidrey - RON

Pitcher Hershiser - OREL

Pitcher Hideki - IRABU

Pitcher Hideo - NOMO

Pitcher LeMarr - HOYT

Pitcher Mario - SOTO

Pitcher Martinez - PEDRO or RAMON

Pitcher Nen - ROBB

Pitcher Ortiz - RUSS

Pitcher Paul - TOTH

Pitcher Quisenberry - DAN

Pitcher Reynolds - ALLIE

Pitcher Robb - NEN

Pitcher Saberhagen - BRET

Pitcher Satchel - PAIGE

Pitcher Seaver - TOM

Pitcher Shawn - ESTES

Pitcher Tiant - LUIS

Place Kicker Benirschke - ROLF

Playwright/Actor Williams - EMLYN

Playwright Akins - ZOE

Playwright Albee - EDWARD

Playwright Anouilh - JEAN

Playwright Ayckbourn - ALAN

Playwright Barstow - STAN

Playwright Beckett - SAMUEL

Playwright Bernard - SLADE

Playwright Bogasian - ERIC

Playwright Brendan - BEHAN

Playwright Burrows - ABE

Playwright Calderon - PEDRO

Playwright Capek - KAREL

Playwright Chayefsky - PADDY

Playwright Chekhov - ANTON

Playwright Clifford - ODETS

Playwright Connelly - MARC

Playwright Coward - NOEL

Playwright David - MAMET or RABE

Playwright Edward - ALBEE

Playwright Eugene - IONESCO or ONEILL

Playwright Federico Garcia - LORCA

Playwright Fugard - ATHOL

Playwright George - PEELE

Playwright Geraldine - ARON

Playwright Goethe - JOHANN

Playwright Hart - MOSS

Playwright Hellman - LILLIAN

Playwright Henley - BETH

Playwrite Henrik - IBSEN

Playwright Horovitz -ISRAEL

Playwright Horton - FOOTE

Playwright Ibsen - HENRIK

Playwright Jean - GENET

Playwright Joe - ORTON

Playwright John - OSBORNE

Playwright Jones - LEROI

Playwright Karel - CAPEK

Playwright Luce - CLARE

Playwright Max - SHULMAN

Playwright Mosel - TAD

Playwright Murray - SCGISGAL

Playwright Norman - MARSHA

Playwright O'Casey - SEAN

Playwright O'Neill - EUGENE

Playwright Paula - VOGEL

Playwright Pinter - HAROLD

Playwright Pirandello - LUIGI

Playwright Rice - ELMER

Playwright Sean - O'CASEY

Playwright Shepard - SAM

Playwright Simon - NEIL

Playwright Spewack - BELLA

Playwright Strindberg - AUGUST

Playwright Victorien - SARDOU

Playwright Wasserman - WENDY

Playwright Wendy - LILL

Playwright William - INGE

Playwright Williams - EMLYN

Playwright Wilson - AUGUST

Playwright Zoe - AKINS

Poet Aiken - CONRAD

Poet Alexander - POPE

Poet _____Alington Robinson - EDWIN

Poet Alfred - NOYES

Poet Alfred_____Birney - EARLE

Poet Alice - CARY

Poet Alighieri - DANTE

Poet Allen - TATE

Poet Amy - LOWELL

Poet Angelou - MAYA

Poet Annibale - CARO

Poet Archibald - MACLEISH

Poet _____Arlington Robinson - ERWIN

Poet Barak - AMIRI

Poet Birney - EARLE

Poet Bradstreet - ANNE

Poet/Cartoonist Silverstein - SHEL

Poet Cary - ALICE

Poet Charles - OLSEN

Poet Clement - MOORE

Poet Conrad - AIKEN

Poet Crane - HART

Poet Cummings - ESTLIN

Poet Dante - ROSSETTI

Poet Dickinson - EMILY

Poet Doolittle - HILDA

Poet Dove - RITA

Poet Dowsen - ERNEST

Poet Earle - BIRNEY

Poet Edgar Lee - MASTERS

Poet Edith - SITWELL

Poet Edward - LEAR

Poet Elinor - WYLIE

Poet Endre - BRETON

Poet Erin - MOURE

Poet Felicia Dorothea - HEMANS

Poet Frank - OHARA

Poet Fredrico Garcia - LORCA

Poet Gallagher - TESS

Poet Gary - SNYDER

Poet Gertrude - STEIN

Poet Ginsberg - ALLEN

Poet Giovanni - NIKKI

Poet Glasgow - ELLEN

Poet Guest - EDGAR

Poet Gunn - THOM

Poet Gwen - HARWOOD

Poet Heamie - SEAMUS

Poet Hart - CRANE

Poet Heinrich - HEINE

Poet Hoyt - ELINOR

Poet Hughes - TED

Poet James Whitcomb - RILEY

Poet John - DONNE or KEATS

Poet Jones - LEROI

Poet Jonson - BEN

Poet Joseph - ADDISON

Poet Kahill - GIBRAN

Poet Karlfeldt - ERIK

Poet Khayyam - OMAR

Poet Khosrow - AMIR

Poet Langston - HUGHES

Poet Laureate Dove - RITA

Poet Laureate Nicholas - ROWE

Poet Laureate Mark - STRAND

Poet Laureate Van Duyn - MONA

Poet Lazarus - EMMA

Poet _____Lee Masters - EDGAR

Poet Levertov - DENISE

Poet Lindsay - VACHEL

Poet_____Lindsay Gordon - ADAM

Poet Lizette - REESE

Poet Louise - BOGAN

Poet Lowell - AMY

Poet Ludovico - ARIOSTO

Poet Mandelstan - OSIP

Poet Mare - WALTER DELA

Poet Marianne - MOORE

Poet Mark Van - DOREN

Poet Markham - IRWIN

Poet Matthew - PRIOR

Poet McKuen - ROD

Poet Millarme - STEPHANE

Poet Millay - EDNA

Poet Milton - ACORN

Poet Moore - CLEMENT or MARIANNE

Poet Muir - EDWIN

Poet Neruda - JAN or PABLO

Poet Nicholes - ROWE

Poet Noyes - ALFRED

Poet Ogden - NASH

Poet Omar - KHAYYAM

Poet Osbert - SITWELL

Poet Oscar - WILDE

Poet Pablo - NERUDA

Poet Percy - SHELLY

Poet Phyllis - WEBB

Poet Pound - EZRA

Poet Rainer - RILKE

Poet Ralph Waldo - EMERSON

Poet Rich - ADRIENNE

Poet Robert - FROST or WACE

Poet Rossetti - DANTE

Poet Rupert - BROOKE

Poet Sachs - NELLY

Poet Salter - MARYJO

Poet Samuel - COLERIDGE

Poet Sandburg - CARL

Poet Sarah_____Jewett - ORNE

Poet Seamus - HEANEY

Poet Sexton - ANNE

Poet Sharon - OLDS

Poet Siegfried- SASSOON

Poet Silverstein - SHEL

Poet Silvia - PLATH

Poet Sitwell - EDITH

Poet Smith - PATTI

Poet St. John_____ - PERSE

Poet St. Vincent Millay - EDNA

Poet Swenson MAY

Poet T. E. - HULME

Poet Tate - ALLAN or NAHUM

Poet Teasdale - SARA

Poet Thomas - DYLAN or GRAY

Poet Torquato - TASSO

Poet Van Duyn - MONA

Poet Voznesenski - ANDREI

Poet W. H. _____ - AUDEN

Poet Walcott - DEREK

Poet Wheeler Wilcox - ELLA

Poet Whitman - WALT

Poet Wilcox - ELLA

Poet Wilfred - OWEN

Poet Wylie - ELINOR

Poet Wystan Hugh - AUDEN

Poet Yevtushenko - YEVGENY

Poet Young - ELLA

Poetic Percy - SHELLEY

Poetic Siegried - SASSOON

Political analyst Meyers - DEEDEE

Political pundit John - SUNUNU

Politician Gary - HART

Politician Gingrich - NEWT

Politico Hollings - ERNEST

Polster Roper - ELMO

Ponselle of opera - ROSA

Pop singer Elliot - CASS

Pop singer Gaye - NONA

Pop singer Hendryx - NONA

Pop singer Phoebe - SNOW

Pop singer Tori - AMOS

Pop star Morisette - ALANIS

Popeye's creator Elzie - SEGAR

Portraitist John Singer - SARGENT

Pot of Cambodia_____ - POL

Primatologist Fossey - DIAN

Producer Adolph - ZUKOR

Producer Brian - ENO

Producer David - MERRICK

Producer De Laurentis - DINO

Producer Hayward - LELAND

Producer Hunter - ROSS

Producer Jack - WARNER

Producer Joseph - PAPP

Producer Phil - SPECTOR

Producer Roach - HAL

Producer Roddenberry - GENE

Producer Schary - DORE

Producer Ziegfeld - FLORENZ

Prohibitionist Carrie - NATION

Prometheus's sister-in-law -
PANDORA

Prynne - HESTER

Psychiatrist Alfred - ADLER

Psychiatrist Jung - CARL

Psychic Edgar - CAYCE

Psychic Geller - URI

Psychoanalyst Feud - ANNA

Psychoanalyst Fromm - ERICH

Psychoanalyst Horney - KAREN

Psychoanalyst Wilhelm - REICH

Psychologist Alfred - BINET

Psychologist Bettelheim -
BRUNO

Psychologist Carl - ROGERS

Psychologist Havelock - ELLIS

Psychologist Jean - PIAGET

Psychologist Jung - CARL

Psychologist Lee - SALK

Psychologist May - ROLLO

Psychologist Pavlov - IVAN

Psychologist Piaget - JEAN

Publisher Adolph - OCHS

Publisher Canfield - CASS

Publisher Chandler - KEN

Publisher Conde - NAST

Publisher William Randolph -
HEARST

Pugilist Tunny - GENE

Pulitzer novelist James - AGEE

Pulitzer poet - AIKEN

Pulitzer winner Huxtable - ADA

Pulitzer Lurie - ALISON

Pundit Coulter - ANN

Puppeteer Fran - ALLISON

Puppeteer Jim - HENSON

Puppeteer Lewis - SHARI

Puppeteer Stu - GILLIAM

Puppeteer Tony - SARG

Puppet master Bil - BAIRD

Quarterback Bradshaw - TERRY

Quarterback Brett - FAVRE

Quarterback Dawson - LEN

Quarterback Dilfer - TRENT

Quarterback Esiason - BOOMER

Quarterback Favre - BRETT

Quarterback Flutie - DOUG

Quarterback Hasselbeck - MATT

Quarterback John - ELWAY

Quarterback Manning - ELI

Quarterback Rodney - PEETE

Quarterback Tarkington - FRAN

Quincy of music - JONES

Racer Andretti - MARIO

Racer Bobby - UNSER or RAHAL

Racer Earnhardt - DALE

Racer Elliott - SADLER

Racer Fabi - TEO

Racer Gordon - JEFF

Racer Jarrett - NED

Racer Lauda - NIKI

Racer Luyendyk - ARIE

Racer Mansell - NIGEL

Racer Petty - KYLE

Racer Rick - MEARS

Racer Stirling - MOSS

Racer Tom - SNEVA

Racer Yarborough - CALE

Racing great Al - UNSER

Radio hostess Hensen - DIANE

Raines - ELLA

Ralph _____ Emerson - WALDO

Rap's_____Kim - LIL

Rapper Elliot - MISSY

Rebecca Romijn - STAMOS

Red Cross founder CLARA - BARTON

Redding of music - OTIS

Reddy of song - HELEN

Reformer Baker - ELLA

Reformer Bloomer - AMELIA

Reformer Jacob - RIIS

Reporter Hume - BRIT

Reporter Stahl - LESLIE

Reviewer Roger - EBERT

Rhodes - CECIL JOHN

Rigby of song - ELEANOR

Rigg or Ross - DIANA

Ring star Dempsey - JACK

Rock star John - ELTON

Rocker Adams - BRYAN

Rocker Bob - SEGER

Rocker Brian - ENO

Rocker Courtney - LOVE

Rocker DiFranco - ANI

Rocker Keith - EMERSON

Rocker Kurt - COBAIN

Rocker Morrison - VAN

Rocker Ocasek - RIC

Rocker Ramone - DEEDEE

Rocker Rose - AXL

Rocker Russel - LEON

Rocker Smith - PATTI

Rocker Steve - EARLE

Rocker Townsend - PETE

Rockney of Notre Dame - KNUTE

Roger of baseball - MARIS

Roh_____Wu - TAE

Roman philosopher - SENECA

Rubik - ERNO

Ruby or Sandra - DEE

Runner Alberto SALAZAR

Runner Boldon - ATO

Runner Budd - ZOLA

Runner Coghlan - EMMON

Runner Devers - GAIL

Runner Johnson - RAFER

Runner Keino - KIP

Runner Lewis - CARL

Runner Mary - DECKER

Runner Mota - ROSA

Runner Rudolph - WILMA

Runner Sebastian - COE

Runner Steve - OVETT

Runner Viren - LASSE

Runner Waitz - GETE

Runner Zatopek - EMIL

Running back Johnson - RUDI

Russian poet Mandelshtam - OSIP

Sally with a fan - RAND

Sarto, Andrea _____ - DEL

Satirist Belloc - HILAIRE

Satirist Bendan - BEHAN

Satirist Mort - SAHL

Satirist Will - DURST

Saxophonist Al - COHN

Saxophonist Coleman - ORNETTE

Saxophonist Getz - STAN

Saxophonist Gordon - DEXTER

Saxophonist John - COLTRANE

Saxophonist Mulligan - GERRY

Saxophonist Parker - EVAN

Saxophonist Zoot - SIMS

Scientist Otto - LOWEI

Scientologist Durkheim - EMILE

Scientologist Hubbard - L RON

Screenwriter Ben - HECHT

Screenwriter Clifford - ODETS

Screenwriter Ephron - NORA

Screenwriter Eric - AMBLER

Screenwriter Hecht - BEN

Screenwriter James - AGEE

Screenwriter Lods - ANITA

Screenwriter Roald - DAHL

Sculptor Arp - JEAN

Sculpror Auguste - RODIN

Sculptor Chillida - EDUARDO

Sculptor Epstein - JACOB

Sculptor Henry - MOORE

Sculptor Hesse - EVA

Sculptor Leoni - LEONE

Sculptor Nadelman - ELIE

Sculptor Noguchi - ISAMU

Sculptor Oldenburg - CLAES

Sculptorr Pisano - NICOLA

Sculptor Sir Jacob - EPSTEIN

Sculptor Taft - LORADO

Sebastian's twin - VIOLA

Seedman Burpee - ATLEE

Senator Hatch - ORRIN

Senator Kefauver - ESTES

Senator Spector - ARLEN

Senator Thurmond - STROM

Sewing machine inventor Howe
   - ELIAS

Sexologist Hite - SHERE

Shaq or Tatum - ONEAL

Sharif or Bradley - OMAR

Shire of Rocky films - TALIA

Shoe designer Maglia - BRUNO

Shore of TV - DINAH

Shortstop Aparicio - LUIS

Shortstop Derek - JETER

Shortstop Garciaparra - NOMAR

Shortstop Peewee - REESE

Shortstopp Walt - WEISS

Shroyer of TV - ENOS

Sicilian code of silence -
   OMERTA

Signor Alighieri - DANTE

Silent actor Novello - RAMON

Silent actress Markey - ENID

Silent actress Normand - MABEL

Silent film star Theda - BARA

Silent star Leeds - LILA

Silent star Naldi - NITA

Silent star, Negri - POLA

Silents star Novello - IVOR

Singer Abdul - PAULA

Singer Acuff - ROY

Singer Adalina - PATTI

Singer Adam - ANT

Singer Adams - OLETA

Singer Aguilera - CHRISTINA

Singer Aimee - MANN

Singer Al - JARREA,
   JOLSON or MARTINO

Singer Alicia - KEYS

Singer Amos - TORI

Singer Anderson - IVIE

Singer Andrews - INEZ

Singer Andy - GIBB

Singer Anita - BAKER, LAURIN or O'DAY

Singer Ant - ADAM

Singer Anthony - MARC

Singer Apple - FIONA

Singer Axton - HOYTE

Singer Bachman - TAL

Singer Baez - JOAN

Singer Bailey - PEARL

Singer Baker - LAVERN

Singer Bandu - ERYKAH

Singer Bandy - MOE

Singer Barbara - MCNAIR

Singer Barry - LEN or MANILOW

Singer Basil - TONI

Singer Beverly - SILLS

Singer Billy - JOEL, OCEAN or VERA

Singer Billy Jo - SPEARS

Singer Black - CILLA or CLINT

Singer Blades - RUBEN

Singer Blakely - RONEE

Singer Bob - DYLAN or SEGER

Singer Bobby - BLAND or DARIN

Singer Bocelli - ANDREA

Singer Bonnie - RAITT

Singer Boz - SCAGGS

Singer Braxton - TONI

Singer Brewer - TERESA

Singer Brickell - EDIE

Singer Bridgewater - DEEDEE

Singer Brightman - SARAH

Singer Brooks - GARTH

Singer Brown - JAMES

Singer Bryson - PEABO

Singer Burl - IVES

Singer C. C. - PENISTON

Singer Calve - EMMA

Singer Campbell - GLEN

Singer Cantrell - LANA

Singer Cara - IRENE

Singer Carey - MARIAH

Singer Carlisle - BELINDA

Singer Carmen - MCRAE or ERIC

Singer Carpenter - KAREN

Singer Carr - VICKIE

Singer Carter - DEANA or NELL

Singer Caruso - ENRICO

Singer Cash - ROSANNE

Singer Cassidy - SHAWN

Singer Celine - DION

Singer Chaka - KAHN

Singer Cherry - NENEH

Singer Chet - ATKINS

Singer Chris - ISAAK or REA

Singer Christina - AGUILERA

Singer Chrystal - GAYLE

Singer Clapton - ERIC

Singer Clark - DEE, ROY or TERRI

Singer Cleo - LAINE

Singer Cocker - JOE

Singer Collins - PHIL

Singer Colombo - RUSS

Singer Cooke - SAM

Singer Coolidge - RITA

Singer Cory - HART

Singer Costello - ELVIS

Singer Crow - SHERYL

Singer Dalton - LACY

Singer Dame Nellie - MELBA

Singer Damone - VIC

Singer Danny - O'KEEFE

Singer David - BOWIE

Singer Davis - MAC

Singer Dee - JOEY or KIKI

Singer Dement - IRIS

Singer Desario - TERI

Singer Diana - ROSS or KRALL

Singer DiFranco - ANI

Singer Donna - SUMMER

Singer Dottie - WEST

Singer Dupree - ROBBIE

Singer Dury - IAN

Singer Eames - EMMA

Singer Easton - SHEENA

Singer Eddie - VEDDER

Singer Edith - PIAF

Singer Eleanor - RIGBY

Singer Enzo - STUARTI

Singer Erykah - BADU

Singer Estefan - GLORIA

Singer Etheridge - MELISSA

Singer Etta - JAMES

Singer Evans - SARA

Singer Falana - LOLA

Singer Farrell - EILEEN

Singer Feliciano - JOSE

Singer Fisher - SHUG

Singer Flack - ROBERTA

Singer Ford - ERNIE or LITA

Singer Foxx - INEZ

Singer Francis - CONNIE

Singer Franklin - ARETHA

Singer Freda - PAYNE

Singer Fricke - JANIE

Singer Gabriel - PETER

Singer Gale - CHRYSTAL

Singer Gary - NUMAN

Singer Gedda - NICOLAI

Singer Gene - PITNEY

Singer Gentry - BOBBIE

Singer George - STRAIT

Singer Gerhardt - ELENA

Singer Gibb - ANDY

Singer Gibbs - TERRI

Singer Gill - VINCE

Singer Glenn - FREY

Singer Gloria - ESTEFAN or GAynor

Singer Gluck - ALMA

Singer Gobbi - TITO

Singer Gore - LESLEY

Singer Gorme - EYDIE

Singer Graham - NASH

Singer Grant - AMY or GOGI

Singer Greenbaum - NORMAN

Singer Greenwood - LEE

Singer Griffith - NANCI

Singer Guthrie - ARLO or WOODY

Singer Haggard - MERLE

Singer Hall - TOM T or DARYL

Singer Halliwell - GERI

Singer Harris - EMMY LOU

Singer Harrison - GEORGE

Singer Havens - RICHIE

Singer Hayes - ISAAC

Singer Hendrix - JIMI

Singer Hendryx - NONA

Singer Hill - DRU, FAITH or LAURYN

Singer Holiday - BILLIE

Singer Holly - NEAR

Singer Horne - MARILYN

Singer Houston - CISSY

Singer Hunter - ALBERTA

Singer Ian - JANIS

Singer India - ARIE

Singer Irene - CARA

Singer Isaac - HAYES

Singer Isadora - PIA

Singer Jackson - ALAN, MICHAEL or MAHALIA

Singer James - ETTA or INGRAM

Singer Janis - IAN

Singer Jaques - BREL

Singer Jarreau - AL

Singer Jennings - WAYLAND

Singer Jenny - LIND

Singer Jerry - VALE

Singer Jerry Lee - LEWIS

Singer Jett - JOAN

Singer Jim - CROCE

Singer Joan - BAEZ or JETT

Singer Joey - DEE

Singer John - ELTON or WAITE

Singer Jon - SECADA

Singer Jones - ALLAN, NORAH or TOM

Singer Joplin - JANIS

Singer Jordan - MONTELL

Singer Josh - WHITE

Singer Judd - NAOMI or WYNONNA

Singer Julio - IGLASIAS

Singer K. T. - OSLIN

Singer Kahn - CHAKA

Singer Kaldor - CONNIE

Singer Kamoze - INI

Singer Karen - AKERS

Singer Kathy - MATTEA

Singer Katie - WEBSTER

Singer Kazan - LAINE

Singer Keith - TOBY

Singer Ketchum - HAL

Singer Keys - ALICIA

Singer King - BENE or CAROLE

Singer Kitt - EARTHA

Singer Kitty - WELLS

Singer Knight - GLADYS

Singer Krause - ALISON

Singer Kravitz - LENNY

Singer LaBelle - PATTI

Singer Laine - CLEO

Singer Lane - ABBE

Singer Lanza - MARIO

Singer Lauper - CYNDI

Singer Laura - NYRO

Singer Lavigne - AVRIL

Singer Lawrence - STEVE

Singer Leann - RIMES

Singer Lehmann - LOTTA

Singer Lehrer - TOM

Singer Lemper - LUTE

Singer Lena - HORNE

Singer Lennon - JOHN

Singer Lennox - ANNIE

Singer Lenya - LOTTE

Singer Leo - SAYER

Singer Leon - REDBONE

Singer Leontyne - PRICE

Singer Leslie - GORE

Singer Lila - MCCANN

Singer Lili - PONS

Singer Linda - EDER

Singer Lisa - LOEB

Singer Loaf - MEAT

Singer Loeb - LISA

Singer Loggins - KENNY

Singer Lola - FALANA

Singer Lonnie - MACK

Singer Lopez - TRINI

Singer Lotta - LENYA

Singer Louis - PRIMA

Singer Love - COURTNEY

Singer Lovett - LYLE

Singer Lovich - LENE

Singer Lyle - LOVETT

Singer Lynn - LORETTA or VERA

Singer Mabel - MERCER

Singer Mahal - TAJ

Singer Makeba - MIRIAM

Singer Manfred - MAN

Singer Mann - AIMEE

Singer Margaret - LEANN RIMES

Singer Maria - MCKEE

Singer Marie - TEENA

Singer Mario - WINANS

Singer Martha - REEVES

Singer Martina - MCBRIDE

Singer Marvin - GAYE

Singer Martin - DEAN or RICKY

Singer Masor - MILA

Singer Mathews - DAVE

Singer Mayfield - CURTIS

Singer McBride - MARTINA

Singer McCann - LILA

Singer McCoy - NEAL

Singer McEntire - REBA

Singer McGraw - TIM

Singer McLachlan - SARAH

Singer McPhatter - CLYDE

Singer Mel - TILLIS

Singer Melba - MOORE

Singer Mercer - MABEL

Singer Merchant - NATALIE

Singer Merman - ETHEL

Singer Michael - STIPE

Singer Midler - BETTE

Singer Mills - ERIE

Singer Minoque - KYLIE

Singer Miriam - MAKEBA

Singer Mitchell - JONI

Singer Moffo - ANNA

Singer Moore - MELBA

Singer Morgan - LORRIE

Singer Morgana - KING

Singer Morissette - ALANIS

Singer Morrison - JIM or VAN

Singer Morse - ELLAMAE

Singer Mouskouri - NANA

Singer Murray - ANNE

Singer Nancy - AMES

Singer Naomi - JUDD

Singer Neil - SEDAKA

Singer Nelson - RICKEY

Singer Neville - AARON

Singer Nicks - STEVIE

Singer Nightingale - MAXINE

Singer Nina - SIMONE

Singer Nixon - MARNI

Singer Norma - JONES

Singer Norman - JESSYE

Singer Nova - ALDO

Singer Nyro - LAURA

Singer Ocasek - RIC

Singer Ochs - PHIL

Singer O'Connor - SINEAD

Singer O'Day - ANITA

Singer Oleda - ADAMS

Singer Ono - YOKO

Singer Orbison - ROY

Singer Osmond - MARIE

Singer Pat - BOONE

Singer Patti - ADELINA or SMITH

Singer Patty - LARKINS

Singer Paul - SIMON

Singer Paula - ABDUL or COLE

Singer Payne - FREDA

Singer Peeples - NEA

Singer Peerce - JAN

Singer Perkins - CARL

Singer Peter - TOSH

Singer Phil - OCHS

Singer Pia - ZADORA

Singer Piaf - EDITH

Singer Pinza - EZIO

Singer Pop - IGGY

Singer Priest - MAXI

Singer Quatro - SUZI

Singer Rabbitt - EDDIE

Singer Randy - OWEN or TRAVIS

Singer Raven - EDDY

Singer Rawls - LOU

Singer Ray - EBERLE or STEVENS

Singer Redbone - LEON

Singer Redding - OTIS

Singer Reed - LOU

Singer Reeves - DEL

Singer Renata - SCOTTO

Singer Rezner - TRENT

Singer Richie - LIONEL or VALENS

Singer Rick - ASTLEY or DEES

Singer Ricky - SCAGGS

Singer Rigby - ELEANOR

Singer Rimes - LEANN

Singer Ritter - TEX

Singer Robbins - MARTY

Singer Rod - STEWART

Singer Rogers - KENNY

Singer Ronan - TYNAN

Singer Ronnie - MILSAP

Singer Ronstadt - LINDA

Singer Ross - DIANA

Singer Roy - ACUFF

Singer Rudgren - TODD

Singer Russell - LEON

Singer Ruth - ETTING

Singer Selena - PEREZ

Singer Salonga - LEA

Singer Sam - COOKE

Singer Samantha - SANG

Singer Sammy - HAGAR

Singer Sayer - LEO

Singer Scaggs – BOZ

Singer Schipa - TITO

Singer Seeger - PETE

Singer Shania - TWAIN

Singer Shannon - DEL

Singer Sharp - DEEDEE

Singer Sheena - EASTON

Singer Sherry - NENEH

Singer Sheryl - CROW

Singer Simms - GINNY

Singer Simon - CARLEY, ESTES or PAUL

Singer Simone - NINA

Singer Skinnay - ENNIS

Singer Sledge - PERCY

Singer Small - MILLIE

Singer Smith - BESSIE or KATE

Singer Snider - DEE

Singer Snow - PHOEBE

Singer Spector - RONNIE

Singer Stranfield - LISA

Singer Starr - IRWIN or KAY

Singer Steve - EARLE

Singer Stevens - CAT, CONNIE or DODIE

Singer Stewart - ROD

Singer Stratas - TERESA

Singer Stritch - ELAINE

Singer Stuarti - ENZO

Singer Stubbs - LEVI

Singer Sumac - YMA

Singer Sommer - DONNA

Singer Susanne - VEGA

Singer Sylvia - SYMS

Singer Taylor - DAYNE or KOKO

Singer Tennille - TONI

Singer Terrell - TAMMI

Singer Thomas - IRMA or ROB

Singer Tillis - MEL or PAM

Singer Tom - JONES or WAITS

Singer Tommy - ROE

Singer Tori - AMOS

Singer Travis - MERLE, RANDY or TRITT

Singer Trisha - YEARWOOD

Singer Tritt - TRAVIS

Singer Tucker - TANYA

Singer Twain - SHANIA

Singer Vallee - RUDY

Singer Vandross - LUTHER

Singer Vanilla - ICE

Singer Vega - SUZANNE

Singer Vic - DAMONE or DANA

Singer Vickers - JON

Singer Walter - EGAN

Singer Warwick - DIONNE

Singer Washington - DINAH

Singer Watley - JODY

Singer Waters - ETHEL

Singer Wayne - NEWTON

Singer Webster - Katie

Singer West – DOTTIE or SHELLY

Singer Whitman - SLIM

Singer Williams - ANDY or DENIECE

Singer Winans - CECE

Singer Winehouse - AMY

Singer Wooley - SHEB

Singer Yearwood - TRISHA

Singer Young - NEIL

Singer Yma - SUMAC

Singing satiriest Tom - LEHRER

Sister-in-law of Prometheus - PANDORA

Sir Laurence - OLIVIER

Sitarist Shankar - RAVI

Skater _____Anton Ohno - APOLO

Skater Babilonia - TAI

Skater Baiul - OKSANA

Skater Berezhnaya - ELENA

Skater Boitano - BRIAN

Skater Bonnie - BLAIR

Skater Brian - ORSER

Skater Button - DICK

Skater Chris - WITTY

Skater Cohen - SASHA

Skater Cranston - TOLLER

Skater Dan - JENSEN

Skater Eldridge - TODD

Skater Hamilton - SCOTT

Skater Harding - TANYA

Skater Heiden - ERIC

Skater Henie - SONJA

Skater Hughes - SARAH

Skater Inoue - RENA

Skater Janet - LYNN

Skater Johann_____Koss - OLAV

Skater Karen - ENKE

Skater Katarina - WITT

Skater Kulik - ILIA

Skater Limpinski - TARA

Skater Michelle - KWAN

Skater Midori - ITO

Skater Oksana - BAIUL

Skater PARRA - DEREK

Skater Paulson - AXEL

Skater Protopopov - OLEG

Skater Rodnina - IRINI

Skater Sasha - COHEN

Skater Slutskaya - IRINA

Skater Sokolova - ELENA

Skater Sonjja - HENIE

Skater Starbuck - JOJO

Skater Stojko - ELVIS

Skater Thomas - DEBI

Skater Tiffany - CHIN

Skater Toller - CRANSTON

Skater Torvill - JAYNE

Skater Uzova - MAIA

Skater Valova - ELENA

Skater Witt - KATARINA

Skater Yagudin - ALEXEI

Skater Yamaguchi - KRISTI

Skater Young - SHEILA

Skater Zayak - ELAINE

Skating great Henie - SONJA

Skating metalist Flemming - PEGGY

Skier Alberto - TOMBA

Skier Girardelli - MARC

Skier Hermann - MAIER

Skier Maentyranta - EERO

Skier McKinney - TAMARA

Skier Phil - MAHRE

Skier Skaadal - ATLE

Skier Tommy - MOE

Sleuth Vance - PHILO

Slugger Canseco - JOSE

Slugger Griffey Jr. - KEN

Slugger Hillenbrand - SHEA

Slugger Killebrew - HARMON

Soccer great Rossi - PAOLO

Soccer star Brandi - CHASTAIN

Soccer star Hamm - MIA

Soccer star Michelle - AKERS

Socialite Maxwell - ELSA

Socialite Mesta - PERLE

Socialite Peggy - EATON

Sociologist Durkheim - EMILE

Sociologist Max - WEBER

Songbird McEntire - REBA

Songstress Laine - CLEO

Songstress McLachlan - SARAH

Song writer Bacharat - BURT

Song writer Bayer Sager - CAROLE

Song writer Blake - EUBIE

Song writer Chris - REA

Song writer Farrell - WES

Song writer Frank - LOESSER

Song writer Greenwich - ELLIE

Song writer Harold - ARLEN or ROME

Song writer Hart - LORENZ

Song writer Jaques - BREL

Song writer Jerome - KERN

Song writer Jimmy - WEBB

Song writer Kahn - GUS

Song writer Keys - ALICIA

Song writer Laura - NYRO

Song writer Leonard - COHEN

Song writer Milton - AGER

Song writer Mitchell - JONI

Song writer Newman - RANDY

Song writer Paul - SIMON

Song writer Porter - COLE

Song writer Raymond - EGAN

Song writer Reed - LOU

Song writer Robin - LEO

Song writer Rogers - JIMMIE

Song writer Silverstein - SHEL

Song writer Sondheim - STEPHEN

Song writer Taupin - BERNIE

Song writer Wilder - ALEX

Sophia of films - LOREN

Soprano Adelina - PATTI

Soprano Anna - MOFFO

Soprano Auger - ARLEEN

Soprano Benzell - MIMI

Soprano Berger - ERNA

Soprano Birgit - NILSSON

Soprano Callas - MARIA

Soprano Calne - EMMA

Soprano Dale - CLAMMA

Soprano Della Casa - LISA

Soprano Emma - CALVE or EAMES

Soprano Farrell - EILEEN

Soprano Flagstad - KIRSTEN

Soprano Fleming - RENEE

Soprano Frances - ALDA

Soprano Gluck - ALMA

Soprano Grist - RERI

Soprano Jenny - LIND

Soprano Kirsten - FLAGSTAD

Soprano Lehmann - LOTTE

Soprano Lily - PONS

Soprano Lucine - AMARA

Soprano Lucrezia - BORI

Soprano Marilyn - HORNE

Soprano Melba - Nellie

Soprano Mills - ERIE

Soprano Mitchell - LEONA

Soprano Moffo - ANNA

Soprano Nilsson - Birgit

Soprano Norma - JESSYE

Soprano Petina - IRRA

Soprano Ponselle - ROSA

Soprano Price - LEONTYNE

Soprano Scotto - RENATA

Soprano Tebaldi - RENATA

Soprano Tekanawa - KIRI

Soprano Tetrazzini - LUISA

Soprano Troyanos - TATIANA

Soprano Upshaw - DAWN

Soul singer Adams - OLETA

Southern of Hollywood - ANN

Spanish artist Salvador - DALI

Speaker of baseball - TRIS

Speed-skater Gustavson - SVEN

Spice girl Halliwell - GERI

Sportscaster Albert - MARV

Sportscaster Allen - MEL

Sportscaster Berman - LEN

Sportscaster Bob - LEY

Sportscaster Cross - IRV

Sportscaster Dick - VITALE

Sportscaster Hannah - AMES
    or STORM

Sportscaster Howard - COSELL

Sportscaster Jim - MCKAY or
    NANCE

Sportscaster McCarver - TIM

Sportscaster Musburger - BRENT

Sportscaster Rashad - AHMAD

Sportscaster Scully - VIN

Sprinter Deevers - GAIL

Statesman Salinger - PIERRE

Statesman Thurmond - STROM

Stimpy's pal - REN

Stoic philosopher - CATO

Stravinski - IGOR

Sufragist Bloomer - AMELIA

Sufragist Carrie Chapman -
    CATT

Sufragist Stone - LUCY

Supermodel Banks - TYRA

Supermodel Bundchen - GIZELE

Supermodel Campbell - NAOMI

Supermodel Carangi - GIA

Supermodel Carol - ALT

Supermodel Carre - OTIS

Supermodel Evangelista - LINDA

Supermodel Heidi - KLUM

Supermodel Moss - KATE

Supermodel Sastre - INES

Supermodel Schiffer - CLAUDIA

Supermodel Taylor - NIKI

Supermodel Veronica - WEBB

Surrealist Joan - MIRO

Surrealist Magritte - RENE

Surrealist Max - ERNST

Surrealist Tanguy - YVES

Surveyor Elmo - ROPER

Surveyor Jeremiah - DIXON

Suzanne of TV - SOMERS

Swedish actress Anderson - BIBI

Swimmer Debbie - MEYER

Swimmer Diana - NYAD

Swimmer Eleanor - HOLM

Swimmer Evans - JANET

Swimmer Gertrude - EDERLE

Swimmer Janet - EVANS

Swimmer Kristin - OTTO

Swimmer Thorp - IAN

Swimmer Vicki - KEITH

Swiss mathematician Leonhart - EULER

Swiss painter Klee - PAUL

Syngman of Seoul - RHEE

Tanner of tennis - ROSCOE

Tarkenton - FRAN

Telejournalist Roberts - COKIE

Television's Gibbons - LEEZA

Tennis Champ Bjorn - BORG

Tennis Champ Fred - STOLLE

Tennis Champ Mandlikova - HANA

Tennis Champ Maria - BUENO

Tennis Champ - Roddick - ANDY

Tennis coach Tiriac - ION

Tennis great Arthur - ASHE

Tennis great Chris - EVERT

Tennis great Gonzolez - PANCHO

Tennis great Keith - EMERSON

Tennis great Marble - ALICE

Tennis great Marie - BUENO

Tennis great Monica - SELES

Tennis player Agassi - ANDRE

Tennis player Andy - RODDICK

Tennis player Becker - BORIS

Tennis player Chandra - RUBIN

Tennis player Coetzer - AMANDA

Tennis player Edberg - STEFAN

Tennis player Emmerson - ROY

Tennis player Fraser - NEALE

Tennis player Goolagong - EVONNE

Tennis player Gustavo - KUERTEN

Tennis player Hingus - MARTINA

Tennis player Hoad - LEW

Tennis player Huber - ANKE

Tennis player Ian - AYRE

Tennis player Irina - SPIRLEA

Tennis player Korda - PETR

Tennis player Kournikova - ANNA

Tennis player Krickstein - AARON

Tennis player LaCosta - RENE

Tennis player Lew - HOAD

Tennis player Likhovtsevva - HELENA

Tennis player Mandlikova - HANA

Tennis player Makarova - ELENA

Tennis player Nadal - RAFAEL

Tennis player Nastase - ILIE

Tennis player Ramirez - RAUL

Tennis player Roddick - ANDY

Tennis player Roscoe - TANNER

Tennis player Rosewall - KEN

Tennis player Rosie - CASALS

Tennis player Safin - MARAT

Tennis player Shriver - PAM

Tennis player Smith - STAN

Tennis player Sukova - HELENA

Tennis player Tilden - BILL

Tennis player Virginia - WADE

Tennis player Wilander - MATS

Tennis player Williams - SERENA or VENUS

Tennis player Yannick - NOAH

Tennis pro Roddick - ANDY

Tennis star Fraser - NEALE

Tennis star Garrison - ZINA

Tennis star Gerulaitis - VITAS

Tennis star Gibson - ALTHEA

Tennis star Gussie - MORAN

Tennis star Huber - ANKE

Tennis star Ilie - NASTASE

Tennis star Kournikova - ANNA

Tennis star Lendl - IVAN

Tennis star Marcelo - RIOS

Tennis star Michael - CHANG

Tennis star Pam - SHRIVER

Tennis star Poncho - SEGURA

Tennis star Sampras - PETE

Tennis star Novotna - JANA

Tennis star Ramirez - RAUL

Tennis star Stefan - EDBERG

Tennis star ZVEREVA - NATASHA

Tennis winner Rafael - OSUNA

Tenor Andrea - BOCELLI

Tenor Bocelli - ANDREA

Tenor Carreras - JOSE

Tenor Caruso - ENRICO

Tenor Domingo - PLACIDO

Tenor Gigli - BENIAMINO

Tenor Mario - LANZA

Tenor Pavarotti - LUCIANO

Tenor Peter - PEARS

Test pilot Chuck - YEAGER

Theologian Charles - HODGE

Theologian John - WESLEY

Theologian Kiergaard - SOREN

Theologian Martin -
    DIBELIUS or LUTHER

Theologian Thomas - AQUINAS

Thermos inventor James -
    DEWAR

Thomas or Herbie - MANN

Tiger great McLain - DENNY

Tomei - MARISA

Tony winner Diana - RIGG

Tony winnner Judith - IVEY

Tony winner Lane - NATHAN

Tony winner Salongna - LEA

Track legend Moses - EDWIN

Track star Devers - GAIL

Track star - Wyomia - TYUS

Trumpeter Baker - CHET

Trumpeter Chuck -
    MANGIONE

Trumpeter Miles - DAVIS

Trumpeter Red - ALLEN

Turkish statesman - INONU

Turner of Hollywood - LANA

Turner of song - TINA

Turner or Koppel - TED

Tushingham or Moreno - RITA

TV actor Gulaher - CLU

TV actor Reiser - PAUL

TV actress Cassie - YATES

TV actress Plumb - EVE

TV anchor Newman - EDWIN

TV anchorman Peter -
    JENNINGS

TV anchorman Roger - MUDD

TV's Degeneres - ELLEN

TV host Gibbons - LEEZA

TV host Hugh - DOWNES

TV host John - TESH

TV host Matt - LAUER

TV newswoman Elizabeth -
    VARGAS

TV producer Arlege - ROONE

TV reporter Van Susteren -
    GRETA

Tyson - MIKE

Uncle Miltie - BERLE

University founder Cornel -
    EZRA

Uriah - HEEP

U.S. Attorney General Janet -
    RENO

U.S. open champ Curtis -
    STRANGE

Van Gogh's brother - THEO

Vanna of TV - WHITE

Vaudeville entertainer Bayes -
    NORA

Ventriloquist Bergen - EDGAR

Ventriloquist Lewis - SHARI

Verdugo of TV - ELENA

Verne's Fogg - PHILEAS

Vibraphonist Hampton - LIONEL

Violin maker Amati - ANDREA or NICOLO

Violinist Bull - OLE

Violinist Camilla - URSO

Violinist Elman - MISCHA

Violinist Francescatti - ZINO

Violinist Georges - ENESCO

Violinist Heifetz - JASCHA

Violinist Isaac - STERN

Violinist Itzhak - PERLMAN

Violinist Jean_____Ponty - LUC

Violinist Kafanian - IDA

Violinist Kavafian - ANI

Violinist Kreisler - FRITZ

Violinist Leopold - AUER

Violinist Menuhin - YEHUDI

Violinist Milstein - NATHAN

Violinist Mischa - AUER or ELMAN

Violinist Niccolo - PAGANINI

Violinist Pearlman - ITZHAK

Violinist Ruggiero - RICCI

Violinist Stern - ISAAC

Violinist Zimbalist - EFRAM

Violinist Zuckerman - PINCHAS

Violin maker Nicolo - AMATI

Virologist Albert - SABIN

Vocalist Vaughan - SARAH

Wallace - MIKE

Watercolorist_____Liu - LENA

Weatherman Willard - SCOTT

Webster or Wyle - NOAH

Welles or Bean - ORSON

Welsh poet Thomas - DYLAN

West or Murray - MAE

Whitlinger of tennis - TAMI

Whodunit's Gardner - ERLE

Williams of tennis - SERENA

Wimbleton champ Fraser - NEALE

Wimbleton champ Gibson - ATHEA

Wimbleton champ Goolagong - EVONNE

Wimbleton winner Novotna - JANA

Wonder of music - STEVIE

Writer Adams - CECIL

Writer Aleichem - SHOLOM

Writer Allende - ISABEL

Writer Almed - SALMAN RUSHDIE

Writer Alther - LISA

Writer Ambler - ERIC

Writer Andric - IVO

Writer Angelou - MAYA

Writer Ann or Elmer - RICE or TYLER

Writer Arch - OBOLER

Writer Arthur - KOESTLER

Writer Ashworth - ADELE

Writer Asimov - ISAAC

Writer Babel - ISAAC

Writer Barker - CLIVE

Writer Beattie - ANN

Writer Bellows - SAUL

Writer Best - EDNA

Writer Betti - UGO

Writer Bierce - AMBROSE

Writer Biggers - EARL DERR

Writer Binchy - MAEVE

Writer Blyton - ENID

Writer Bochco - STEVEN

Writer Borges - JORGE

Writer Bova - BEN

Writer Bradbury - RAY

Writer Bruckner - ANITA

Writer Buchanan - EDNA

Writer Buntline - NED

Writer Burrow - ABE

Writer Buscaglia - LEO

Writer Caldwell - ERSKINE

Writer Calvino - ITALO

Writer Canetti - ELIAS

Writer Capek - KAREL

Writer Carroll - LEWIS

Writer Cendrars - BLAISE

Writer Chekhov - ANTON

Writer Chomsky - NOAM

Writer Christie - AGATHA

Writer Claude - ANET

Writer Cleaver - ELDRIDGE

Writer Cocteau - JEAN

Writer Connell - EVAN

Writer Conrad - AIKEN

Writer Conroy - PAT

Writer Cynthia - OZICK

Writer Dahl - ROALD

Writer Damon - RUNYON

Writer Daniel - DEFOE

Writer Danielle - STEELE

Writer David - GROSSMAN or MAMET

Writer de Balzac - HONORE

Writer de Beauvoir - SIMONE

Writer de la Roche - MAZO

Writer Defoe - DANIEL

Writer Deighton - LEN

Writer Derr Biggers - EARL

Writer Dinesen - ISAK

Writer Dominick - DUNNE

Writer Dorothea - SAYERS

Writer Dostoevsky - FYODOR

Writer Drummond - IVOR

Writer Drury - ALLEN

Writer du Maurier - DAPHNE

Writer Elaine - MAY

Writer Ellison - HARLAN

Writer Elmer - RICE

Writer Ephron - DELIA or NORA

Writer Erik - POHL

Writer Eugene - FODOR

Writer Fallaci - ORIANA

Writer Fannie - HURST

Writer Felix - ADLER

Writer Ferber - EDNA

Writer Fleming - IAN

Writer Follett - KEN

Writer France - ANATOLE

Writer Francoise - SEGAN

Writer Frederico Garcia - LORCA

Writer Frederik - POHL

Writer Gardner - ERLE

Writer Gallant - MAVIS

Writer George - ADE or PERAC

Writer Georgette - HEYER

Writer Germaine - GREER

Writer Gertrude - STEIN

Writer Gide ANDRE

Writer Gilbert - ADAIR

Writer Gogol - NIKOLAI

Writer Gordiner - NADINE

Write Grafton - SUE

Write Grey - ZANE

Writer H. H. - MUNRO (SAKI)

Writer H. L. - MRNCKEN

Write Hamsum - KNUT

Writer Hannah - ARENDT

Writer Harte - BRE

Writer Helen - BEATRIX POTTER

Writer Heinrich - HEINE

Writer Henley - BETH

Writer Henry - ROTH

Writer Hentoff - NAT

Writer Hilaire - ELLOC

Writer Hobson - LAURA

Writer Hoffer - ERIC

Writer Hubbard - LRON

Writer Huffington - ARIANNA

Writer Hughes - LANGSTON

Writer Hunter - EVAN

Writer Huxley - ALDOUS

Writer Huxtable - ADA

Writer Irwin - SHAW

Writer Isaac - ASIMOV

Writer Ishmael - REED

Writer Ivan - BUNIN

Writer Jack - ABBOTT

Writer Jacob - RIIS

Writer James - AGEE

Writer Janowitz - TAMA

Writer Joe - HAN

Writer John DICKENSON - CARR

Writer John Le - CARRE

Writer Jones - LEROI

Writer Josephine - TEY

Writer Kathleen - NORRIS

Writer Kerouac - Jack

Writer Kesey - KEN

Writer Kilmer - JOYCE

Writer Kingsley - AMIS

Write Klima - IVAN

Writer Kureishi - HANIF

Writer Lardner - RING

Writer Lathem - EMMA

Writer Laura - NYRO

Writer Laurie - ALISON

Writer Lebowitz - FRAN

Writer Leo - ROSTEN

Writer Leonard - COHEN

Writer LeSage - ALAIN

Writer Leshan - EDA

Writer Leslie - EGAN

Writer LeGuin - URSALA

Writer Leshan - EDA

Writer Levin - IRA

Writer Lindbergh - ANNE

Writer Lofts - NORAH

Writer Lola - MONTEZ

Writer Lowell - AMY

Writer Ludwig - EMIL

Writer Madame de - STAEL

Writer Madeleine L'_____ - ENGEL

Writer Maksirr - GORKI

Writer Mansfield - KATHERINE

Writer Marcel - PROUST

Writer _____Maria Remarque - ERICH

Writer Mario Vargas - LLOSA

Writer Marsh - NGAIO

Writer Martin - AMIS

Writer Marx - KARL

Writer Maurice - SENDAK

Writer Max - BEERBOHM

Writer Maxim - GORKI

Writer McEwan - IAN

Writer Monroe - ALICE

Writer Montagu - ASHLEY

Writer Moravia - ALBERTO

Writer Morrison - TONI

Writer Mumford - THAD

Writer Murdock - IRIS

Writer Ngao - MARSH

Writer Nicholas - ROWE

Writer Nikolai - GOGOL

Writer Nora - EPHROM

Writer Norman - MAILER

Writer Novello - IVOR

Writer O'Brien - EDNA

Writer O'Casey - SEAN

Writer Octavio - PAZ

Writer O'Faolain - SEAN

Writer O'Flaherty - LIAM

Writer Oscar - WILDE

Writer Oz - AMOS

Writer P. J. - PROURKE

Writer Paresky - SARA

Writer Pascal - BLAISE

Writer Paten - ALAN

Writer Peggy - NOONAN

Writer Pera - PIA

Writer Peters - ELLIS

Writer Philip - ROTH or WHALEN

Writer Phillpotts - EDEN

Writer Plath - SYLVIA

Writer Pollitt - KATHA

Writer Primo - LEVI

Writer Proust - MARCEL

Writer Quindlen - ANNA

Writer Rand - AYN

Writer Raymond - CHANDLER

Writer Rendell - RUTH

Writer Roald - DAHL

Writer Robb - INEZ

Writer Robinson - EDEN or SPIDER

Writer Rogers StJohns - ADELA

Writer Rohmer - SAX

Writer Rolland - ROMAIN

Writer Rombauer - IRMA

Writer Rosten - LEO

Writer Roth - PHILIP

Writer Runyan - DAMON

Writer Sackville West - VITA

Writer Samuel - DASHIELL HAMMETT

Writer Santha Rama - RAU

Writer Sarah_____Jewett - ORNE

Writer Schoemperien - DIANE

Writer Segal - ERICH

Writer Seton - ANYA

Writer Sewell - ANNA

Writer Sexton - ANNE

Writer Shaw - IRWIN

Writer Sheehan - NEIL

Writer Shelley - MARY

Writer Shere - HITE

Writer Sholem - ASCH

Writer Shreve - ANITA

Writer Shute - NEVIL

Write Sidney - SHELDON

Writer Sillitoe - ALAN

Writer Silverstein - SHEL

Writer Sinclair - LEWIS or
UPTON

Writer Sir Richard - STEELE

Writer Solzhenitsyn -
ALEKSANDR

Writer Sontag - SUSAN

Writer St. Johns - ADELA

Writer Steel - DANIELLE

Writer Stout - REX

Writer Syner - OMARR

Writer Talese - GAY

Writer Tarbell - IDA

Writer Terkel - STUDS

Writer Tertz - ABRAM

Writer Toffler - ALVIN

Writer Tom - CLANCY

Writer Turgenev - IVAN

Writer Turkel - STUDS

Writer Tyler - ANNE

Writer Umberto - ECO

Writer Uris - LEON

Writer Victor - HUGO

Writer Vittorini - ELIO

Writer Vonnegut - KURT

Writer Wallace - LEW

Writer Walton - IZAAC

Writer Waugh - ALEC or
EVELYN

Writer Welty - EUDORA

Writer Wiesel - ELIE

Writer Wilder - LAURA
INGALLS

Writer Wilhelm - KATE

Writer William - INGE

Writer Willy - LEY

Writer Wister - LOESS or
OWEN

Writer Yutang - LIN

Writer Zimmer Bradley -
MARION

Writer Zora _____Hurston -
NEALE

Whodunit writer Gardner -
ERLE

Wimbleton champ Gibson -
ATHEA

Wimbleton champ Goolagong -
EVONNE

Wimbleton winner Novotna -
JANA

Wrestler Flair - RIC

Yachtsman Dennis - CONNOR

Yeats - WILLIAM BUTLE

Yeltsin - BORIS

Zedong - MAO

Zola - EMILE

PHUNNY PHRASES

Ab_____ - OVO

_____Ababa - ADDIS

ABU_____ - DHABI

_____accompli - FAIT

_____acid - IODIC or PICRIC

_____acte - ENTR

Ad_____per aspera - ASTRA

Addis_____ - ABABA

Adrien_____ - ARPEL

_____Adronicus - TITUS

Agni_____ - DEVA

"Agnus_____" - DEI

_____Alamitos - LOS

_____Alba - TERRA

_____Alcohol - METHYL

_____Alegre - PORTO

_____Alighieri - DANTE

Alla_____ - BREVE

_____Alla scala - TEATRO

_____Alle - PAS

Allegro_____ - ASSAI

Allegro con_____ - BRIO

Allegro non _____ - TROPPO

_____-Aller - PIS

_____Alte - DER

_____Alto - PALO

_____Amatoria - ARS

Amino_____ - ACID

Amious_____ - CURIAE

Amo, Amas, _____-AMAT

_____and penates - LARES

_____and Principe - SAOTOME

Andria_____- DORIA

_____Andronicus - TITUS

_____Angelico - FRA

_____Anglais - COR

Ankor_____ - WAT

Apres_____- SKI

_____Apso - LHASA

Aqua_____ - PURA, REGIA
    or VITAE

Arroz con_____ - POLLO

Ars_____Artis - GRATIS

Ars_____,vita brevis - LONGA

_____Artery - ILIAC

_____Aryan - INDO

_____Atque vale - AVE

_____au lait - CAFE

Au_____ - NATUREL

_____aurhum - BABA

Aurora_____BOREALIS

Auto_____ - DA-FE

_____-Au-vent - VOL

Ave_____Vale - ATQUE

_____Avis - RARA

Avant_____ - GARDE

_____Aviv - TELE

A votre_____ - SANTE

Baba au_____ - RHUM

_____Bagatelle - AMERE

_____Ballerina - PRIMA

Bali_____ - HAI

Ballet_____ - RUSSE

_____-Barr virus - EPSTEIN

Basse_____ - Mer (low tide)

_____Bator - ULAN

_____bean - FAVA

Beau_____ - IDEAL

Beaux_____ - ARTS

_____-beche - TETE

_____Bede - ADAM

Bel_____cheese - PAESE

Bel_____- AMI or CANTO

_____Belli - CASUS

_____bene - NOTA

Beta_____ - CAROTENE

Bete_____ - NOIRE

_____bien - TRES

Billet_____ - DOUX

Biscuit_____ - TORONI

Bitter_____- ALOES

_____Blanc - CHENIN

_____Blanco - OSO

_____Blas - GIL

Bois_____ - DARC

Bon_____ - MOT

_____Bono - CUI

Bono_____ - DEA

_____Borealis - AURORA

Bouquet_____ - GARNI

_____Brava - COSTA

_____breve - ALLA

_____brevis, ars longa - VITA

_____B'rith - BNAI

Broccoli_____ - RABE

_____broche - ALA

Broom_____ - HILDA

Bryn_____ - MAWR

_____Bucci - OSSI

_____Buco - OSSO

_____Buena (herb) - YERBA

Buenos_____- DIAS

_____Buffa - OPERA

Buona_____ - NOTTE or
SERA

Burkina_____ - FASO

Cabo_____Lucas - SAN

Cafe au_____- LAIT

Cafe_____ - NOIR

Calcium_____ - NITRATE

_____Cantata - MISSA

_____Canto - BEL

Carpe_____ - DIUM

_____Carta - MAGNA

_____carte - ALA

_____cava - VENA

Cave_____ - CANEM

Caveat_____ - EMPTOR

Cedant_____Togae - ARMA

_____Central – MASSIF

Cest_____ - AVIE

Chacun a son_____ - GOUT

Chaise_____ - LONGUE

Champs_____ - ELYSEES

_____ - Chandon - MOET

_____chango - PRESTO

_____Chat - PASDE

Chemin de _____- FER

Chennin_____ - BLAC

_____Chi - TAI

Childe_____ - HAROLD

Chou en _____ - LAI

_____Choy - BOK

_____Ciria - AMICUS

_____Citato - OPERE

Citta_____vaticano - DEL

Claire de_____ - LUNE

_____Coast - ADELIE

_____- Coburg - Gotha - SAXE

_____ - Cochere - PORTE

_____Codicil - ADDA

Coeur d'_____,id -ALENE

_____coeur - SACRE

Coq au_____- VIN

Cogito_____sum - ERGO

_____Comic - SERIO

Commedia dell'_____ - ARTE

Comme il_____ - FAUT

Como_____ - ESTA

_____Compos mentis - NON

Concerto_____ - GROSSO

_____concors - HORS

_____Contendere - NOLO

_____Corda - UNA

_____Cordiale - ENTENTE

Cordon_____ - BLEU

Corgi_____ - WELSH

_____Corner - AMEN

_____corpus - HABEAS

Cosi fan _____ - TUTTE

Cote_____ - DOR

Cote d'_____ - AZUR

Coup d'_____-ETAT or OEIL

_____Creole - ALA

_____Crayon – CONTE

Creme_____ - FRAICHE

_____CRI - DERNIER

Croix de_____ - GUERRE

_____Cuantos - UNOS

_____culotte - SANS

_____Culpa - MEA

Cum grano_____ - SALIS

_____cum laude - MAGNA

_____Cupid - DAN

Curriculum_____ - VITAE

Da_____ - CAPO

_____Dahaka - ASI

_____Dame - NOTRE

_____d'Amore - OBOE

_____Dance - ANITRAS

Dar Es_____ - SALAAM

_____d'art - OBJECT

_____d'Athur - MORTE

_____d'azur - COTE

_____Darya - AMU

Das lied von der_____ - ERDE

_____Dazs - HAAGEN

_____de Balzac - HONORE

_____de-boeuf - OEIL

_____de camera - SONATA

_____de-camp - AIDE

_____de chose - PEU

_____de coeur - CRI

_____de cologne - EAU or BOIS

_____de combat - HORS

_____de corps - ESPRIT

_____de deux - PAS

_____de escrivir - ERTE

_____Deferens - VAS

_____de foie gras - PATE

_____de Force - TOUR

_____de Fraise - CREME

_____de Frannce - TOUR

_____de Gourmond - REMY

_____de Guerre - CROIX or NOM

_____Dei - AGNUS

_____de javelle - EAU

_____de-lance - FER

_____de la societe - ILES

_____de la paix - RUE

_____Del Corso - VIA

_____Del Este - PUNTA

_____del fuego - TIERRA

_____de - LUXE

De_____ - NOVO

De_____(sumptuous) - LUXE

_____de mayo - CINCO

_____de mer - MAL

_____de parfum - EAU

_____de pascua - ISLA

269

_____de siege - LETAT

_____de soie - PEAU

_____de toilette - EAU

De_____ - TROP

_____del fuego - TIERRA

_____del sol - COSTA

Depeche_____ - MODE

_____de plume - NOM

Der_____ - ALTE

Dernier_____ - CRI

_____Desperandum - NIL

_____de tourne - DEMI

_____de veau - RIS

_____de Viande - GLACE

_____de vivre - JOIE

_____Dhabi - ABU

_____d'honneur - AFFAIRES

_____Diavolo - FRA

_____Dicit - NIHIL

_____Dicta or Dictum - OBITER

_____die - SINE

Dies_____- IRAE

_____Diem - CARPE

_____dieu - PRIE

_____di Lammermoor - LUCIA

_____dimittis - NUNC

_____Dinh Diem - NGO

_____Dire - VOIR

_____Disant - SOI

Ditat_____ - DEUS

_____dium - CARPE

_____dixit - IPSE

_____d'oeuves - HORS

_____doble - PASO

Dolce far_____ - NIENTO

_____Dolorosa - VIA

_____Domingo - SANTO

_____Domini - ANNO

Dona_____Pacem - NOBIS

_____donna - PRIMA

_____d'Orsay - QUAI

_____dos aquas - ENTRE

Duchess of _____ - ELBA

_____du Diable - ILE or SACRE

_____du jour - CARTE or
   PLAT

_____du lieber - ACH

_____du Salut - ILES

_____du seigneur - DROIT

_____du tout - PAS

_____du Vent - ILES

_____Eberhart - FABER

Ecce_____- HOMO

_____ed euridice - ORFEO

Emerald Point _____ - NAS

_____Emptor - CAVEAT

_____En Lai - CHOU

Enola_____- GAY

_____en Rose - LA VIE

_____en scene - MISE

Entr'_____(intermission) - ACTE

Entre_____- NOUS

_____equinox - VERNAL

ESSE_____Percipi - EST

_____-Es-Salaam - DAR

Et_____ - ALII

_____Et Laboro - ORA

_____et mon droit - DIEU

_____ex machina - DEUS

Ex_____(one-sided) - PARTE

_____Face (turnabout) - VOLTE

_____Facia - SCIRE

_____facto - IPSO

_____faire - LAISSEZ or SAVOIR

Fait_____ - ACCOMPLI

_____fan tutti - COSI

Fata_____ - MORGANA

_____Fatuus - IGNIS

Faux_____ - PAS

_____Favor - POR

_____Fein - SINN

Femme_____ - FATALE

Feng_____ - SHUI

Festina_____ - LENTE

_____Fide - MALA

_____Fideles - ADESTE

_____Filipinas - ISLAS

Fin De_____ - SIECLE

_____firma - TERRA

_____fixe - IDEE or PRIX

_____Flask - DEWAR

Fleur de _____ - LYS

_____Flow - SCAPA

Fontana de_____ - TREVI

_____Forma - PRO

_____Fortis - AQUA

Fra_____Lippi - LIPPO

_____Franca - LINGUA

_____Francaise - COMEDIE

_____fratres - ORATE

Fruits de_____ - MER

Fur_____ - ELISE

_____Garde - AVANT

_____Gatherum - OMNIUM

_____Gatos - LOS

_____Gauche - RIVE

_____generis - SUI

_____Gestae - RES

_____ghanouj - BABA

_____Giorno - BUON

Gloria_____ - PATRI

_____Go Bragh - ERIN

_____Gorda - PUNTA

_____Gorde - OLDUVAI

Graf_____ - SPEE

Grand_____ - CRU

_____gratia artis - ARS

_____gratia - DEI

_____gratias - DUO

_____gravure - ROTO

_____grecque - ALA

Gregorian_____ - CHANT

Gum_____ - ARABIC

_____Guofeng - HUA

Guy de _____ - MAUPASSANT

_____Habilis - HOMO

_____Hashana - ROSH

Haute_____ - MONDE

_____Heights - GOLAN

_____homo - ECCE

Hors_____ D'OEUVES

Id_____ - EST

Idee_____ - FIXE

_____impasse - ATAN

_____Incognita - TERRA

_____In Egitto - MOSE

In_____ - ESSE (living)

_____In Horto - URBS

In medias_____ - RES

In_____ - SITU

In_____(completely) - TOTO

In_____ - UTERO

In_____Verites - VINO

In_____ - VIVO

_____Incognita – TERRA

Inter_____- ALIA

Inter_____ - ALIOS

In vino_____VEDITAS

_____Ipsa Loquitur - RES

_____Irae - DIES

_____Irish rose - ABIES

Iron_____OXIDE

Itar_____ - TASS

_____Jacet - HIC

_____Jahan - SHAH

Jai_____ - ALAI

Jeanne d'_____ - ARC

Je ne_____quois - SAIS

Johnny_____- REB

_____Jong - MAH

_____judicata - RES

_____Jure - IPSO

Junipero_____ - SERRA

_____Juris - SUI

Kama_____ - SUTRA

Karmann_____ - GHIA

Knight_____ - ERRANT

Kofi_____Annan - ATTA

_____Kogo - JINGU

Kol_____ - NIDRE

_____Kum (desert) - KARA

_____Kwon do - TAE

La_____gauche - RIVE

Lag B'_____ - OMER

La_____Bonita - ISLA

_____Lahm - BATU

Laissez_____ - FAIRE

_____Lama - DALAI

_____Lance - FERDA

Land o' - GOSHEN

Lao_____ - TZU

_____la paix - RUE DE

Lapis_____ - LAZULI

_____la-Vallee - MARNE

_____la vie - CEST

_____la vista - HASTA

La_____vita - DOLCE

_____law - SALIC

_____lazuli - LAPIS

Le belle et la_____- BETE

Le_____du Printemps - SACRE

_____Lepton - TAU

_____Lescaut - MANON

Lesages_____Blas - GIL

Lignum_____ - VITAE

_____lily - SEGO

Lingua_____ - FRANCA

_____Lingus - AER

Linzer_____ - TORTE

_____Lisa - MONA

_____Lisboa - NOVA

Livin' la_____Loca - VIDA

Lobster_____Diavolo - FRA

Logum_____ - TENENS

_____L'oeil - TROMPE

_____Longa - ALBA

_____Longa, vita brevis - ARS

_____Lorraine - ALSACE

_____Longue - CHAISE

_____Luego - HASTA

_____Lumpur - KUALA

Luna_____ - MOTH

_____macabre - DANSE

_____ - Mache - PAPIER

Madam De_____ - STAEL

_____Magica - ARS

Magister_____ - LUD

Magna_____- CARTA

_____Magnon - CRO

Magnum_____ - OPUS

_____Mahal - TAJ

Mai_____ - TAI

Mais_____ - OUI

_____majesty - LESE

_____major - CANIS or URSA

Major_____-DOMO

_____Mal - PETIT

Mal de_____- MER or TETE

_____Malvinas - ISLAS

Mens_____ - REA

Mao_____tung - TSE

_____Marbles - ELGIN

Mardi _____- GRAS

_____Martin - ASTON

_____Masque - BAL

Mata_____- HARI

_____mate - YERBA

_____Mater - ALMA, DURA, PIA or STABAT

Mato_____ - GROSSO

Mauna_____ - KEA or LOA

_____Mawr - BRYN

Mazel_____ - TOV

Mea_____ - COLPA

_____Medica - MATERIA

_____Membrane - TYMPANIC

Memento _____- MORI

Meno_____ - MOSSO

Mesa_____ - VERDE

_____Metabolism - BASAL

_____me tangere - NOLI

_____minerale - EAU

_____minor - LEO

_____Mirabilis - ANNUS

_____Mitzvah - BARor BAS

Mobutu_____ SEKO - SESE

_____moi le deluge - APRES

Molto_____ - BENE

_____Momento - UNO

Mon_____ - DIEU

_____Monde - HAUT

_____monster - GILA

Moon_____Zappa - UNIT

_____morgana - FATA

_____Mot (wittism) - BON

_____mundi - ANNO

_____Nacht - STILLE

Ne plus_____ - ULTRA

_____ - Neisse Line - ODER

_____Nidre - KOL

_____Nisi Bonum - NIL

_____Nitrate - AMYL

_____Noir - BETE

Nom de _____ - GUERRE

_____Nome - CARO

_____Nostra - COSA

Nota_____-BENE

Nous_____ - ENTRE

Nouveau_____ - RICHE

_____nova - ARS or BOSSA	_____Pei – SHAR
_____nui - RAPA	_____Penee - ARRIERE
_____oblige - NOBLESS	_____Penh - PHNOM
Oder_____Line - NEISSE	_____pentameter - IAMBIC
_____of Iwo Jima - SANDS	Per_____Ad astra - ARDUA
_____of Kashmir - VALE	Per_____ - CAPITA
_____of Lebanon - CEDAR	_____perpetua - ESTO
Olla_____ - PODRIA	_____personae - DRAMATIS
_____Omnia vincit - AMOR	Personae non _____ - GRATAE
_____on parle Francais - ICI	Peut_____ - (perhaps) ETRE
Opera_____SERIA	_____Philippe - PATEK
_____operendi - MODUS	_____Phraya - CHAO
_____orange - OSAGE	Pico de_____ - ANETO
_____ordinaire - VIN	Pie_____mode - ALA or CAPA
_____Oro - RIO de	Pied_____ - A-TERRE
_____Ovo - LACTO	_____perpetua - ESTO
_____Paese (cheese) - BEL	Pis_____ - ALLER
_____Pareil - SANS	_____Plaid - GLEN
_____Park, Cal. - BUENA	_____Plaisir - AVEC
Pas de_____ - DEAU	_____platter - PU PU
_____Pasa - QUE	Plaza de _____ - TOROS
Pasta_____ - FASOOL	_____podrida - OLLA
Pater_____ - NOSTER	_____poetica - ARS
Pathet_____ - LAO	_____Pointe- DEMI
_____patriac - AMOR	Poli_____ - SCI
_____Paulo - SAO	_____polloi - HOI
Pearl_____ - DAIO	_____pompilius - NUMA
Peau de _____ - SOIE	_____populi - VOX

Por_____FAVOR

_____Porsena - LARS

Port_____ - SALUT

Post_____ - MORTEM

Pot-au-_____ - FEU

Pousse _____ - CAFE

_____Pradesh - UTTAR

Prie_____(kneeler) - DIEU

Prima_____ - FACIE

_____Prius - NISI

Prix_____ - FIXE

Pro bono_____- PUBLICO

Procol_____ - HARUM

_____Profundo - BASSO

_____ pro nobis - ORA

_____pro quo - QUID

Pro_____- RATA

_____prosequi - NOLLE

Pro_____-TEM

_____Publica - RES

Punta del _____-ESTE

_____Pura - AQUA

_____Purchase - GADSDEN

_____qua non - SINE

_____quam videri - ESSE

Quattro cinque_____ - SEI

Que_____ - SERA or TEL

_____Qui Peut - SAUVE

Quid pro_____- QUO

Quod____Demonstradum - ERAT

Quod_____Faciendum - ERAT

Raison d'_____- ETRE

Rapa_____ - NUI

Rara_____ - AVIS

Rarae_____ - AVES

_____Rasa - TABULA

_____Razor - OCCAMS

_____Rea - MENS

_____Regni - ANNO

_____relief - BAS

_____Relievo - ALTO

Res_____Loquitur - IPSA

_____Restartus - SARTOR

Richard_____de Lion - COEUR

_____Riche - NOUVEAU

_____Rima - OTTAVA

Rio de La_____ - PLATA

Rio_____ - NEGRO

_____Rios - OCHO

_____Rivera, CA - PICO

_____Rogas - UTI

_____Romagna - EMILIA

_____Roman - GRAECO

_____Romana - PAX

_____Rosenkavalier - DER

_____Rouge - BATON

_____Royale - ISLE

Sacro_____ - ILIAC

_____Sahib - PUKKA

San_____ , CA - ANSELMO

_____sana in corpore sano - MENS

_____Sanctorum - ACTA

_____Sanctum - INNER

Sang_____ - GROID

Sans_____ - EGAL

_____Sans in corpore sano - MENS

_____Sanskritt - VERIC

Sao_____- PAULO

_____Sapians - HOMO

_____Saud - IBN

Sauve_____Peut - QUI

_____Savant - IDIOT

Savoir_____ - FAIRE

_____scale of hardness - MOHS

_____segno - DAL

_____Semper tyrannis - SIC

_____sequitor - NON

_____serif - SANS

_____Seul - PAS

_____show - RAREE

_____Shue - FENG

_____ Shuffle - LIDO

Sierra_____ - LEONE or MADRE

_____Signum - ECCE

_____Simbel - ABU

Sine_____non - QUA

_____Ski - APRES

Soave_____ - BOLLA

_____soda - SAL

_____Soit qui mal y pense - HONI

_____solemnis - MISSA

Soto_____ - VOCE

Sphagnum _____ - MOSS

_____spumante - ASTI

Status_____QUO

Status quo_____ - ANTE

St. Philip_____ - NERI

Sturm_____drang - UND

Sub_____ - ROSA

Suma cum_____ - LAUDE

Sun_____ - YAT-SEN

_____Supuesto - POR

Sword of _____ - DAMOCLES

Tabula_____- RASA

_____Tafari - RAS

_____-Tass - ITAR

_____Tai - MAI

_____Tartare - STEAK

Te_____ - DEUM

Tel_____ - AVIV

Temple of _____ - ARES

Tempus_____ - FUGIT

_____Tenure - UDAL

_____Terrier - CAIRN or SKYE

Tersa_____ - RIMA

Tetro alla_____ - SCALA

_____Thule - ULTIMA

Tierra del_____ - FUEGO

_____Tiki - KON

_____Tome- SAO

_____Torte - SACHER

_____Tranquillautis - MARE

_____Trasit gloria mundi - SIC

Tres_____- BIEN

_____Triste - VALSE

_____Trouve - OBJECT

_____Tse or Tzu - LAO

_____Tsu - SHIH

Tu_____ - ERI

_____Tu - ERES

Ulan_____-BATOR or UDE

Una_____ Poco Fa - VOCE

_____un drang - STURM

Val d'_____ - ISERE

Valse_____ - TRISTE

_____vapeur (steamed) - ALA

Vega_____ - ALTA

Vena_____ - CAVA

_____Veneto - VIA

Veni_____Vici - VIDI

_____Venner (Holmes work) - ELSIE

_____vera - ALOE

Verbum_____ - DEI

_____Verde - PALO

_____Verte - TERRE

Vidi_____ - ISAT

_____vie - EAUDE

Villa d'_____ - ESTE

_____vincit omnia - AMOR

Vingt_____ - ETUN

Viola da_____ - GAMBA

_____virumque cano - ARMA

Vissi d'_____ - ARTE

_____Vital - ELAN

_____Vivant - BON

_____Vive - QUI

Vive le _____- ROI

_____Voce-SOTTO

_____voce (orally) - VIVA

Voir_____ - DIRE

_____volatile - SAL

_____Volens - NOLENS

_____volente - DEO

_____Von der erde - LIED

_____Vore - EATE

Vox_____ - DEI or POPULI

_____Vu - DEJA

_____way - APPIAN

_____whale – SEI

_____Wiedersehan - AUF

_____Xiaoping - DENG

_____Yoga - HATHA

_____Zedong - MAO

Zend_____ - AVESTA

Zeno of_____ - ELEA

Zhou_____ - ENLAI